whole music

PROPERTY OF
MARCELLA SMITHERS

whole music

a whole language approach to teaching music

lois blackburn

HEINEMANN • Portsmouth, NH

Heinemann
A division of Reed Elsevier Inc.
361 Hanover Street
Portsmouth, NH 03801-3912

Offices and agents throughout the world

© 1998 by Lois Blackburn

All rights reserved. No part of this book may be reproduced in any form or by any electronic or mechanical means, including information storage and retrieval systems, without permission in writing from the publisher, except by a reviewer, who may quote brief passages in a review.

The author and publisher wish to thank those who have generously given permission to reprint borrowed material:

Excerpt reprinted from William Walker, edited by Glenn C. Wilcox, *The Southern Harmony and Musical Companion*, copyright 1993 [© 1854] by The University Press of Kentucky, by permission of the publishers.
"Elena Nikolaidi gives . . .," by William Mootz. Copyright by The Courier-Journal. Reprinted with permission.

Library of Congress Cataloging-in-Publication Data
Blackburn, Lois.
    Whole music : a whole language approach to teaching music/Lois Blackburn.
      p.   cm.
    Includes bibliographical references.
    ISBN 0-435-07043-6
    1. Music—Instruction and study.   2. School music—Instruction and study.
I. Title.
MT1.B643   1998   97-41403
780'.71—dc21   CIP
                                                                                          MN

Editor: Lisa A. Barnett
Production: Vicki Kasabian
Cover design and illustration: Jenny Jensen Greenleaf
Manufacturing: Louise Richardson

Printed in the United States of America on acid-free paper

01 00 99 98   DA   1 2 3 4 5

Contents

	Acknowledgments	vi
1	Whole Language and Whole Music	1
2	The Whole Music Environment	15
3	Movement: The Root of It All	30
4	Singing	42
5	Whole Music Activities for Musical Understanding, Part 1	57
6	Whole Music Activities for Musical Understanding, Part 2	81
7	Listening	97
8	Creating	103
9	Standard Notation and Music Reading	113
10	Whole Music Across the Curriculum	144
11	Summing It Up	163
	Bibliography	167
	Appendix A: Suggested Book List	171
	Appendix B: Songs	179
	Appendix C: Classical Music for Listening Activities	207

Acknowledgments

I am deeply grateful to Marilyn Billups (one of the world's best school music teachers) for being my first editor and critic; to P. K. Northcutt for his expert computer rendering of the scores for the songs; to Ellen Perconti for examples of children's invented notation from her fine dissertation for the University of Idaho; and to Yetta Goodman for giving me my first glimpse of the world of the psycholinguistics of reading.

1

Whole Language and Whole Music

This book offers a fervent message to teachers. Since the message concerns teaching music to children, I hope that readers of the book will include both elementary classroom teachers and music specialists.

To Elementary Classroom Teachers

For elementary classroom teachers, my primary missionary goal is to proclaim the word that music can be integrated into many classroom activities, and that this can be done effectively by people with neither musical training nor musical knowledge. "Music lessons" are not necessarily limited to the popular conception. Without being able to read music, or sing, or dance, a person can nurture musical interest and creativity in children. (In saying this, I am making a token acknowledgment of the conviction of many adults that they "have no musical talent and cannot sing." Actually, my belief, based on many years of research and experience, is that there is no such thing as a "tin ear" or tone deafness—except in cases of hearing impairment—and that the Zimbabwean proverb is correct: if you can talk, you can sing. If you can walk, you can dance.) A "music lesson" does not have to involve quarter notes or clefs, or even singing. It can be thumping on the bottom of a wastebasket or playing "follow the leader." This kind of activity not only nurtures music in children but makes valuable contributions to their development in other ways. Illustrations of this are part of the content of this book.

Classroom teachers are thoroughly familiar with the whole language approach. For them, the review of that concept here is probably superfluous. However, it is a necessary prelude to the discussion of the many relevant parallels between language and music, including the adaptation of a whole language approach to bring music into the classroom.

For classroom teachers, all of this book, taken from the beginning and in order, is relevant and sequential. Chapter 6 addresses the more advanced concepts in the sequence and is intended mainly for music specialists. Any of the adventures in this book can also be effective when isolated from the sequence and used in any order; they can also be constructive "time fillers."

To Music Specialists

For music specialists—people who specifically teach music in *any* context—my message is that the kinds of activities in this book are profoundly valuable as beginning and intermediate levels in a music-skills-and-concepts sequence. They can also be used out of sequence, to address particular subjects or problems. The thumps on the wastebasket and deliberate imitation of physical activity in "follow the leader" can be developed into the skills necessary for participation in the high school marching band. It is part of my mission to chart this exciting progression for music specialists. It is effective as a broad and lasting foundation, it is developmentally sound, and it nurtures music in such a way that children are profoundly engaged rather than bored and intimidated.

Music teachers are not necessarily familiar with whole language and the implications of it in any learning situation. Moreover, because only small and localized innovative movements have as yet reached music education, music teachers have a tendency to duplicate their own musical training with their students. When I see a general music teacher begin every class by passing out the basic music series books, or when I see a teacher of beginning strings introduce music reading in the lesson following the one on holding the violin, or a teacher of beginning band spend the second week of lessons trying to explain a "tree" of eighth, quarter, half, and whole notes, I want to jump up and shout, "No—*wait!*" For music specialists, this book is about what they should be waiting for.

I urge music specialists to consider *all* these ideas as interrelated steps in a sequence of musical development from initial exploration of sound and movement to performance and music reading skills.

Music Is Not a Liquid

Music deserves to be included in the category of "solid" subjects. It would be a great boon if my missionary message were somehow also to reach any school administrators who look at music classes out of the corner of their eyes whenever budget cuts are required. Music is not an "extra"; it is not a specialty for an elite minority. Music is clearly as much a part of human inheritance as language. No known culture has ever been without it. Inherent in the study of any human endeavor is a connection to music: history, language, sociology, anthropology, science, and mathematics. The exploration of music has a positive and demonstrable halo effect on achievement in other subject areas, as well as on self-esteem and creative thinking. The public school emphasis on linguistic and mathematical/scientific subject matter not only excludes artistic experiences that make us human but also denies children with artistic capabilities the achievement and recognition that they deserve.

Children are born with cognitive structures for the development of music perception; the uniquely human ability to construct and perceive symbols includes artistic symbols as well as linguistic ones. Research on the eve of the twenty-first century suggests that cognitive structures appropriate to specific learning tasks will, if not exercised, be taken over for other tasks or will die out. In other words, the evidence implies, "Use it or lose it." The windows of opportunity for developing both language and music must be exploited early and throughout the development of children.

Help! We're Marooned in a Time Warp!

A serious problem with "music lessons," in any setting, is that teaching music has gotten stuck in a particular time period (the nineteenth and early twentieth centuries) and a particular place (Western Europe). If it was good enough for Beethoven and Sousa, it must be fine for our school-aged children now. People teaching "music lessons" are laboring along without the benefit of all the late-twentieth-century discoveries made by researchers in learning theory and in music's parallel discipline, language. Based on the work of psycholinguists and other language researchers, techniques loosely and collectively described as "whole language" have made reading and writing more relevant and accessible to a generation of children. In fact, these approaches have been more universally applied in learning situations and can now be labeled "whole learning." The whole learning philosophy is ideally suited to the teaching of music. In this book, I propose *whole music*.

Language Acquisition and Music Acquisition

Language Acquisition is a common expression among educators and others interested in child development. A computer database search using those words will unleash a flood of references. But how about *Music Acquisition?* Few educators—even music specialists—would use such a term. A musician would probably define it as the purchase of new sheet music. Nevertheless, there is a musical counterpart to the developmental phenomena collectively described as language acquisition. Beginning with specific cognitive programming at a particular period of a child's development, many parallels exist between the way a child internalizes the language of a culture and the music of a culture. And every known human society does have a mother tongue and a mother music.

Most parents spend a great deal of time assisting their children in the development of language. Although a disproportionately small amount of thought is given to the development of music (at least in the Western World), children are equipped by nature for music acquisition in much the same ways that they are programmed for language. There are significant implications in this about the vital importance of learning the mother music as well as the mother tongue, and about effective ways to teach music. The goal of this book is to emphasize the child-centered, (w)holistic ways that are used in nurturing language skills and analogous ways of nurturing music.

Whole Language

A description of whole language could be as follows: the initial exposure to written language through whole segments of meaningful text, rather than beginning with letters and isolated words. Emphasis is on a search for meaning within a context, often without reference to sound. Therefore, phonics and "sounding out" are not a part of this *initial* experience.

Learning activities are designed to capitalize on the life experience that each child brings to the classroom, and through which each child seeks to make sense of his or her world , including written language. Thus, whole language is a child-centered approach that seeks to involve the whole child—including the child's sensory and kinesthetic modes of perception—in the learning process. *Whole* also includes whatever environmental influences have shaped that child, including family, community, and native language. Explorations of any subject take advantage as much as possible of any connections with other subjects. Children are encouraged to express themselves freely in written and spoken language, at first inventing spellings or grammatical constructions when necessary. Creativity and individual thought are fostered in the absence of fear of immediate and embarrassing correction.

When tensions arise about the quality of schools and education, worried parents often take up the cry of "Back to Basics" (a nebulous goal, at best). To many people who learned to read through (or in spite of) phonics and flash cards, those tools constitute *The Basics*. Whole language is sometimes seen as a high-flown, newfangled idea, which is responsible for all problems that develop when a child is learning to read. Consequently, whole language has received some negative coverage by the news media, which have capitalized on the phonics-vs.-whole language *war*.

The truth is that whole language is not an exclusive method but a flexible approach that can be combined with others. It is simply a whole-to-part way of introducing information to children: context first, details later. And, except in cases of misinterpretation of the approach by teachers, details do indeed follow later. Children in whole language classes *do* learn standardized spelling and grammar, but within the context of appropriate literature and their own writing and speaking rather than from isolated examples in textbooks.

A Brief History of Whole Language

The ideas embodied in the term *whole language* existed long before the term itself. There were whole language teachers long before they were called that. They just courageously pulled their wagons in a circle and taught in a way that seemed right for them. An elementary teacher in the 1960s, Nina Fallon, gave my daughter the one year of elementary school she remembers with happiness. When no other teachers in that school were doing such things, Ms. Fallon taught her class about other countries by arranging for the children to cook ethnic food in the classroom, write plays, make costumes, sing songs, and learn phrases in the appropriate language. Fallon was a revolutionary; she was a whole language teacher.

The values motivating whole language have affected public education before, beginning with the powerful influence of John Dewey (1859–1952), American philosopher and educator. Dewey is often referred to as the father of the progressive education movement, a pioneering incarnation of child-centered education. In its prime in the late 1940s and early 1950s, progressive education was strongly influenced by Dewey's writings on the importance of the individual and of tailoring instruction to each child's interests, abilities, and life experiences.

Dewey's own education had been one in which students were seen as receptacles into which teachers poured knowledge: theoretical, academic facts and conclusions which they would presumably apply to their own experiences and explorations—*later*, in the "real world." Progressive education, and later whole language, embraced Dewey's belief that learning should *begin* with the concrete real world, the experiences the child brings to school and those provided by the teacher to motivate the child to develop his or her own questions. As the child is helped by the teacher to find the answers, the facts and academic knowledge are *derived* from the experience. The process is one of the child and teacher working together to develop practical theory and knowledge from concrete life experiences.

Progressive education made use of such revolutionary ideas as having the children help plan the subjects and activities of their own school day, and permitting individual students to pursue their own projects or courses of study. Some progressive private schools offered courses from which the students could select; alternatively, they could choose to attend no classes at all.

My early pre-music-specialist days as an elementary classroom teacher were in the atmosphere of progressive education. With the impetus of Dewey's warm-blooded views on teaching and learning, the movement was maturing and developing after the kind of bumpy start that new endeavors often undergo: some misapplication and zealous tendencies to throw the baby out with the bath water. The movement, however, was thriving until the trauma of the 1957 launching of the Russian satellite "Sputnik." The perceived superiority of the space program of the U.S.S.R. and its implications in the Cold War were attributed to a perceived superiority of the Soviet education system. Panic dictated that U.S. education should be refocused on science, mathematics, and the "Three R's." We were back to theoretical and academic knowledge for its own sake.

The 1970s saw a brief return to a vision of a child-centered education system. This revolution promised to be a big one, at all levels. It involved the development of many new programs and the building of new facilities, all financed by allocation of a great deal of federal and foundation money. But big revolutions, administered from the top down, are very expensive. Idealism faded. Pragmatism became the rule, until whole language appeared.

The whole language revolution is not a ponderous, expensive administrative project. It is teachers using their own imagination and intuition to help children learn the same way in school as they learn out of school. It means an attempt to lessen the impact of mandated standardized tests. It can mean teaching and learning without "basals," weekly spelling tests, tracking, and workbooks.

Above all, a whole language environment is a *safe* environment for learning. Experimentation and creativity are basic. Children are encouraged to explore, to take risks based on their own intuition and judgment. The questions they are attempting to answer are their own. They are not nervously waiting to be corrected.

Among the founders of whole language as a recognized process and philosophy are Kenneth and Yetta Goodman and Frank Smith. Their vital, prolific work is ongoing and central to this return to the child as the center of education.

The *whole* in whole language refers to a (w)holistic, contextual approach to learning experiences. The importance of *language* as a descriptor is that it is a basic medium for learning of many kinds. The ability of humankind to encode information into agreed-on symbols and manipulate them has made it possible to store and transmit generations of knowledge so that each generation need not start from scratch. Learning the signs and symbols operating in one's culture gives one access to the collective accumulated knowledge of that culture. There is an interdependence between learning language and learning *through* language. *Whole language* has now been replaced in some contexts by the term *whole learning*, since it is a philosophical approach that is appropriate to other learning situations as well as to the teaching of reading.

Nonlinguistic Symbols

Language, however, is only one of the many symbol systems operative in human interaction. During the second half of the twentieth century, attention has been increasingly given to the vast number of other symbolic competencies of which human beings are capable. Much has been written about different modes of cognition, about individual cognition according to dominance of right or left brain hemisphere functions, or about location in specific areas of the brain, unique in each person, of specific capabilities. Psychologist Howard Gardner proposes the existence within each individual of multiple intelligences.

Gardner points out that until very recently, human brain capacity was viewed in the Western world as a single, measurable entity possessed in some degree by every human being. This entity has been tested and confidently assigned a number representing the Intelligence Quotient, or IQ. This model of the human brain as a single mechanism with a measurable amount of some general problem-solving capacity is incompatible with current knowledge of how the nervous system works. Moreover, standard IQ tests feature linguistic and/or mathematical/scientific questions with only one correct answer. This, of course, makes the tests easier to score, with no messy variables in the final numerical judgment. However, there is no room here for inventiveness or ability to approach problems with multiple solutions. Persons with abilities other than linguistic or mathematical/scientific are off the scale. The knowledge tested is isolated, out of context, and culturally exclusive. Worse yet, schools sometimes take the practical approach and teach students strategies for taking these tests.

In his significant body of work investigating the arts in education, Howard Gardner proposes the existence within each individual of multiple intelligences (1993a and b). According to Gardner, some capacities, such as language, evolve in all normal persons; others, like music, are strikingly different in individuals. For a variety of reasons, each individual has his or her own set of intelligences. Gardner makes clear that there can never be a definitive list, since "intelligence is not a measurable entity . . ." but proposes his own listing:

1. Linguistic
2. Logical/Mathematical
3. Spatial
4. Bodily/Kinesthetic
5. Personal
   Interpersonal: the capacity for satisfying interaction with others
   Intrapersonal: the capacity to know oneself

Some nonlinguistic forms of symbolization, sometimes called *artistic symbols*, are visual-spatial, aural-temporal symbols. They are woven into the fabric of every culture, although little importance has been attached to them in the education systems of the Western world. These are languages of the "other" intelligences. The symbols of musical, spatial, and bodily/kinesthetic intelligences are probably based predominantly in the right hemisphere: the analogue system, the metaphorical brain. A characteristic of these symbols is that they are images which must be perceived as a whole, through nuances and associations. They are proof of the triviality of the old argument that thinking cannot take place without language. Elliot Eisner wrote (1992, 592), "In the beginning there was the image. It is the image that gives meaning to the label." In some way (unexplainable in words!), these symbols express profound feelings and emotions. Where words leave off, the music begins. Isadora Duncan said, "If I could say it, I wouldn't have to dance it." A painting or sculpture has its effect through different perceptions from those used to apprehend either spoken or written language.

The extensive and profound body of work of philosopher Susanne K. Langer encompasses her theories of the human mind and symbolism, particularly in the arts. From her assertion that "symbol and meaning make man's world, far more than sensation . . ." (1951, 34), Langer developed first a theory of symbolism in music in *Philosophy in a New Key* (1951) and then published an expanded theory of symbolism in all the arts, *Feeling and Form* (1953).

For linguistic symbols, Langer adopted the term *discursive*; nonlinguistic symbols are *presentational*. To Langer, the very limitations inherent in discursive communication gave rise to artistic expression through presentational symbols. In fact, the power of artistic symbols lies in their ambivalence.

Memory is to human beings what programming is to a computer. Memory is composed of an internalized database that we can build on, interconnect, and apply to new situations. The brain stores information in many forms, only some of which are linguistic. Information is programmed through all of the sensory receptors, including taste, touch, smell, and movement. Stored memory is an essential component of an individual's sense of self. What we are is in part derived from accumulated memory. Included in our image of ourselves is the itch of that worst case of poison ivy, the taste of salt water on the first ocean-beach trip, the pain and panic of touching the tongue to the frost on the metal schoolyard fence, the feel of the satin first-place ribbon, the smell of the dentist's office. Visual images are especially strong and can be evoked without language. They can appear unbidden.

Memory is a vital component in the internalization and synthesis of information and experience. Memory is not learning; it is an indispensable *tool* for learning. Harnessing the power of memory requires skill not only at facilitating storage but at retrieving it. This means manipulation of symbols: visual, tactile, olfactory, and aural, as well as linguistic.

For example, researchers have found ways of committing to memory even numerical data by associating them with visual, rather than linguistic or logical/mathematical, images. This is an excellent example of consciously gaining access to specific areas of the brain. It is yet another instance of incorporating all types of symbol systems into classroom experience.

Children can be helped to develop the capacity to perceive the vast array of extralinguistic symbol systems. They can learn to understand them, reflect on them, and to create them. This is not done through an accumulation of facts or bodies of verbal knowledge. This kind of knowing cannot be entered into a notebook and regurgitated for an examination. Instead, children must have the opportunity to work intensively with concrete materials, to learn the characteristics and possibilities of the media and what part the arts can have in their lives. They must begin by arriving at their own questions, and the answers that they seek must not necessarily be prescribed adult ones.

It is essential that these other symbol systems have a vital place in the schools, both for children whose individual intelligences give them special capacities for perceiving these symbols and for children whose lives will be enriched by understanding them.

Any classroom is a fertile place for artistic symbols so long as its environment encourages exploration and discovery, learning in context, and working with whole, real materials. The arts can also be tailored to the needs and interests of the child, embedded in the culture and social expressions of the community.

Whole Music

Whole music is my term for music introduced through a whole language (whole learning) approach.

Music has many striking parallels to language beyond the obvious one of being a form of communication with syntax and both aural and written modes. The music of a culture is another vital symbol system. As with language, an interdependence exists between learning music and learning *through* it. Learning music gives another access to the collective learning and wisdom of a culture.

Because of the "whole" in the whole language approach, this educational philosophy provides a perfect environment for learning musical perception. John Dewey would likely have ecstatically approved whole language. He would have endorsed whole music, as well. One of Dewey's philosophical concerns was the nature of symbols and of human interaction with them. He was especially interested in artistic symbols, which he believed could bring about "the sense of disclosure and heightened intelligibility of the world" (Dewey 1958, 319). He observed that we know ourselves "reflected in the mirror of art," and as we know ourselves "are transfigured" (1958, 77).

Music is at least as ubiquitous as language in human society. Anthropologists have discovered, as previously mentioned, that every culture has music in some form. It has been called the universal response of humankind, a world phenomenon. Just as children are born with cognitive structures specific to language acquisition, so are they also equipped—possibly in a different way—for music acquisition. Some of the components of speech are common to music. In fact, during the first year of life, emerging speech and incipient music production are indistinguishable. An infant is often able to match specific pitches. Early babbling imitates the "song qualities" of speech such as intonation and phrase-like pitch sequences and is closer to musical chanting than to language (Gardner 1981).

This intimate relationship between language and music makes them compatible cornerstones for a whole learning classroom. In whole music as in whole language, the word *whole* is taken seriously and applied liberally. It is the starting point. Learning is from whole, real experience. Learning is in context, from whole to part, with details (*facts*) inferred and derived. This is the ideal way to explore and learn music.

Each child will bring to this classroom his/her own previously internalized experiences with life, language, music, and other symbol systems of the culture. It is through this programming (*schemata*) that a child goes about the business of trying to make sense of the world; a person solves problems by referring to what he/she knows already. This is the way learning takes place in situations other than the classroom, and it is the goal of a whole learning classroom that the same process will be operative there. Music instruction should begin with the music experiences which the child brings to the classroom and should proceed from there.

Selective Perception

It is vital for educators to be aware of the phenomenon of *selective perception*. It is a profound component of the learning process and is a basic reason for the need to individualize instruction. Selective perception refers to *perception mediated by experience*. It is described in depth in the writings of cognitive psychologists in the areas of visual perception, information processing, and the acquisition of symbolic skills.

Robert Gagné (1977) wrote that when a stimulus is received, certain features of it are *selected* by the perceiver, according to the perceiver's disposition to attend to them. Jerome Bruner (1973) described perception as a decision process in which events are placed into mental categories previously developed through experience. Ulric Neisser said, "Whatever we know about reality has been *mediated* . . . by the organs of sense and by complex systems which interpret and reinterpret sensory information" (1967, 3–4).

A child brings to school a mental database of experience with language. By the time he/she is in kindergarten or first grade, a child has acquired a functioning vocabulary of between two thousand and four thousand words, depending on home environment. Noam Chomsky, the grandfather of all linguists, called this *linguistic competence*: the result of unconscious internalization of the vocabulary and the rules of the native language. This competence enables people to understand and produce an infinite number of new utterances. Chomsky proposed *generative grammar* as the process through which a child, hearing language all around, stores enough samples to unconsciously generalize rules (*transformation rules*). Sometimes children overgeneralize, as in assuming that the "house/houses" rule applies also to "mouse/mouses." (Only in a language as inconsistent as English are there so many opportunities for errors through overgeneralization.) A child who has developed linguistic competence can do more than repeat word-for-word the utterances he/she has heard. Through unconscious application of transformation rules, he or she can produce an infinite number of new combinations (Chomsky 1965, 1977). One of the absorbing pleasures of being around young children is listening to them in the process of generating and exploring these rules. Any new experience with linguistic symbols is mediated by or filtered through these linguistic schemata.

The process of musical perception is a close parallel to language. Music can be defined as *organized sound* (as could spoken language), and its sounds, like those of language, become symbols through familiarity. From the time of birth (or before), a child is surrounded not only by language but by music. Whatever the musical idiom is in that environment is then automatically programmed into the child's mind. Composer/conductor Leonard Bernstein, inspired by Chomsky, suggested that there are cognitive generative grammars that enable people to store musical samples and unconsciously generate transformation rules (1973). The development of these musical samples and internalized rules can be observed as young children explore and develop.

From early musical babbling, children progress to short, disjointed musical phrases, then to recognizable fragments of songs they have heard, then to ability to sing entire songs, and finally to short improvised, original songs—all characteristic of the musical idiom of their own environment. Children develop both linguistic competence and musical competence. Bernstein's theory has been reinforced and confirmed by other scholars, including Fred Lerdahl and Ray Jackendoff in *A Generative Theory of Tonal Music* (1983) and John Sloboda in *The Musical Mind* (1985). Both linguistic and musical competencies become a part of the preprogrammed schemata that filter the information a child encounters.

Whole to Part

Another aspect of whole learning besides consideration of the influence of individual schemata is the whole-to-part orientation. Human perception, through any or all of the senses, naturally begins with the whole.

In all of the proliferating studies of the human brain, it is still generally conceded that in most individuals the right hemisphere processes information (w)holistically, while the left hemisphere deals with analysis and details. The right hemisphere, in addition to its other functions, is part of our primitive survival system: perceiving the whole situation first is essential to alertness and readiness to react. Picture the familiar scene from an old movie of a person walking through a jungle. Jungles in old movies usually featured quicksand below, boa constrictors above, and man-eating plants in the middle. The intrepid traveler certainly must focus the right brain hemisphere for surveillance of the whole environment. In situations like these, time devoted to a left-brain analysis of a footprint results in a lapse of the right-brain scanning process. That's when the snake drops on one's neck.

A more current situation is that of the driver of an automobile approaching an intersection. This is another situation calling for the survival hemisphere. It is vital to get the whole picture at once: the traffic light, the approaching automobile turning left, the dog wandering across, the child who might dart into the street. Focusing on details like a window display could be dangerous.

FIGURE 1-1: *Partitioning in visual perception*

It is a basic human instinct to ascertain the whole first, with everything in context. Only later do we switch to an analysis of details. It makes a great deal of sense to organize the classroom learning activities in the same way.

Another aspect of "whole" as it applies to learning: human perception, through whatever sensory receptor, takes place through identification of patterns and relationships. If no pattern is apparent, the would-be perceiver will, either consciously or otherwise, try to construct one.

This phenomenon was studied by Gestalt psychologists beginning in the early part of the twentieth century. Studies by Kohler, Koffka, Ehrenfels, and Wertheimer explored the way in which eye and brain perceive stimuli through *grouping* (Katz 1950). The Gestalt term for this was "partitioning in visual perception." By the "law of proximity," a person can efficiently count lines which are grouped; counting is more difficult in arrays of equidistant lines (Figure 1-1).

In a music text, an array of eighth notes (as they are sometimes written in vocal music, in order to conform exactly with the words) indicates no observable rhythmic pattern. Pairing the eighth notes with beams makes the pattern jump out for the reader (Figure 1-2).

Whole language teachers train readers to search for meaning by sampling chunks of text. Beginning readers who can read and

FIGURE 1-2: *Beaming eighth notes makes rhythm pattern observable*

understand language in context often do not recognize the same words in isolation, not part of a unit.

Betty Edwards (1979) documented success in teaching her art students to draw by "open[ing] the access by conscious volition to the right side of the brain . . ." (4). Edwards trains prospective artists to look first for positive shapes, negative spaces, and format, with details as a secondary consideration.

Cognitive psychologists have also studied the implementation of grouping or organization in cognitive information processing. Robert Gagné noted that information is transferred from short-term memory to long-term memory through encoding; it is *organized* in some semantic, meaningful way involving topical, verbal or visual coding (1977). Jerome Bruner described perception as a *categorization* process (1973). In Ulric Neisser's model of visual perception, the perceiver constructs an appropriate visual object for storage by first segregating *units*, then constructing details through a pattern-recognition process (1967).

What if a person is confronted with signals which, after all schemata have been applied, still present no observable pattern and make no sense at all? In language, this would be either signals with which the would-be perceiver has had no experience, such as a foreign language, or something like nonsense syllables or poetry of the absurd. In the realm of the visual arts, most museumgoers could recall examples. In music, this occurs to listeners in the presence of the more random forms of twentieth-century music, such as music composed by the roll of dice. According to Bernstein, Sloboda, and Lerdahl and Jackendoff, these signals are inaccessible to cognitive processing. In an opposing view, composer Roger Sessions attributed to the human ear the ability to discover some kind of pattern in *any* musical signal (1970). In most cases, however, if the human mind fails to discern a pattern after using all of its strategies, it will give up in despair and frustration. This may account for a large body of twentieth-century music literature that still has no substantial fan club.

Human perception takes place through organization of signals, seeking out units, groups, or patterns and applying internalized schemata. It follows that in introducing information, we should present our students with an organized signal in the first place; that is, a meaningful whole with information in context.

A final reiteration of another aspect of *whole* in whole music, as in whole language: it implies opportunities to access information through all of the senses, beginning with structured, large-muscle movement of the whole body. Historically in the Western world, perception through sensory experience has been ranked far below rationality on the intellectual scale. This bias, reflected in school systems, closes out many different ways of knowing, and has a limiting and even crippling effect on the development of human minds. I propose whole music as part of the solution.

2

The Whole Music Environment

.... In the whole music classroom, the definition of music is *organized sound*. Musical experiences are therefore opportunities for exploring ways to organize sound: ways that a child can organize sound in child-initiated, child-directed activity, as well as the ways other people have organized sound to make music. The environment is a safe one in which children can use their own judgment and inventiveness. Exploration means not expecting to be corrected. Music is a highly appropriate subject for this approach, since musical problems invariably have a range of possible solutions.

Learning is an *interactive* process. In a classroom, this interaction takes place in three general categories of student activity: interaction with materials, interaction with adults, and interaction with other children.

Interaction with Materials

In every whole music classroom, for learners of every age from early childhood to adulthood, the learning environment should have a wide variety of materials available for individual exploration, as well as enough *time to explore them*. (Materials need not be expensive; time, however, is expensive, scarce, and precious.)

In early childhood and elementary classrooms, music materials can be at learning centers or simply available throughout the room. Objects can be in boxes or in large, brightly colored plastic tubs (big enough to climb into). There should be plenty of things that children can use freely: objects that are rugged or easily replaceable. A child's developing ideas do not and should not necessarily correspond to established adult ones. What is "banging" on the drum to the teacher is legitimate experimentation for a child, so the drum should be tough or have a replaceable plastic head. Just dumping out instruments on the floor is an experience in sound. Remember that widely accepted twentieth-century composers have composed music incorporating glass being smashed in a bathtub, recorded dog barks played backwards, and ensembles of radios and vacuum cleaners.

A sample list of materials:
1. "Found" objects, such as a metal wastebasket
2. Objects from home that make good sounds, such as pan lids and graters, for example. A good class project is having children bring things from home selected on the basis of an interesting sound they can make (and with the permission of a parent!).
3. Home-made instruments, such as plastic bottles, paired paper plates, or cardboard tubes filled with dried beans, rice, pennies, and the like. Making these instruments is a good class project.
4. A box of funny hats and varied costumes
5. Traditional folk instruments such as spoons, a washboard with a metal thimble as strummer, or a washtub bass
6. Sturdy classroom instruments: triangles, bells, agogo bells, sandpaper blocks, oatmeal-box drums, plastic maracas, and rugged xylophones
7. Commercially available musical toys
8. Puppets. A class project can be the construction of puppets out of materials such as paper lunch bags. The folded-over bottom of the bag becomes the mouth, with the rest of the face on the bottom of the bag. The straight part of the bag is the body, with the puppeteer's hand inside.
9. Books, audio recordings, and videos (see Appendix A)

In addition to these objects, which can be used with limited intervention from adults, children should experience more fragile instruments such as keyboards and Orff instruments: drums of various sizes and mallet instruments such as xylophones and metallophones. With their versatility and beautiful sound, Orff instruments enlarge the child's horizons and concepts of possibilities. (If a teacher can, alas, afford only *one* such instrument, my personal suggestion would be a metallophone.) However, for these, the children must be instructed in the vulnerability, use, and care of the instruments, for which a special time and place should be reserved.

Such opportunities for experiencing sound should not be limited to very young students. Older elementary children can benefit from all of the foregoing suggestions, with more elaborate additions like tape recorders, electronic keyboard instruments, and computers with music programs. Wind instruments, such as recorders, present the problem of possible transmission of colds and other diseases; this problem can be minimized with a can of disinfectant spray formulated for this purpose and available at music stores.

Other sources of musical sounds make good tools for individual and group projects; that is, they are made available at learning centers with do-it-yourself instructions. These can include:

1. Well-used orchestral, band, and folk instruments. Fingering charts and pictures showing how the instruments are held and played will help.
2. A couple of cleaned-up brake drums with a mallet
3. A jug to blow on. This is a quiet instrument with a long history in folk music. Instructions should include a brief mention of hyperventilation and caution against persisting in the presence of symptoms like dizziness or faintness.
4. A set of bottles, which can be filled with water to various levels, producing different pitches when the bottles are blown or tapped with a spoon. A group of bottle players can invent compositions or play tunes. This can be integrated into a lesson in acoustics: a study of the relationship of pitch to the size of the vibrating column of air that has not been displaced by water. A more elaborate experiment is a set of thin water glasses (better store them with Orff instruments) to be filled to varying water levels. These can be "played" by running a moist finger (moistening with water with a little detergent is best) around the rim of the glass. If the player is successful, the resulting sound is ethereal. As with bottles, several players, each equipped with a glass "tuned" to a different pitch, can produce a group composition or play melodies. This could lead to some research on the glass harmonica, an instrument based on this principle, for which Mozart composed special music.

Junior high and high school students also need time and opportunity for free interaction with music materials. This is a wistful suggestion, however, since so little time is allocated in school schedules even for more traditional music activities that the idea of reflective or creative time is usually out of the question. But in case it should be possible, equipment can be any kind of electronic equipment, pianos, guitars and banjos, percussion instruments, and any available band or orchestral instruments. It can even be a pad of manuscript paper and a calligraphy pen.

At any level, it is profoundly important for a young child or an adolescent to experience something that in any classroom is a scarce and precious commodity: the opportunity to work alone, as an individual, on his or her own. This could mean interacting with materials, working on individual projects such as original composition or research, watching a tutorial videotape by a famous jazz musician, listening to recordings through earphones, or practicing his or her own instrument. The outcomes of this are many: exercise in self-motivation; progress at one's own pace, at one's own level, according to one's own interests; reflection and creativity; and skill with materials not available at home.

Individual and group musical activities involving materials

This treasure trove of sound generators can provide inspiring tools for individuals and groups working on projects. Here are some of the ways this can be used:

Learning centers. Special areas at the periphery of the classroom can be dedicated to musical exploration. They might be related to a music concept or to a unit of study in another area of the curriculum (see Chapter 9, "Whole Music Across the Curriculum"). This center can be equipped with objects to manipulate and instructions or explanations. One term for a set of instructions like this is a *learning activity package* (sometimes familiarly abbreviated to LAP). An example of this might be playing a jug, as in a jug band. The LAP gives detailed, step-by-step explanation, including how to position the jug and hold the mouth, what alterations to make if no sound is produced, and when it's time to rest to avoid hyperventilation.

A short form of a LAP is a *job card*. A job card is used when only brief instructions are called for. A courageous teacher might want to have a day when learning centers of various kinds are set up in various parts of the room, with job cards and materials provided at each center. The class is divided into groups, with a group assigned to each center. If the job cards direct the participants into some sort of performance, the conclusion of the adventure could be performances of each of the groups for the others. Here is an example of a learning center with a job card: the materials at the learning center consist of a poem with definite rhythmic patterns (see Appendix A for suggested literature) and five percussion instruments: a drum, a triangle, maracas, castanets, and a wood block. The job card instructs the group to devise rhythmic accompaniment for the poem, with the drum providing the macrobeat. Students not playing instruments read the poem aloud together.

Classroom recorder playing. The recorder is a small wind instrument with a long history; it is a "real" instrument, rather than a toy. Its advantages, besides availability and low cost, include versatility. It can be played with satisfaction at many levels: by children using only one hand and playing simple tunes, and by adults playing complex Renaissance and Baroque music. Recorders and a fingering chart can, like orchestral and band instruments and guitars, be available for individual exploration; however, as with those instruments, proficiency is best attained through instruction, and there can be great enjoyment in playing with a group.

(Similar instruments are the tonette and the song flute; these, however, are very limited, with no "upward mobility" possible, since they can play only in the key of C and have shallow tone quality.)

There are ways to use the recorder simple enough so that almost all students can experience some success. Although there are many exceptions, it is usually wise to wait until children are in the fourth or fifth grade before the recorder is introduced. At this age, they can learn simple melodies and even two-part pieces with good results and much satisfaction.

Almost any adult can find a method book and become proficient enough to introduce children to the recorder. The teacher can then stay "a page ahead" of the students and keep the process going. It is not unusual for adults who learned this way to find themselves becoming members of a community recorder group.

The whole class can learn to play recorders together, with some attention given to the following guidelines:

1. As in learning any other instrument, the children should learn a tune or two by rote before learning to respond to notes in standard notation; *Rain, Rain; Mary Had a Little Lamb; Au Clair de la Lune;* and *Hot Cross Buns* are the most accessible. (I change the title on that last one when I introduce it, to avoid some giggles and hooting.) "Twinkle" is *not* simple on a recorder.
2. "Squeaks" invariably result from one of two problems: overblowing, and failing to cover the holes completely. Describe the breath technique by asking the

children to "blow *warm* air. Warm your hands or clean your glasses." Describe the inappropriate way to blow by having the children blow *cool* air, as if cooling hot cocoa or soup. Describe the fingering technique by asking children to "use the soft pads of your fingers, not the tips. Be sure you feel the *whole* round edge of the hole so that you are completely covering it."

3. Introduce note-reading very slowly, with much repetition. Method books usually have a good sequence, except that they move too fast and progress too soon to playing notes with both hands. Stay with only the notes of the *left hand* for quite some time. This can include several familiar songs, and repetition is important.

Many music specialists who teach elementary band instruments find that working with an elementary band class for six weeks on recorder—before the trumpets, trombones, and other instruments are brought to class—is excellent preparation. With this simpler instrument, the children have an orientation to breath control, "making a nice sound," coordinating their fingers, and responding to printed notation. For this topic, see Chapter 9, Standard Notation and Music Reading.

Project contracts. A contract can be negotiated and written out between the teacher and an individual student. In the contract, the student agrees to complete a project, which is described in detail along with materials needed, final form of the project, resources that will be tapped, projected date of completion, and grade anticipated if certain standards are met. This kind of individual activity can be used as an alternative form of learning for a child who, for whatever reason, cannot participate in the current work of the class. It also allows for a gifted student who is ahead of the class, or a student with special intelligences that need to be exercised. A project can take any form that is related to the unit of study.

Interaction with Adults (Teacher's Role)

Preschool, kindergarten, first grade

The role of the teacher or other adult is twofold: the first is to set up the classroom environment. However, simply turning a child loose in a room full of sound sources has limited potential as a learning activity. The teacher must also act as a mediator and model. This role varies with circumstances. For example:

1. Some children find it difficult to explore things on their own. The teacher can reassure the child that he or she is free to do this and can make suggestions about getting started.
2. During periods of child-initiated activity, the teacher can move among the children, encouraging each child to talk about what is happening. "Kid talk" should be highly valued in the classroom, not only because this respect engenders a sense of worth but also because talking about things helps a child to clarify and sort out his or her ideas. It also gives the teacher a window through which to observe the child as a person, as well as each child's individual cognitive processes, strategies, inventiveness, and development.
3. The teacher can also ask questions and make neutral, leading suggestions. For example, "What is the difference between the sound of the top bar on the xylophone and the bottom one?" "What is it about the bars that makes them sound different?"
4. The teacher can play instruments for the children. Any kind of instrument would be good. Simple demonstrations are valuable, such as the different ways to play a drum: "zinging" it with a snap of the thumb or tips of the fingers, "thwacking" it with the palm of the hand, brushing the flat hand in a circular motion over the drumhead, playing it in the middle or near the rim, or using a soft mallet.
5. In talking with young explorers, the adult can provide them with vocabulary for concepts. Naming things makes it easier to think about them. "How would you play that instrument to get a higher (or lower, louder, softer, different kind of, etc.) sound?" All these words embody musical ideas. As children have more experience, more advanced musical words can be added, such as accent, crescendo, tempo, dynamics, timbre, or whatever fits the situation.
6. These activities can lead to others. The teacher can ask, "What does that sound make you think of?" One little girl answered my question about her castanets with, "They're like clams." I asked her what rhymes with "clam," and she made up a little poem about a clam, with the castanets as both protagonists and sound effects.

The Clams, by Erin Morra, age 6
This is Pam.
This is Sam.
Pam and Sam sit on the sand.

7. Last on my list but of equal importance is for the teacher to act as organizer of ensembles. Children can take turns being the conductor while the others play sound-makers in free improvisation or to a macrobeat with chants, songs, and recordings. The student conductor can model elaborations of rhythm patterns and "riffs" for the players to imitate. Players can alternate solo and group improvisation.

The class can provide sound effects for a story read aloud. For example, in "The Gingerbread Man," different sounds can be assigned by the class to represent each of the characters, with the reader pausing briefly for the sound each time a character's name is read. (Before beginning, the teacher can demonstrate a "scissors" motion with the thumb and fingers of both raised hands, to "cut off" the sound effect so that it doesn't go on too long. Children enjoy this if it is practiced in advance.) The usual favorite sound effects for this story are for "Run, run, run, as fast as you can . . ."

Elementary grades 2–6

For children beyond first grade, the teacher's role is still that of mediating and modeling, and the role of the children is still exploring and creating. Older children, however, can work together in groups with a more organized focus. They can assume the roles of organizer, consultant, and demonstrator/illustrator. The general goal of the adult is to motivate children to assume leadership in developing questions and finding answers. During this process, the teacher helps the class deduce information about music. The following sample lesson plan is an extended example of how this works.

Lesson Subject: Creating drawings, poems, and songs to "I am a maker of . . ."

Anticipated Outcomes in the form of concepts and skills: Information that can be deduced and emphasized from the lesson. This depends on whether the teacher is, for example, working on music or featuring language arts, and the levels or areas being developed. Here is a partial list of concepts which can be highlighted from this lesson:

visual art	rhyming words	rhythm and accent in language
macrobeat	meter/accent	
pitch	melody/tune	playing instruments
creating poems	composing songs	working in groups
audience courtesy	performing in public	creative listening movement

musical terms: dynamics, tempo, timbre, etc.

Lesson Schedule: Six days, twenty to twenty-five minutes each day, depending on the age and characteristics of the class.

Procedures

> DAY 1: After a demonstration by the teacher, each child will draw, under a heading of, "My name is . . . . I am a maker of . . .," a picture of himself or herself making or building something.
>
> *Teacher's role on day 1:* To demonstrate the activity, equip the students with large crayons and very generous pieces of clean newsprint, and encourage large, free, open drawings. The teacher should *demonstrate* on a piece of paper on an easel or affixed to the chalkboard, since the cognitive styles or attention spans of many young children make verbal instructions incomprehensible, especially in a sequential series. The teacher writes at the top of the page, "My name is . . . I am a maker of . . . ." and asks the class, "What shall I be a maker or builder of?" One child's suggestion, when I recently did this, was "butterflies." The teacher quickly draws himself/herself making butterflies of various sizes and colors, incorporating some of the suggestions that are offered. The children then go to work drawing themselves as builders or makers of something.
>
> DAY 2: After practicing the task as a class, the children work in groups to create a poem from one or more of the drawings: "I am a maker of . . . (boxes, cakes, boats . . .). Each child's idea can be a new stanza. The poem is performed as a chant with percussion instruments and/or movement and sound gestures.
>
> *Teacher's role on day 2:* To first demonstrate the task by having the class create a poem from "I am a maker of . . ." Leading questions could be, "Do we want this poem to rhyme? Do poems have to rhyme?" "What could I make

butterflies from?" Here is the poem that one of my classes made from "butterflies:"

> I am a maker of butterflies.
> I make them from paper and glitter and glue.
> I make them to sell at the market,
> And people will buy some, too.

Before the students adjourn to groups, their instructions are to appoint a group scribe to write down the poems. If there is time (and attention span), the groups can write a stanza for each child in the group. Movement can be added to the poems. If there are to be five groups, the teacher can have students "count off" to five. (Remind them in advance to remember the number they say.) Then designate places in the room for "all the ones," "all the twos," and so forth. The teacher visits each group briefly, to help them get started, if necessary.

DAY 3: The class will make up a tune for the "Butterflies" poem, using xylophones or Orff mallet instruments, with the option of adding movement, percussion, and sound gestures. On the Orff instruments, using only the bars of the pentatonic scale will simplify the process.

Teacher's role on day 3: To demonstrate the task by working with the whole class in making up a tune for a poem. For example, using the "Butterflies" poem, the teacher walks among the children rhythmically chanting "I am a maker of butterflies" and asking for a tune. Usually children will volunteer something. The teacher then sings the first line with that tune and chants the second line, for tune suggestions, and so forth for all the lines of the poem. Singing it from the beginning each time helps children think of what could follow next, and to learn the whole song.

If there is discomfort about singing on the part of either teacher or students, mallet instruments can be used to compose the tune, which can be written using the letter names from the bars of the xylophone. (In the regrettable absence of expensive Orff instruments, small, serviceable xylophones are available at very reasonable prices.) Moreover, the tune can be recorded on a cassette player. A teacher who has autoharp, piano, or guitar skills can get melodic ideas started by playing chords in a beat pattern ("OOM—pah—pah" or ONE—two—three; "BOOM—chick" or ONE—two).

Most elementary children will readily make up tunes, so a teacher need not be too uneasy about trying this. Often, the children's tunes are a variation of the "calling tune" or the "neener-neener" tune. This is normal and useful. (See "The Ur-song and the pentatonic scale" in Chapter 4.)

DAY 4: Groups will compose their tunes and practice singing their poems with their tunes.

Teacher's role on day 4: To circulate among the groups to give support where needed.

DAY 5: Groups will take turns performing their songs or chants for the class.

Teacher's role on day 5: To help a student who will serve as master/mistress of ceremonies and to get the class to talk about listening skills and audience courtesy, thus soliciting the children's ideas about this and about how it feels to perform in front of other people. The teacher might mention that when music starts, people often begin to talk. Why? Do television and radio have anything to do with this? Stress the importance of applause and firmly prohibit "boo's," referring to the discussion about how it feels to be in the spotlight.

DAY 6: The class and teacher will talk about "what we did and what we learned."

Teacher's role on day 6: To make an art display from the children's drawings and to get the children to talk about their drawings, the poems and songs, how their groups worked together, and how decisions were made. At this point, information can be derived from the students' poems and songs, with emphasis on the original objectives. This is a versatile lesson which can be used for many purposes.

Students were the visual artists, authors, and composers in this activity, working either as individuals or as members of a group. The context of the students' own creation/composition is rich with opportunities for inferring concepts. Moreover, a lesson of this kind provides the basis for subsequent activities in many different directions.

Grades 7 to 12

In the upper grades, exploration of and composition with sound generators are just as valuable. With these students, even more than with younger ones, the most important criteria for a lesson are that the lesson:

1. is not "stupid" or "silly";
2. does not underestimate or "talk down" to students;
3. challenges, but is free from too many pitfalls leading to failure;
4. is relevant to the student's own life and expectations.

In short, if it isn't "cool," it may bomb. If it does, the only learning to take place may be negative.

Student involvement is still central. Even instrumental lessons may be given with the student(s) at the center, without much lecturing from the teacher. I believe that as teachers, we all talk too much. I once observed a demonstration of a first lesson for a beginning junior-high-age string bass player given by renowned bassist and author Barry Green (1986). Green taped his own mouth shut and approached the lesson with only the string bass and bow, plus an empty soda can. The entire lesson took place without a word from Green. He placed the student's hands (grasping the soda can demonstrated the approximate hand position for both hands). He then demonstrated stance, holding and drawing the bow, and so on, in short increments, pausing periodically for the student to imitate. The student occasionally asked a question, which Green answered by demonstrating the answer. In less than ten minutes, the student could play *Mary Had a Little Lamb* and *Twinkle, Twinkle,* with acceptable position, tone, and intonation—all without one word from the teacher. Now, *that's* whole music!

Here are some samples of whole music lessons for grades 7 to 12. These are recipes very recently tested using current classroom ingredients: students who struggle for self-esteem and image and who reject any activity, however educational, which may threaten their self-image and self-esteem.

1. Original commentary to a background of music: The student chooses a piece of music—*any* music that is instrumental, with no words—and creates a text to be read as a voice-over to this music. The text may be poetry or in prose and could be, for example, social commentary or personal opinion, a narrative vignette from childhood, an original poem or short story, a short item from a newspaper, or favorite works by another author. The text and music could be matched either because the student feels that the text and the music are mutually appropriate, or, conversely, because of the

irony of a mismatch. Auxiliary sounds could be incorporated. The end product is a recording of the student reading the text with the music as background.

2. Reviews of recordings: The first part of this lesson is research by the student to bring in examples of reviews of recent CDs. A requirement might be to bring several reviews from a variety of sources (magazines, newspapers, record store advertisements) with a range of types of music. The second step could be an outline of which aspects of the recordings are covered in these reviews: choice of material, quality of performance, integrity or intent, background/training of performer(s), overall effectiveness, and target audience. The end product will be a review written by the student incorporating the outline and using the professional reviews as models. The recording reviewed could be either one of the student's choice or one assigned by the teacher, depending on the objectives of the lesson. If the class has been studying musical theater, for example, the recording reviewed should be a musical, but could be chosen by the student. Or reviews could be written contrasting musical theater of two different periods.

3. Constructing original musical instruments and scores: The construction of original sound generators works well in conjunction with a study of twentieth-century composers who have explored compositions using nonstandard sound sources: stones, vacuum cleaners, and recordings—played forwards or backwards—of environmental sounds. The student devises sound sources, composes a score (in either original or standard notation or a combination), and presents a performance. Other students may be enlisted as performers as needed. If computers are available with such capabilities as sampling, this is of course ideal, but this equipment is not standard issue in all schools.

4. Exploring the history of music in the community: The musical history of a community or larger local area can be fertile ground for research. Sources could include old newspapers and library or historical society archives. For example, mining communities in many states had bands and even orchestras with personnel who had brought their instruments and skill when they came from other places to work in the mines. In

West Virginia, railroad workers had bands, with separate organizations for white and African-American railroad employees. High school students might research earlier yearbooks of their school for musical organizations and their performances. Early photographs can enhance the final research paper.
5. Original composition: Depending on the class and the objectives, various forms of original composition and performance can be incorporated. If training in standard notation is not part of the class or the background of the students, the student composers can devise original notation or charts, or record the performance of the composition to preserve it.

Interaction with Other Children

For a prolonged period in early childhood, a child is in a stage known as *egocentrism*, during which the child is cognitively unable to understand that another person might have a different point of view. During this stage, individual child-initiated and child-directed activities are especially effective. However, one of the goals of preschool and kindergarten is helping children grow from this developmental stage to greater awareness of other people. Circle games and other activities are effective for this. On this subject, I have had nursery school and kindergarten teachers suggest that the music teacher should just start a little game in the corner, with the children who are attracted to it wandering over to participate while other children go on about their individual business. This ignores several aspects of human group dynamics. First of all, too much distraction makes it impossible for even mature persons to concentrate. More important, however, is the phenomenon of group experience. The impact of a game played with others is a completely different experience from playing solitaire or bouncing a ball against a wall. The effect of a film or play is heightened by sharing it with a group, even if the rest of the audience are strangers. This phenomenon can be exploited to smooth the transition from egocentrism to awareness of the feelings of others. A large part of the advantage of group education is the process of socialization that can take place.

Children learn from each other as well as from their teachers. This is nothing new, but new studies have shown that children as young as ten months old, children who cannot yet communicate with words, can learn things from each other and retain what they have learned (Hanna and Meltzoff 1993). Researchers are also finding that attendance at stable, high-quality day care programs can have a strong positive influence on both social and academic development later (Field 1991).

For older children, the benefits of interaction with each other are even greater. In musical activities, this can be making music together with voices or instruments, or creating poetry, music, and drama as a group. Many voices or instruments together, alternated with solo ones, offer richness and variety. In this group activity, the children apply many of the concepts that were internalized in individual, child-directed exploration. For individual skills such as playing an instrument, a child who has mastered the skill can then help a classmate with it.

As children interact with each other in the classroom, they can begin to assume the roles that the teacher has modeled: mediator, organizer, consultant, and demonstrator. Children become the composers, scribes, conductors, drum-beaters, performers, choreographers, and organizers. The teacher's task is to set up activities with new challenges and to motivate the development of new skills and knowledge necessary for these creative tasks.

Every new learning experience in a whole music class begins with *making music*. From these encounters with whole, real music, we infer and extract the "facts" about music. The remaining chapters are examples of whole music in action. They are offered, not as a compendium of ideas, which can be found in many other sources, but as *samples* of the kinds of activities which can be used in a whole language approach to teaching music.

3

Movement: The Root of It All

Movement: A Nonlinguistic Symbol System, A Path for Learning and Information-Processing

The collective wisdom of a culture is preserved for its posterity in its symbol systems, such as spoken and written language and music. Another of those symbol systems is inflected movement, as in ritual and dance.

Dances and ritualistic motions can preserve and communicate history, myths and folk tales, social values, laws and taboos, aesthetic standards, and spiritual ideas. They can motivate, unify, move, and control people. Dances are also expressive and entertaining and serve to synchronize and organize the body and the mind, either as a direct goal or as a beneficial side effect. This power of physical movement as a liaison between mind and body and as a tool for learning make it vitally important in the classroom.

Current research involving brain function concludes that it is an oversimplification to consider exercising an individual brain hemisphere (however great the need may seem to be). However, it is possible to train individuals to find ready, voluntary access to specific functions of the brain, such as the centers that process information (w)holistically. One of the effective training experiences that require such processing is structured, large-muscle movement, which broadens the focus of attention to include the whole body in relationship to the space immediately surrounding it.

I use the adjectives *structured* and *unstructured* to make the following distinction: unstructured large-muscle movement describes behavior exhibited by children flinging themselves after each other in an improvised chase, tussling, reacting to anger or frustration in physical ways such as kicking objects or stamping the foot, and any other movements that are not the result of prior thought or planning, however brief. Unstructured movement, as I define it, probably originates in the limbic brain, the primitive "animal brain," rather than in the cerebral hemispheres.

Structured large-muscle movement is preceded, if only for a split second, by planning on the part of the mover; it involves some kind of pre-formed mental image of the movements to be performed. The image may be an improvised, original creation that is constructed in the person's mind or an imitation of an instructor or a television performer. A child who is engaged in some kind of structured, large-muscle movement unconsciously forms a mental picture of himself or herself doing this movement, and proceeds to act on it. The mental image is probably formed in the right cerebral hemisphere, and the entire mind-body complex is mobilized to accomplish it. The activity is structured: planned, deliberate, and the result of a split-second advance mental rehearsal.

Skill in *voluntary* coordination of the large-muscle movements of the body develops in several stages. Most of these, in the normal course of things, precede or accompany maturation of the ability to think symbolically. Historically, in all known cultures, children have engaged in outdoor, physical games. These have been either loosely organized by the children themselves or structured by the adults of the community with specific goals, such as the teaching of physical skills needed in hunting or battle. Anthropologists have found these games fertile ground for study, since they often reveal a body of children's folklore, transmitted not from adult to child but somehow from child to child on the playgrounds of the world. Examples of this in the United States are children's jump rope chants. Structured physical movement appears to be a part of natural human development.

But now television is with us. It has become central to the lives of most children in so-called civilized countries. In conjunction with video games and movies, it monopolizes much of children's time at home and even some of it at school. Few children now begin their after-school time by grabbing a snack and running out to play street baseball. It is rare today to see a hopscotch pattern chalked on the sidewalk. In some neighborhoods, it is not safe for children to play on the sidewalk or even in a neighborhood park. Instead, children go home, get the latchkey from its hiding place, and head for the television. They do not move, except to the refrigerator and back. Structured, large-muscle movement, a natural human developmental stage, is being substantially eliminated from children's lives.

The brain and the body are not separate entities but parts of the same system, with synchronous, interdependent growth of parts programmed in advance. Each infant slides from the womb with a brain-body system equipped with its own individual set of potential capabilities. Unused, they atrophy. "Use it or lose it" is an appropriate description of the process. Consider the probable deprivation to the culture of the Western world if Beethoven and Dickens had spent their formative years in front of a television set.

But, wait. It is obviously untrue that if the body is not exercised and coordinated, then the brain will not develop. There are individuals of great brilliance and accomplishment who have triumphed in spite of severe physical challenges. Itzhak Perlman, crippled in childhood by polio, became a great violinist. Stephen W. Hawking, trapped in a wheelchair from his midtwenties and crippled by amyotrophic lateral sclerosis to the point of his inability to speak or write, is widely regarded as the most brilliant theoretical physicist since Einstein. If the mind and the body are one system, how do we account for the many examples of people who function superlatively with incomplete equipment? The answer lies in the multiple paths connecting brain and body. All the senses are receivers and transmitters of information. If any of these are incapacitated, or a majority of them, as in the case of Helen Keller, the remaining ones serve as backup. Moreover, challenged individuals are able to develop the remaining faculties to an abnormally high level. They make maximum use of what they have.

However, the more routes of access and the better coordinated the system is, the better it functions. All available perceptual sensors must be used to promote learning and to provide experiences that will help children make the most of their inborn capacities and to learn with their whole mind/body systems.

Most of the daily business in the average public school classroom is conducted in a way that severely limits body movement and most certainly does not use it as a learning tool. The standard procedure in most classrooms is to immobilize the body as much as possible, releasing only the eyes and ears, and to a limited extent, the hands. Thus, many components of the perceptual centers of the mind/body complex are imprisoned in a desk and thereby rendered inoperable. Senses other than sight and hearing are ignored, including touch, taste, smell, bodily kinesthetic perception, and whatever mysterious perceptual mix results in intuition. Information that could easily be assimilated through chanting, singing, or movement is presented by lecture, written into notebooks, and squeezed out on tests. Nevertheless, it might be a safe wager that the teacher, when trying to write the correct date in his/her checkbook, chants surreptitiously, "Thirty days hath September . . ." This uses beat and rhythm, which are underlying components of motion, for recalling data. In the "real world," that is, outside of the classroom, both children and adults assimilate information through all the avenues of the body/mind. Learning in the classroom should take place the same way. A classroom should be a microcosm of the positive parts of the real world.

The natural way that learning takes place begins with the whole and moves to parts; the first perception is of the *whole* stimulus via the *whole* mind-body complex. Unconsciously, a human being seeking information activates every perceptual avenue of the body at once; all systems are "go." Stepping into a place that is unfamiliar evokes reaction from much more than the eyes and ears: the surface of the skin (temperature and density of the air), the feet (texture and rigidity of the ground surface), the nose (smell and relative humidity), and even the voice. At a high level of alertness, calling out, "Anybody home?" or "Who's there?" may function like radar or bat squeaks to detect another presence. These are powerful learning tools, which are available to educators but are usually untapped.

Beginning in early childhood, classroom use of movement of the body, particularly large muscles, is a natural and important avenue for learning. The curiosity of a child, nature's built-in motivation for exploration, is expressed by manipulating things with the hands (haptic touch), pushing and moving with hands and feet, putting objects into the mouth and ears, climbing and exploring with the whole body. And this process is not limited to early childhood. Just as toddlers learn music by jumping to a beat or "banging" on a xylophone, so do high school students learn by improvising a dance or "noodling" on a keyboard.

The relationship between movement and music is so close as to make the two almost inseparable. Young children automatically respond to music by moving. Historically and in most cultures, music and movement are intertwined. Music unaccompanied by movement, as in a symphonic concert setting, is only a very recent phenomenon, and again is largely an invention of Western tradition. However, even formal concert music of the Western world projects an analogue of motion: sound that imitates motion through variations in tempo and dynamics. There is such a thing as symbolic movement without music, of which a sophisticated example is the choreography of Merce Cunningham, whose work explores movement in space without relationship to music. However, the basic human instinct to connect the two is the basis for my use of movement as a foundation for whole music.

There have been many practitioners of whole music in the history of music education. All functioned quite well without the availability of my term for them. Two of the best known are Emile

Jaques-Dalcroze, usually referred to by the single name of Dalcroze, and Carl Orff. Dalcroze (1865–1950), a Swiss music educator, was concerned about the preoccupation of music teachers with "dry facts" of music, and about the resulting shallow understanding of musical ideas. Believing that people should internalize music by experiencing it with their whole bodies, Dalcroze developed a system of kinesthetic assimilation of music, which he called "Eurhythmics." In music classes for adults as well as children, students were taught to respond to music—specifically, music improvised on a piano—with appropriate improvised body movement. For example, students would respond to fast eighth or sixteenth notes by running or taking fast little steps. Quarter notes were denoted by walking; dotted notes were skipping; half and whole notes implied continuous slow motion. The work of Dalcroze had a profound and healthy influence on philosophies of music education, including that of Carl Orff. Dalcroze practitioners, associations, and classes are still alive and well, and most of us who are devoted to vitality and innovation in music teaching owe a great deal to Dalcroze.

Carl Orff (1895–1982), a German music educator, arrived quite naturally at his devotion to movement in music education. His early teaching associates were dancers, and his early teaching was in a school of dance he founded with Dorothee Gunther. One of his interests was the incorporation of musical accompaniment provided by the dancers themselves, usually with percussion instruments. In fact, he worked toward a unified "elemental music," of which dance, drama, and music were all vital components. In his work with children, he emphasized creativity. Convinced that children should explore and learn on musical instruments that are easily played and make beautiful sounds, Orff commissioned the manufacture of barred percussion instruments of various timbres—all of high quality, with a resulting aesthetically-pleasing sound. These, along with various kinds of unpitched percussion instruments, form the "Orff instrumentarium." With these, children can explore and invent their own music as well as experiment with the ideas and conventions of music in general. If I were even a little bit rich, I would give an Orff-type barred instrument to each of my students, who now are all prospective elementary classroom teachers or school music specialists. Orff and Dalcroze were the embodiment of whole music teaching.

Some Examples of Movement in Whole Music Learning

Structured, large-muscle movement is actually a whole learning activity. It can be a music lesson—or a reading lesson or a math lesson or a language lesson. Development of each of these skills is facilitated by the mind-body organization involved in the internalization of beat and rhythm or the deliberate choreography inherent in physical games. The functioning of the human kinesthetic and cognitive structures is in itself an inherent natural rhythm: a kind of dance of muscle tissue and cortical synapses that profits from synchronized rehearsal.

In any classroom situation there are space considerations. Whenever possible, children should experience large-muscle movement with as few space constraints as possible. Outdoors would be excellent, when weather permits. However, *any* movement, even while standing beside desks, is better than none. The best way to begin in a way that minimizes self-consciousness is with children scattered about the space; they can be asked to "find your own personal space somewhere in the room." There is a little privacy this way, since attention is not focused on any one child. Later, when the students feel more at ease with these activities, a circle is effective as a kind of stage for small dramas. Children take turns as performers, learning to express themselves in front of others. The onlookers are expected to applaud, which adds self-esteem and satisfaction to the outcomes for individuals and esprit de corps for the group.

The following suggestions for movement activities are intended only as ideas for getting started. They can serve as "seeds" to evoke the children's own creative scenarios.

Free exploration

Free improvised movement to a story or to music can take the form of "follow-the-leader" type games, in which children take turns making motions for others to imitate. This can be done in a line or in a circle. A good example is "Monkey see, monkey do, monkey do the same as you," sung to the two pitches of the "calling tune," sol-mi. Classroom or percussion instruments could be incorporated. Also, children can stand in a circle taking turns contributing motions for the class to imitate to recorded music or a song.

One of the best ways to get children to move freely is to have them move while holding an object, which diverts their attention from their own bodies. With recorded music at first (instrumental music improvised by the children can be used in succeeding events), the students move to the music waving scarves, crepe paper streamers, or paper plates. Scarves and streamers lend themselves to flowing music; paper plates are good with marches or jazzy music. The usual favorite thing is shuffling to music with a paper plate under each foot. Dixieland or ragtime music is great for this.

For movement which encourages improvisation while highlighting a musical concept, the children can improvise their interpretation of suggestions such as, "Make a low, small shape. Open up the shape. Make it bigger. Make it higher." Children can take turns suggesting other shapes.

Using pantomime, children can play new roles. They can become:

- bubble gum, popcorn, a can of soda
- an appliance, such as a toaster, a blender, a washing machine
- a cough, a sneeze, a hiccup

They can walk:

- like a robot
- with one leg shorter than the other
- as if they are very sad (happy; angry; shy; afraid; guilty; etc.)
- over rapids in a wide stream, on moss-covered rocks
- on a tightrope
- as if they were pushing something heavy

Or you can have them pretend that:

- they are carrying a cup of hot coffee on an icy sidewalk out to their father, who is working in the garage.
- they are late to church, but must walk up the aisle to the front row, making as little disturbance as possible, because they are participating in the service.
- they are in a jetliner, trying to make their way back to their seat during turbulence.

Movement games

These games may overlap other categories, especially those in Chapter 5, "Whole Music Activities for Musical Understanding." Here are some of my students' favorites:

Class sculpture: Distantly related to the rowdier old game of "Statues," this activity uses the members of the class as components of a sculpture. If the class is large, a smaller group of ten or fifteen is ideal. The sculpture is "composed" by a sculptor (a student, after the initial demonstration by the teacher), who beats a drum as each student walks to the sculpture site to take his or her place. The speed at which each student walks is determined by the tempo of the drumbeat. When the drum stops, the walker stops. The sculptor then instructs the student to make a high, medium, or low shape (or a happy, sad, triumphant, etc. shape) and "freeze." Each succeeding student connects in some way to his or her adjoining component in the sculpture: hand on shoulder, back-to-back, etc. Thus, both the sculptor and the students design the resulting connected human shape. Some student sculptors enlarge the possibilities by asking students to make such shapes as a tree, a fireplug, a truck, and the like. Many of the "components" will unconsciously make graceful movements which they wouldn't dream of doing under other circumstances. The teacher should photograph the result for later display.

Along with the experiences in structured movement and spatial creativity, the sculpture game subliminally explores some musical concepts: tempo (fast and slow) and a macro-beat on the drum.

Mirror: The leader (the teacher, at first) stands in front of the room, with the students in individual spaces around the room. The students "mirror" the movements of the leader. The teacher's initial demonstration should be slow movements, one body part at a time, the more graceful, the better. The group members, intent on "mirroring," are usually quite unselfconscious about imitating these dance-like motions, and succeeding student leaders will make similar ones. The teacher can even design an extended "routine" which students will recognize and memorize after a few repetitions. Incidentally, this is an amazingly *quiet* activity.

A variation of this activity puts the students in pairs, with the partners taking turns being the mirror while the other controls the action. A signal from the teacher, such as a tap on a drum, can indicate the time to switch roles. (This is much noisier than the previous variation!)

Body machines: Students work as partners, each pair constituting a machine with two cycles. Each student decides what his or her motion will be; they then alternate their individual motions, possibly with some physical connection to each other, such as holding hands or bumping feet, for example. After a little practice at this, a drumbeat is added, with the motions done to a spoken count of "one-rest-two-rest." One of each pair of students will move on "one," the other on "two," with rests in between. For the second run-through, the leader will say aloud only the one and two, because a rest really means silence. Both leader and students will "think" the rest. On the third try, there is only a drumbeat—no spoken words—on "one" and "two," with participants "thinking" the rests.

After the machines are practiced at their two alternated cycles, each student invents a vocal or other mouth sound to accompany his or her motion. Each couple then demonstrates their motions and accompanying sounds to the rest of the group. After that, with the drumbeat to keep them together, all the machines are "turned on" at once, to the internalized count of "one-rest-two-rest."

For the full effect, the participants should be encouraged to listen to the combination of sounds and watch each other out of the corner of their eyes. The machines should be tape-recorded (or, better yet, recorded on videotape). The result is a class sound picture: a composition. Children enjoy hearing the resulting clamor, which is a musical composition: organized sound. Variation: two or more machines can be combined, or more than two students can form a machine.

Musical concepts experienced with "body machines" include timbre (quality or kind of sound), conforming to a regular beat, composing (organizing sound), and cooperating in ensemble music-making.

Movement can be devised to accompany nursery rhymes (a part of Western European heritage that is an endangered species) or other poetry for children such as that of Shel Silverstein, Dr. Suess, or A.A. Milne. (See also Appendix A.) Other vocal exercises that can be accompanied by music and motion include jumping rope to jump-rope rhymes or to original poetry by the children in the class. (See Chapter 8, Creating.)

Movement to accompany songs

There is no clear boundary between musical games, dance, and songs using motions. All of them could actually be in one category. However, I have highlighted separate categories to illustrate the various possibilities. Movements accompanying a song are simply illustrating the words. Almost any children's song could be outfitted with accompanying motions, but my examples are songs traditionally sung with gestures. See Appendix B for: *Plant My Garden, The Bus Song, Scotland's Burning,* and *Tony Chestnut.*

Musical games

In a musical game, some kind of structured game is played while the song is being sung. The game components do not always correspond with the song words. For example, in the song/game *A-Tisket, A-Tasket,* the child who is "it" is skipping around the outside of the circle while the beginning of the song is sung, an action not described in the words. There are many other possibilities.

Hand-jive

This African-American term refers to movements of the arms and hands—usually complex—to contribute a background of rhythmical movements to singing or instrumental music. Sounds are also added by clapping, snapping fingers, or slapping thighs. A relatively easy hand-jive sequence is illustrated with the song, *Miss Mary Mack,* in Appendix B. This sequence of motions is very versatile and can be used for many other children's songs.

Dance

Again, there is no exact point at which musical games or songs with gestures can be categorized as dance. In fact, with some groups of children, especially those who have become "terminally cool," such as sixth graders (and sometimes sooner), it may be better to avoid using the word "dance" altogether. The teacher of the class is the best judge of this, and of whether to stick with circle dances or incorporate dances which involve partners.

The activity mentioned earlier in which children stand in a circle, taking turns making motions to music for the group to imitate, *is* a dance. Moving to music while waving crepe paper streamers, scarves, or paper plates is also a dance. And very much a dance are the movements children do when they shuffle to *Salty Dog Rag* with a paper plate under each foot.

Some other simple songs with motions that are a dances include *Hokey Pokey, Tideo,* and *The Elephant* (see Appendix B).

Some folk dances can be taught in a very simple form. One is a simple, repetitive step that fits polka and schottische music. This is it: 1—2—3—hop, 1—2—3—hop, step—hop, step—hop, step—hop, step—hop. That's it, over and over. Children can just hop around the room singly, or can dance with partners, adding elaborations (without altering the step) such as spinning each other around, holding hands side-by-side or facing each other, etc.

Phyllis Weikart (Appendix A) suggests that children "say and do, whisper and do, think and do."

Another dance which is a favorite with everyone who tries it is a simple, repetitive step to do to any hora (Jewish, Israeli) music. This is it: 1—2—3—4—5—6—7—8, hop—kick, hop—kick, hop—kick, hop—kick. This is done in a circle with the participants' arms over each other's shoulders. The eight steps are in one direction, followed by the hop-kicks in place (kicking toward the center of the circle); then the whole thing is repeated, going the other direction.

If the teacher knows a dance and can perform it in front of the group for them simply to imitate, that works very well also. I can do some jig steps, and children love to just watch and do what I do. Repeat one step for a while until everyone is with you; then change to a different one. You can make steps up as you go along. "The chicken," the Charleston, or whatever else the teacher (or one of the children) can demonstrate are excellent dance experiences.

There are just a few things to keep in mind when introducing dance in the classroom, beyond the aforementioned considerations of whether to involve partners or mention the word "dance":

1. Keep it very simple, so that everyone can experience some success.

2. Use demonstrations and walkthroughs as well as verbal instructions. Since the venture is body movement, a symbol in itself, for some people it is confusing to translate it to linguistic symbols which must be translated back again. Others do better with verbal cues to speak—and later just think—to themselves. Other factors influence this, including immaturity, self-consciousness, and other distractions.
3. Begin very slowly, and use repetition freely.
4. If children are permitted to bring recordings to school, listen to the recordings in advance, to make certain that the lyrics are acceptable. However, in general, one of the jobs of teachers is to introduce children to *new* experiences. That includes types of music that are new to them. They really have no need to listen *again* to the music that they listen to all the time, anyway.
5. Above all, remember that it is essential for each child to feel safe and secure in the classroom. Many children do not feel good enough about themselves to move or dance in a group setting. Children should never be forced to participate, or to feel that they are being excluded or have offended the teacher if they are uncomfortable about moving their bodies in public. The teacher can be reassuring and good-natured, but continue to invite the child to join in.

For excellent guidance on teaching dance to children, refer to the works of Phyllis Weikart (see Appendix A).

Drama

Actions that tell a story are *drama*. This could include the pantomime situations described under "Pantomime" in this chapter. It could include *The Bus Song*, if children set up chairs in the form of the interior of a bus and get involved in characterizing the driver and the passengers. Funny hats and other "props" encourage dramatic touches. Songs with a cast of characters, such as *Little Rabbit Foo Foo*, can become small dramas.

Children love to act out their favorite stories. There are various ways to do this. One is to have a cast of characters in the front of the room to act out the story in pantomime while the text is being read. The story can be read aloud by the teacher, by a competent student reader, or by the class. Reading aloud as a group is a special experience and has several advantages: everyone participates, the story must be read at a moderate speed for everyone to read together, and the volume and pace of this make the reading clear and understandable. At its best, this becomes choral reading, with prearranged pitch changes according to the events in the story. A simple example would be the very low voice for Papa Bear, the medium voice for Mama Bear, etc. With an entire group doing this together, the effect is striking. An example that children love is *Possum Come a-Knockin'*, by Nancy Van Laan (see Appendix A). The cast of characters is large and appealingly rich in possibilities for characterization. (The wonderful illustrations by cartoonist George Booth are unforgettable.) Best of all, from a whole music standpoint, the whole story is written as a poem with toe-tapping, unerring beat and rhythm. A bonus learning experience is the important concept of sequence: events or words that occur in order. Like other cumulative songs and poems that progressively add new items and then review the whole collection of items in order (*The Twelve Days of Christmas*, for example), the narrative poem, *Possum*, keeps adding things, then reviewing them.

Another favorite is Maurice Sendak's *Where the Wild Things Are* (see Appendix A). The cast includes Max, his mother, and as many as seven Wild Things.

All books by Dr. Suess are excellent for reading aloud and/or dramatization. Like *Possum*, Dr. Suess's books are usually in catchy, rhythmic poetic lines. The all-time favorite of children with whom I have worked is *Horton Hatches the Egg*. This one is a good start toward making up songs; one recurrent line just *begs* to be sung: "I meant what I said, and I said what I meant. An elephant's faithful, one hundred percent." A class can make up a tune for those words, whether or not anyone, including the teacher, can write it down. For the technique, see Chapter 7.

Another possibility for dramatization is to have the children write their own story, then write a script incorporating as much as possible of the original text of the story. The story can be generated by the whole class or a smaller group (see Chapter 8, "Creating").

Movement can be used to illustrate a musical concept, as described in Chapter 5, and can be incorporated across the curriculum, as discussed in Chapter 10.

It is intriguing to imagine early hominids beating on logs and improvising a dance. Or did they improvise a song first, or did it happen simultaneously? We can never know. I have given movement a higher rank in the anthropological hierarchy by discussing it first. But singing definitely comes next.

4

Singing

Singing deserves a chapter to itself because, as Hungarian music educator Zoltan Kodály observed, the voice is the one instrument available to everyone. Moreover, that which is experienced through one's own voice is as intimate and personal as that which is experienced through movement of the rest of the body. Singing has been characterized as "heightened speech." The voice as a medium of expression is an essential avenue for whole learning. Finally, the major body of literature available for teaching music to children consists of songs.

My personal feeling is that songs and singing are overused when they are the principal, or only, musical experience offered as music instruction. When music period is invariably introduced by the distribution of song books, music becomes boring, distasteful and even dreaded by children. One could lead children through a great many valuable experiences relevant to music without having the students sing at all.

At one point in my teaching career, I did just that. The class was a group of thirty-five or so ninth grade boys, all of whom had been "dumped" into what was designated as a "boys' choir class" for a variety of reasons, none of which included interest on the part of the boys. The wall of resistance from this group was fortified by the natural insecurity about even *speaking*, let alone singing, on the part of boys with changing voices. Without comment, I constructed the class as a crash course in music fundamentals, including notation, leading to original compositions as a final project. The group became deeply involved with the class and the composition study. The compositions, performed by school performing groups and soloists at a school assembly, were impressive and in some cases amazing. The students were never required to sing a note, but the "Boys' choir class" was a smashing success. Under a different name and no longer gender-exclusive, it became a popular class for the rest of my five-year tenure at that school.

Of course, under most circumstances, omitting singing altogether is as misguided as including no music except songs. But a balance of varied musical experiences is essential: Whole music, across a wide spectrum; hence, some observations about singing.

A proverb from Zimbabwe states, "If you can walk, you can dance. If you can talk, you can sing." There is more truth to this than most people realize. The United States is not, in general, a nation of people who sing. A depressing number of people insist that they cannot sing, and many claim to be tone-deaf, or to have a "tin ear." As I mentioned earlier, I sincerely believe, after many decades as a musician and music educator, that there is no such thing as inherent tone-deafness or a "tin ear," except in cases of actual hearing loss. The essential factor in singing is *experience*: practice. The vocal cords are controlled by muscles; facility involving muscles is acquired through repetitive and focused practice. Someone who wants to excel at a physical activity *works out*. North Americans are reluctant to attempt to sing. They are timid about it, afraid of being humiliated, embarrassed about exposing something so intimate as themselves singing. In many other countries, singing is a vital part of the culture and is essential to conducting daily social business. In others, singing is an unabashed means of expression. In some countries, students walk down the street arm-in-arm, singing at the top of their lungs; people in bars and cafés burst into spontaneous, raucous, song. Not so in the United States. The only segment of the population which sings even occasionally are churchgoers. Lip-sync is in; song is out. In fact, North Americans do not even know many songs. Group-singing sessions around a piano or a campfire usually fizzle out after the first line of a song, after which no one knows any more words. The shared repertoire of most citizens of the United States (of Western European background) is *Happy Birthday; Amazing Grace; Mary Had a Little Lamb; Twinkle, Twinkle; Old MacDonald;* and some Christmas carols.

This is not a nation of tone-deaf people with tin ears. It is a culture which, after early childhood, does not sing, which explains the immaturity of the repertoire. To be able to sing, one must *do* that. The only persons in a position to reverse this trend are probably school teachers and parents—a heavy responsibility, indeed.

It is true that some people seem to be able to sing without effort. It is unclear why this is so, although Gardner's theory that one of the intelligences is musical intelligence may be a partial answer. However, anyone can learn to sing, even people with hearing loss.

The Development of Singing in Children

Howard Gardner has done a great deal of research on the development of singing in children. The following is a brief summary of his findings (Gardner 1981). Children at the age of . . .

- up to one year: imitate the intonational patterns, or "song qualities," of speech. Many infants can match specific pitches with far greater than chance accuracy.
- one year to 15 months: produce wave-like melodic fragments with no strong musical identity. This is analogous to the babbling that introduces language development.
- one-and-a-half years: can produce, for the first time, discrete pitches. This is analogous to early babbling developing into production of specific words.
- one-and-a-half to two-and-a-half years: are able to sing their first intervals: seconds, minor and major thirds.
- second and third years: sing a repetitive drill of those intervals in fragments and begin development of intervals of a fourth and fifth. Their spontaneous song, like the early subsong of birds, is undefined, unorganized, and rhythmically irregular.
- two-and-a-half years: demonstrate awareness of the tunes sung by others in their environment. Fledgling efforts to reproduce these tunes are mostly fragments, often recognizable only by the lyrics. The tune is still spontaneous song.
- end of third year: show awareness of the rhythmic structure of music in the environment. There is now both a lyrical and rhythmic resemblance to the cultural model. Three-year-olds explore the building blocks of learned song. Characteristic bits are repeated over and over, as a young bird does at this stage.
- three or four years: experience a sea change: they attempt to reproduce the overall learned song, which replaces spontaneous song. Listeners must still rely on lyrics and rhythm to recognize the song, since these singers still lack a sense of key, except for ups and downs.
- five years: can produce particular intervals and are aware of an organizing key.

Gardner concludes that ". . . children seem predisposed at a certain point in development to acquire the forms of the culture. In the absence of cultural instruction, it seems likely that development would cease altogether" (1981, 103).

Thus, according to Howard Gardner, does Nature take care of the early development of song. After that, a great deal is dependent on nurture. Children need to be sung to, to hear other people sing, to sing with other people, to sing and be encouraged by others.

I have heard many adults describe their childhood experience of being asked by a teacher or a choir director to "move your lips, but don't sing, so you won't spoil the program." Others have described music class groupings with names like "Larks, Sparrows, and Crows." The children classified as crows probably never again tried to sing. We can hope that today's more enlightened educators would never do these things, but more subtle attitudes can silence budding singers. Even a mild display of amusement on the part of an adult listener when a child sings can cause the child to burn with humiliation. Singing has been called "heightened speech." When there is something too serious, profound, or urgent for speech, human beings often use song: for hymns and religious chants, for love songs, for mourning, for expressions of deep joy. When we sing, we expose our inner selves, which are tender and vulnerable. It takes courage to do that. When a listener reacts with amusement, derision or criticism, a kind of internal bleeding takes place. It is important, then, to handle a child singer with care. In fact, that goes for a singer of any age.

According to Gardner's chronology of singing development, the last element to emerge is an awareness of pitch. Infants can often match pitches, but seem to lose that ability before the end of the first year. When a child has reached the age of about five, when this perception reappears, is the perfect time for some "pitch-nurture" to take place. Both classroom teachers and music specialists can help.

The "Ur-song" and the Pentatonic Scale

In 1973, composer/conductor Leonard Bernstein was invited to give the Norton Lectures at Harvard University. His theme, inspired by the work of linguist Noam Chomsky, was the possibility of an innate human cognitive system for the acquisition of music (Bernstein 1976). Bernstein hypothesized that such a system is parallel to or related to the cognitive system for language acquisition described earlier by Chomsky.

As evidence of the existence of this innate musical processing system, Bernstein cited the nearly universal vocative tune or calling tune: the two or three pitches used when a name is called out. These pitches incorporate the descending minor third interval (*sol-mi*), with sometimes an added lower, but unfixed, pitch to accommodate more syllables.

[Musical notation showing names fitted to calling tune: John, San-dy, A-lo-y-sius, A-lon-zo, Pam-e-la, A-ber-na-thy]

FIGURE 4-1: *Fitting names to the calling tune*

Phonologist Mark Liberman (1979) hypothesized that internalized *grammars* prescribe *transformation rules* for fitting utterances to the "tunes" of a language. Virtually every speaker of English, and many other languages as well, uses the same transformation rules for fitting names to the vocative (calling) tune (Figure 4-1).

A related "tune," also cited by Bernstein, is the children's "taunting chant" ("Neener, neener, neener!" "Johnny's got a girlfriend!"), which consists of the same notes as the calling tune—the descending minor third interval (sol-mi)—plus one higher pitch (la). This tune, like the calling tune, is a cultural component of every society with some connection to European tradition, and it has appeared in others as well. Howard Gardner (1981) refers to this tune as the "Ur-song," a reference to the "Ur-language," a hypothetical primal language from which all others may have evolved (Figure 4-2).

Although controversy exists about the assumption that the vocative tune and the Ur-song are basic components of human behavior, the assumption is certainly applicable to beneficiaries of a Western European or Northern Mediterranean inheritance. Many children's songs that seem to materialize in children as child folklore (learned from each other rather than from adults) are based upon the Ur-song and on the pentatonic scale, which adds to sol, mi, and la two additional pitches, do and re. The pentatonic scale, *Do Re Mi Sol La*, has only whole steps (major second intervals) and no half steps (minor second intervals) and embraces the minor third (Figure 4-3).

[Musical notation of the taunting tune]

FIGURE 4-2: *The "taunting tune"*

FIGURE 4-3: *The pentatonic scale*

Cultures whose music uses the pentatonic scale include, among many others, Asian and Native American. (Native Americans may have carried pentatonic music across the Bering Strait from Asia.)

English language Ur-song and pentatonic songs are so common that we could add them to the previously-enumerated song repertoire in the United States. These include *Goodnight, Sleep Tight; Ring Around the Rosy; Rain, Rain; It's Raining; A-Tisket, A-Tasket; See-Saw, Margery Daw;* and *Teddy Bear, Teddy Bear.* Some not-so-obvious ones are *Bow-Wow-Wow* and *Shortnin' Bread* (which has a long history and may have originated in Africa). *Amazing Grace,* and *Michael, Row Your Boat Ashore* have only one pitch each that is outside the pentatonic scale.

Before Bernstein, renowned music educators Zoltan Kodály (1882–1967) in Hungary and Carl Orff (1895–1982) in Germany both used music instruction sequences that introduced music-making by beginning with sol-mi and sol-mi-la, then progressing to the pentatonic scale. In the United States, the innovative Pillsbury Foundation for the Advancement of Music Education (1977; reprint 1993) observed and utilized the universality of the vocative tune and the Ur-song.

This constitutes historic, fully-researched reassurance that there is a natural, accessible way to help young children learn to match a pitch. The teacher who asks children to sing the calling tune or the Ur-song is not asking too much, since all children use them on the front porch and the playground, anyway.

Uses for the "calling tune" and the "Ur-song"

At the beginning of each of these exercises, it is important to emphasize a starting pitch first, giving the children time to try to match it.

Calling the class roll, singing the children's first names to the calling tune. The class will be asked to respond, imitating the teacher's tune and (as closely as possible) pitches, singing, "He's here," "She's here," or "Ab-sent." (Children know who is absent.) Later, children can be asked to respond alone to their own names; the class fills in "ab-sent." At first, if the children even approximate the pitches and interval (the first pitch higher than the second), progress is being made. The next step is to direct the child toward the correct pitch with hand gestures to indicate, "make it higher" or "make it lower," nodding emphatically and happily when the child approaches the correct pitch. (See "Exploring the Voice" later in this chapter.)

Composing original songs. When children "make up" a song or a tune for some words, they often use the "Ur-song." This is natural and satisfying. Later, the teacher can gently encourage some wider melodic horizons.

Singing pieces of information, such as spelling or multiplication tables. Examples of this could include "c-l-e-f, that spe--ells treble clef." "Everybody hear me: seven-times-nine is 63!"

Participating in a story being read by singing a recurrent phrase to the Ur-song. A story that has this built in is *Mortimer*, a delightful story by Robert Munsch about a little boy who won't be quiet (see Appendix A). Children love to join in with Mortimer's cheeky little song, "Cling, clang, rattle-bing-bang, going to make my noise all day." There are other opportunities for participation in this story, including stamping feet when the various protagonists clump up the stairs, and joining in with the recurrent admonition, "Mortimer, be quiet!" The illustrations are appealing and are printed opposite each page of text so that the teacher can display the illustration while reading.

Creating small pieces of drama in which the protagonists sing something to each other in the Ur-song. This is a good activity with puppets, which the children can make out of paper lunch bags, using the folded (bottom) part for the mouth. A little conversation that already exists in children's folklore is the following:

Puppet 1	**Puppet 2**
Hello, sir!	Hello, sir!
Won't you come out and play, sir?	No, sir.
Why, sir?	Because I have a cold, sir.
Where did you catch a cold, sir?	At the North Pole, sir.
What were you doing there, sir?	Catching polar bears, sir.
How many did you catch, sir?	One, sir, two, sir, three, sir, and That's enough for me, sir!

This has the additional advantage that children who are otherwise too timid to sing will sing when it is the puppet who is singing and not the child.

Whole Music and Singing

The antithesis of a whole music approach to singing is the hypothetical (but still, alas, all too common) teacher who conscientiously includes music in the classroom but accomplishes that with an invariable routine of passing out basic music series textbooks and occasionally having the class listen, with minimum preparation, to a recording. Whole music is *making* music. Note the deferred position of notation and music-reading in the sequence of this book. Hands-on (or, rather, voice-on) experience with singing and *hearing oneself singing* (not covered up by a recording or piano) should precede the introduction of music reading, just as children learn to read language only after experience with language.

Exploring the voice

An essential step in learning to sing is exploring the workings of one's own voice, and how it "feels" to make the pitch go higher or lower:

Making glissandos (sliding, waving sounds) and sooping sounds. Since this activity could unleash chaos in an elementary class if it were unstructured, the teacher can invent scenarios of which the sounds are a part; for example, a story that incorporates sound effects provided by the students. The best kinds of sounds for exploring are imitations of sirens, wave-like sounds, insect noises, and airplanes. The teacher can improvise a story which uses these sound effects, rehearsing them before the story begins. A rehearsed "cut-off" signal is also needed, such as a thumb-and-fingers scissors motion. The teacher then reads the story, pausing for the appropriate sound effects. (This is a rather awkward story because it attempts to incorporate *all* the above sounds.)

> Once upon a time, a sailor was working on his ship during a storm. The waves were *very* high, making the ship go up and down, up and down. [pause for wide, wave-like vocal sounds. Cut-off.] Suddenly, he heard the siren [pause for siren noises. Cut-off.] that meant to abandon ship. He grabbed a life-preserver and jumped overboard from the high deck, way down into the water. [pause for sound that begins high and swoops down low. Cut-off.] When he was afloat again, he could see the other sailors all around, bobbing around on life rafts and life preservers. [pause for wave-like sounds. Cut-off.] Everyone stayed this way for a long time. Once, a mosquito landed on the sailor's arm. [pause for high mosquito noise, with the sudden stop that means it has landed.] The sailor wondered, "What is a mosquito [pause for mosquito noise] doing way out here?" Just as he realized that this meant that land was near, he heard an

airplane. [pause for level airplane sound. Cut-off.] The pilot saw the sailors in the water and made a pass over them [pause for sound of airplane swooping down, then back up. Cut-off.] Soon a rescue ship arrived [pause for low sound of ship's motor. Cut-off.] and picked all of the sailors safely out of the water.

Making a bulletin board of pictures (drawn by the children or cut from magazines) of things which make high and/or low sounds. The teacher can prepare a bulletin board with three available blank sections labeled "High Sounds," "Low Sounds," and "High and Low Sounds." Each student holds up what he or she has brought, identifying it as a high sound (bird), low sound (automobile), or something that can make high or low sounds (piano). In each case, the class then makes a sound corresponding to the picture. (Individual children are often too timid to make the sound but enjoy being the motivation for the exuberant sound effects provided by the class.) While making the sounds, the children put their hands on their own throats to explore what the muscles are doing to make the sound, and how it "feels," both inside and out, to make a high or low sound. The student then posts his or her picture under the appropriate heading on the bulletin board.

Group reading (aloud) of stories that can illustrate particular characters or events by changing pitch levels. "Goldilocks and the Three Bears" is an obvious example, but many children's stories can be read this way.

Rhythmic chants incorporating pitch. The class can be divided into three groups, each group chanting the name of one of the group members (George, Nancy, Melissa). The teacher drums a steady macrobeat and demonstrates the rhythm and approximate pitch that will be used for each name. The pitch need not be exact; high, medium, and low will do. One name might be drawn out in a low pitch over two beats (Geo--orge) Another might be repeated in a high voice twice on each beat (Nancy-Nancy). "Melissa" fits into two beats very well, with the first syllable as a pick-up note. Exaggerating the sibilance of the esses contributes to an interesting sound texture. Beginning with one name, the other two are added consecutively. The effect is invigorating; the students usually like to hear their own names used; rhythm and conforming to a macrobeat are incorporated; and the children explore their voices and pitch. (See also "Beat, Rhythm, and Pitch," in Chapter 5.)

Kazoos. Children can make their own kazoos from an empty toilet paper roll. The teacher cuts squares of waxed paper about 4" × 4".

One of these is stretched over the end of each toilet paper roll and held in place with a rubber band. The teacher takes a pocket knife around the class, making a little slit about a quarter of an inch long in the middle of each piece of waxed paper. The kazoo is "played" by humming (not blowing) into the open end of the kazoo. After a little experimentation, the children can find the right volume level to get the kazoo to "buzz" with their voices. This is another way to cajole timid children to sing. *O, Susanna* sounds very funny through a kazoo and will receive enthusiastic participation. The voice explorations can also be done through a kazoo.

Singing along with a chant is discussed under "Harmony" in Chapter 5.

Matching a pitch. This is the process of ear-training, and it includes three skills which can be difficult to develop without outside help, that is, someone to monitor:

1. Perceiving the pitch the leader is singing and ascertaining if what one is singing oneself is the same as the target pitch (what the leader is singing)
2. Perceiving if one's own pitch is higher or lower than the target pitch
3. Learning how the larynx (voice box) feels when the pitch goes higher or lower, and learning to control it

As with any other kinesthetic task, all of this requires focus and practice. It is a great help to have someone listening and pointing whether to sing higher or lower to match the target pitch, then confirming when it is reached. However, practice and progress can and do take place without the direct attention of the teacher, particularly if a few suggestions have already been made. Children who sing with a group in which are all singing (approximately!) the same thing have an opportunity to learn to match the others without the pressure of the spotlight. A comfortable beginning can be using the natural, familiar tunes with which they call to or jeer at their friends (the "calling tune" and the "Neener-neener" song. See "The Ur-song and the pentatonic scale" earlier in this chapter.)

Movement with singing

The whole body can take part in singing. While even a very formal choir is usually instructed by its director to look pleasant when that is appropriate, a gospel choir really gets "into" the music physically. As a result, gospel groups usually produce music of great vitality, with the energy of the whole body behind it.

Zoltan Kodály was a whole music practitioner, in that he incorporated body language: he used hand signals for the relative pitches of the scale, beginning with sol-mi, then sol-mi-la, then the pentatonic scale, and finally the entire diatonic scale (Figure 4-4).

Although Englishman John Curwen probably originated this particular set of signals, Kodály appropriated and popularized them. Today, all over the world, Kodály educators and other teachers train their students to use and follow these signals. The specific hand motion for each pitch incorporates movement up or down in space relative to the size of the interval between pitches. This is a kinesthetic reinforcement of the aural perception and the sensation of making the vocal cords match it. A teacher who is willing to train his or her students with this method will be giving the students a solid background in understanding pitch and intervals (see also Chapter 5).

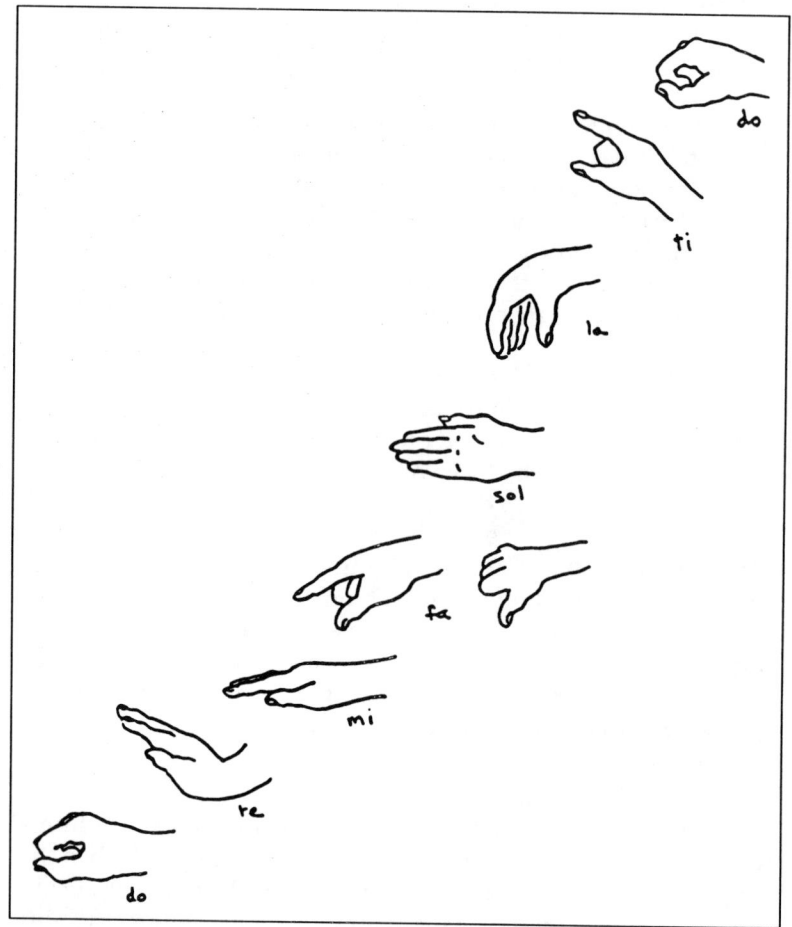

FIGURE 4-4: *Hand signals for pitch*

If the teacher feels unprepared for this task, the time-honored method of "lining-out" can be used. Song leaders in rural churches have used this method for centuries: the leader sings one line at a time (hence the term *lining out*), pausing for the congregation or choir to repeat it. Along with singing the song, the leader often maps out with his or her level hand in space the direction of the melody and the approximate size of the intervals. Sometimes the singers follow along with their hands, mirroring the leader's hand motions. The pitch indications of a good leader anticipate the actual pitch change by a second or two, giving the singers time to prepare their voices and follow along with their hands. Lining out is less sophisticated and precise than Kodály's hand signals, but it provides kinesthetic reinforcement.

Kinesthetic reinforcement for beat and tempo can be shared by a group. With the group standing in a circle or a line, the teacher indicates the target beat; each student taps this beat on the shoulder of his or her neighbor until the whole group is tapping and feeling the beat together. Wherever appropriate, body movements should be incorporated into singing. In addition to songs which traditionally include motions (see "Movement to accompany songs," in Chapter 3), motions can be devised by the class and the teacher for other songs, including original songs by the students. Rounds are very effective with motions, since the motions are in canon as well as the music and words. My example is *Scotland's Burning* (see Appendix B).

Using sign-language from the repertoire of the hearing-impaired can be a profound experience for both the singers and the audience. Sign language is beautiful and graceful to perform and observe; it can internalize the meaning of the song far beyond simply singing the words.

Directors of secondary school swing choirs or jazz choirs incorporate choreography with their routines, often paying sizable fees to professional choreographers for help. Although this occasionally gets out of hand and obscures the music and/or good vocal technique, the movement part is vitalizing for the singers and pleasing to the audience. Elementary teachers and students can devise their own choreography.

Pictures, props, and costumes

Other visual effects can also be a part of singing. That includes appropriate pictures, "props," and costumes. Pictures can add to the enjoyment of the song and help children remember the sequence of the words. To repeat the example of *The Twelve Days of Christmas*, children can make pictures to cue and illustrate each of the verses, holding up each picture when appropriate, displaying them in succession during the cumulative part. "Props" or objects (from the theatre term, "properties" for objects used in the stage business) can also enliven the experience; an example would be all members of an early childhood class bringing teddy bears to participate in singing and dancing *Teddy Bear*. Costumes are as versatile as imagination can make them. They enrich songs from specific cultures, about seasons, community life, history, or almost any other theme. They can merely be hats, or the entire class can wear white gloves to highlight the motions accompanying the song. Costumes can be as elaborate as authentic costumes of a historical period. Singing can be an integral part of a unit that also incorporates drama (with costumes and props), models, ethnic food, creative writing, and visual art.

Music literature/repertoire

Kodály, in his splendid sequential and comprehensive curriculum plan for the public school music program in Hungary, spent a great deal of time on sol-mi, sol-mi-la, and pentatonic scales. At that time, the now-ubiquitous media were not a factor. Moreover, Hungary has geographic and consequently cultural ties to Asia, where traditional music was pentatonic.

However, I believe that in the United States, where children are virtually bombarded with the musical idiom of their culture (including some fine positive examples, such as the Sesame Street television programs), they are thoroughly programmed with music of the entire scale. After—and during—the use of Ur-song and pentatonic music for work on matching pitch, children are certainly ready to sing music using the entire diatonic scale. Much of the music of the Western world is *Do-Re* based, rather than *Sol-Mi*. Remaining too long with limited pitch range will frustrate and bore children in the United States.

There is no shortage of repertoire for children of all ages. Take into consideration what the group might think is silly or un-cool, but don't be constrained too much by that. Children like songs with which they are familiar. If they know a song, they feel secure singing it. Conversely, they will groan and complain whenever anything new is introduced, *whatever* it is. When you have chosen a song for your own reasons, stand by your plan and go on with it in a cheerful but businesslike manner, ignoring negative reactions. If you yourself are positive about the song, the class will come around. Provided that you have the good judgment not to try to teach *Would That I Were a Tender Apple Blossom* to sixth grade boys, your song will not be a bomb.

Finally, search outside the Western European tradition for the untapped wealth of songs from other cultures. Elementary school children are still at the age when their cognitive structures are programmed for assimilating language as well as music. They learn utterances from other languages as well as new sound sequences with much greater ease than adults do. My examples are *Mi Chacra* and *l'Araña Pequeñita* (*Eensy, Weensy Spider*) in Spanish, and the *Navajo Happy Song* (see Appendix B). This is excellent enrichment as social studies illustrative material. However, it becomes more than enrichment if students in the class represent particular cultural groups such as African American, Iranian, or Hispanic. It is essential. Whole music, like whole language, is a contextual approach to learning experiences, drawing from the broadest frame of reference relevant to the child: the culture of the family, the community and beyond. The songs explored in the classroom should reflect all of that.

Some general aspects of classroom singing

To reiterate, song-leaders should keep in mind when pitch-matching/ear-training: Sing the starting pitch in isolation first, using the first syllable of the song. (For instance, for *Twinkle, Twinkle,* use "Tweng—".) Move around the room, repeating this pitch with the syllable, giving everyone a chance to match it. Then return to the front of the room and proceed with the song. Many people who are leading songs assume that if they just start off, the group will join in. For children (or adults) just learning pitch-matching, this is not a valid assumption. The singers must have a chance to explore the target pitch and analyze how it *feels* to make the correct pitch.

In teaching a song, it is usually a good idea to teach the *words first*. The singers will have already internalized the rhythmic structure, which is determined by the words. Incorporating the melody after that is much easier. Having said this, I must explain the reason for this contradiction of the usual whole music philosophy of presenting the whole first, with its elements in context. Teaching the words first has less to do with whole music than with accommodating singing anxiety. If the words (hence also the rhythm) of the words are secure, the singer has more confidence about embarking on the tune.

One way to teach song words is to write them on a chalkboard, having the children chant them. Then begin to erase a few words each time the words are repeated until all are erased, by which time the group has memorized them (the *Cloze procedure*). The teacher then sings the tune, which the children add by rote to the rhythmic framework already prepared.

Any teacher, whether musically-trained or not, can work with tone quality and voice production with children. Influenced by some popular singers on television, children often seem to feel that good singing is shouting. Children's voices should not be strained. Their teacher should be working toward the unique, lyrical sound of children's natural, light voices rather than a full, adult sound. The tone should be the unforced "head voice" rather than a "chest voice" forced up into the children's range. The children can be helped to visualize their voices as coming from the top of the mouth or the top of the head. Many instructors use the metaphor of pulling the voice out the top of the head with an imaginary piece of string. Use whatever image produces results.

Children can also learn breath control. The teacher can demonstrate filling the diaphragm area with air, which pushes the abdomen out. This idea must replace their image of "taking a deep breath," in which the chest comes out, or the shoulders come up. They can practice feeling their diaphragms pushing the breath up through the vocal cords. They can learn to breathe between phrases rather than in the middle of them. The teacher can amuse and illustrate with an exaggerated demonstration: sing "My country [huge, audible intake of breath], 'tis of thee . . ." and ask them what is wrong with that. Then have them speak the words to a song, identifying where it would make sense to pause for breath.

Singing: About as Whole as We Can Get

Whole music: involving the whole child, the whole body, the whole environment relevant to the child; beginning with a whole context and working from that to the components. An overview of this chapter on singing confirms that singing is about as whole as we can get. As heightened speech, it originates from an intimate place in the depths of the person. It is a facet of natural human development, probably with cognitive structures programmed to receive it and demonstrably predictable stages. Entire populations share the vocative tune and the Ur-song as basic components of behavior. The voice, along with other avenues of perception, is a valuable learning tool. Singing can involve not only the vocal cords, auditory apparatus, and respiratory system, but also the whole body, with illustrative motions, exuberant body language, hand signals for pitch, and dramatization. Singing can incorporate visual devices, such as pictures, props, and costumes. Songs can reflect the demographics of the family and community; repertoire can come from all over the world. Musical concepts include beat, rhythm, pitch, intervals, dynamics, tempo, tone quality, form, and phrasing. Although singing should not be the only musical activity in the classroom, it does involve an instrument which everyone has, and there really is no such thing as a tin ear, except in the case of actual hearing loss. Singing touches all the whole music bases, which is why it rated a chapter all to itself.

Whole Music Activities for Musical Understanding, Part I

The musical explorations in this chapter constitute a sequence that leads to a basic understanding of musical concepts, which are the components of music.

For Elementary Classroom Teachers

For elementary classroom teachers, the material in this chapter is a step-by-step sequence so that you and your students can become familiar with music terms and concepts together. Chapter 6 represents a point at which your objectives diverge from those of music specialists so that, after Chapter 5, you will probably want to skip directly to Chapter 7.

For Music Specialists

For the objectives of music specialists, Chapters 5 and 6 constitute a step-by-step sequence that explores most of the fundamentals of music through a whole music approach. Each step in the sequence can lead to the next; the outline can serve as a framework for curriculum and lesson planning.

This chapter provides the basic foundation, the "whole" end of the whole-to-part sequence. Chapter 6 develops the sequence in greater detail. The explanations of music terms and concepts are not intended for you, but instead will serve as a "script" for explaining things to your students.

For Both Music Specialists and Elementary Classroom Teachers

These activities can be plucked out of sequence and either integrated into work in another subject area or used as a mini-music lesson. For *both* music specialists and classroom teachers, these exercises can be *fillers*. I bring this up without apology, because in the real world, we have all experienced that five minutes before recess when the lesson plan has run out, or a Monday morning after a weekend out of town. The following are little adventures in musical concepts, and they are no less valuable when used *detached* to fill a time period that would otherwise be traumatic for the teacher.

Rhythmic Organization: Beat, Rhythm, and Meter

Music is organized sound. One of the ways in which it can be organized is by duration: long and short sounds and silences, and sounds at regular intervals. This was probably the original way that early humans began to organize sound, using some resonant object, such as a hollow log, and only later developing drums and other percussion instruments.

Beat

Beat can be defined as the *basic pulse*. Our own bodies acquaint us with beat in the form of heartbeat and pulse. Children can be introduced to the concept of beat through awareness of these bodily functions. When we find ourselves tapping our feet to music, that is keeping the beat.

Jumping rope. Children can experience the underlying regular beat, or macrobeat, by jumping rope. Whether novice or athlete, a rope-jumper keeps a steady beat. Although he or she may go faster or slower, the swinging of the rope cannot be erratic. It must be steady. People jumping rope often add a little mini-jump between jumps; this is the *offbeat*. By subdividing the pulse, this in-between jump adds an additional structure to the framework, helping to keep the beat steady. Clapping can be kept steady in the same way: by adding a gesture (usually throwing the hands out to the side, palms up) on the offbeats, between the claps (beats).

Bouncing a ball. Bouncing a ball is another demonstration of beat. The most skillful handlers of a basketball cannot bounce it erratically, as in Morse code. A ball is bounced with a steady beat, or macrobeat, even if the *tempo* (or *speed*) changes.

Singing songs with motions. Motions added to a song usually fall on the beat. For an example of this, see Appendix B for *Miss Mary Mack*.

Playing "beanbag switch." Participants stand in a circle, shoulder to shoulder, each holding out his or her right hand. To a steady drumbeat, a beanbag is passed clockwise around the circle, right hand to right hand. The objective is to place the beanbag in one's neighbor's hand exactly on the beat, which requires, on a slow beat, moving the beanbag in an arching motion to its destination. The drumbeat can vary in tempo, as long as it is not so fast as to be physically impossible. For very young children, this is advanced enough. For older children, there is higher level. When the drummer gives the order to "switch!" the person holding the beanbag puts it into his or her own left hand on the beat. The other participants raise left hands instead of right hands. Without missing a beat, the beanbag is now passed from left hand to left hand, counterclockwise around the circle. Even junior high and high school students enjoy this, and it is a *trainable* skill. The students improve with practice.

Rhythm

Rhythm may be defined as *sound patterns superimposed over a beat*. The regular beat, or macrobeat, is the underlying pulse. Rhythmic patterns are embroidered on top of the beat. Every language has characteristic rhythmic patterns in individual words as well as phrases. The words of a song usually dictate the rhythmic patterns of the music. In fact, the instrumental music of a culture, although it has no words, often reflects the rhythmic and intonational patterns of the native language. Some whole music examples of exploring rhythm:

Chanting rhythmic patterns with a jump rope or a bouncing ball. A student or several students bounce balls or jump rope together at a steady pace at the front of the room. When they are embarked on a unified, steady beat, the class can superimpose rhythmic patterns by chanting a poem or words to a song. Example:

Blackbird, blackbird, sittin' on a rail,
Pickin' his teeth with the end of his tail.

[Or, for a syncopated, jazzy rhythm:]

Got along without ya before I met ya, gonna get along without ya now.
You ran around with every gal in town.
You'll never know how it got me down.
Got along without ya before I met ya, gonna get along without ya
now. (old blues song)

The teacher can point out that the ball bouncers or rope jumpers cannot make the jump rope or the ball perform to a rhythm such as . . . Pickin' his teeth with the end of his tail." The swinging of the rope or bouncing of the ball must remain steady (on the beat) while the voices distribute the rhythm over the beat. To highlight the distinction between rhythm and beat, the rhythm can be translated from spoken words to clapping; the children think the words and clap out the syllables over the beat. See Joanna Cole's *Anna Banana* for a compilation of 101 jump rope rhymes (see Appendix A).

Playing the "string string bass." Each student is given a piece of string about a yard long. One end of the string is held taut under the foot while the other end is stretched over the end of the index finger and held in the ear (see illustration in Appendix B). The child then strums the string with the other hand, with the resulting effect in the ear of a string bass. Tightening the string raises the pitch; loosening lowers it. The "bass player" can start by keeping a beat, then progress to "riffs" (rhythmic patterns). A recording of country-and-western music is satisfying to strum to. Young children and those with physical limitations sometimes cannot manage the physical coordination required to hold a string in their ears. They can, instead, just press the string right in front of the ear canal, or on the bone behind the ear.

Chanting rhythmic word patterns in three parts. This activity makes use of the innate rhythm of spoken words. The class is divided into three groups, each one chanting one of the student's names. Each can be a different rhythmic pattern; variation is accomplished easily by using names with different numbers of syllables. Variations in dynamics and pitch may be added. (See also "Rhythmic chants incorporating pitch," under "Exploring the voice," in Chapter 4.) In addition to names, the chants can utilize descriptions of the weather ("cold," "cloudy," "raining-raining-raining"), food items ("french fries," "pizza," "apple pie"—This technique has been exploited by McDonald's in advertising), or automobile brand names. Drums or other percussion instruments are a good addition, and a student conductor can keep everything all together.

Making rhythmic sound gestures. The sound gestures originated by Carl Orff may be used to help students internalize rhythmic patterns. The sound gestures are clap, snap, *patsch* (slap thighs), and stamp. Orff's original German term describing these activities translates to "body sounds" in English, but any teacher can predict the class reaction if the teacher asks for *body sounds;* hence, *sound gestures* is a good substitute.

A leader produces rhythmic patterns with sound gestures, first with only one (such as clapping), then incorporating two types such as clapping and patsching), and finally three and four. After each rhythmic pattern (to a steady beat), the class imitates the pattern, without losing the beat. It is a good idea to introduce patterns initially using three or four sound gestures by going from the top down, or vice versa (snap, clap, patsch, stamp). This is a *trainable* skill, both on the part of the leader and the class. As the skill level increases, the children can advance to the stage of doing the rhythmic patterns and imitations in canon. While the students are imitating one pattern, the leader is producing the next one, and so on. Children can become quite competent at this.

A word about handclapping: there are actually several different types. The most exuberant involves the entire arms/hands moving as units from the shoulder down, fitting the entire flattened hands together (the "seal" clap, observable in the inventors at Sea World). This requires quite a bit of large-muscle coordination and is really very difficult for young children. A much easier gesture is holding one hand stable, palm up and slightly cupped, and striking the palm with the closed fingers of the other hand. This can be just as satisfyingly loud as the seal clap. A variation with lower volume and different timbre is the "alligator clap," which is striking the cupped palm with two fingers of the other hand.

Meter

Meter refers to *measured beat*. In other words, measuring out beats into sections of two, three, or four, depending upon the *accent*. The characteristic rhythm patterns of languages also are determined by accent; consequently, the meter of a song is usually determined by the stresses of its words. Even the meter of music without words often similarly reflects the cultural speech rhythms.

Meter can be *duple*: "ONE – two, ONE – two" or "ONE – two – THREE – four." Most children's songs and the majority of "pop" or folk songs are in duple meter. Many theories exist about the reason for this, most alluding to the fact that the natural beats of the human body, the pulse and the heartbeat, can be said to be in duple meter. (You are in trouble if your heartbeat or pulse sounds like "ONE – two – three, ONE – two – three" rather than "ONE – two, ONE – two.") An example of a song in duple meter is "TWINK – le, TWINK – le, LIT – tle STAR . . ." Early pop musicians referred to duple meter as "BOOM – chick, BOOM – chick." This is a good phrase to use to give children an illustration of duple meter.

Meter can be *triple*, as in "ONE – two – three, ONE – two – three." The early pop musicians' phrase for this was "OOM – pah – pah, OOM – pah – pah," another good example of triple meter for

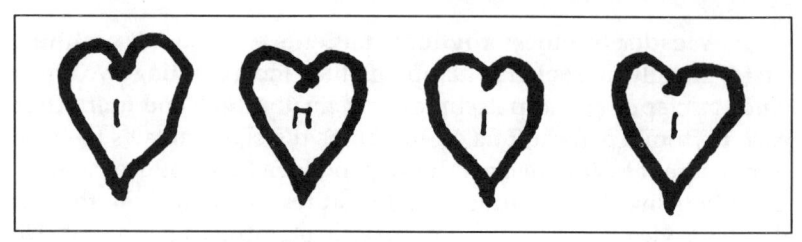

FIGURE 5-1: *Meter expressed in heartbeats*

FIGURE 5-2: *Meter (or time) signature and measure lines*

children. This is the meter of a waltz and a few common songs like *Happy Birthday* and *The First Noel*.

Although the heartbeat can be said to be in duple meter, Kodály educators introduce meter by using a heartbeat symbol to represent individual beats, whatever the meter. Meter is introduced with these symbols in groups of two, three, or four, with a number beside the grouping to confirm the meter (Figure 5-1):

This leads to the introduction of *measures*, the sections in notated music which divide the beats into groups of two, three, four (or more), according to the meter. The meter is indicated by the *meter signature* (also called the *time signature*), which looks like but is not a fraction. Lines which divide the music into measures are called *measure lines* or *bar lines*. The top number of the meter section indicates how many beats are in each measure. The bottom number specifies what kind of note in this composition gets one beat (Figure 5-2):

Music specialists who are going to teach the significance of the bottom and top numbers of the meter/time signature should understand that explaining the meaning of these—at least the bottom number—will be one of the most difficult challenges you will face in the area of music concepts. It is important to emphasize that this is not a fraction because it will be further complicated if the students think that it is. Please take my word for it! Explanation of the bottom number of the meter signature is among the last of the "parts" after the sequence of building the whole. (See "Meter" in Chapter 6.)

Here are a couple of whole music activities for exploring meter:

Chanting duple-meter poems to "BOOM – chick" (or "ONE – two") and triple-meter poems to "OOM – pah – pah" (or "ONE – two – three). The class is divided into two parts; one group will chant "BOOM – chick, BOOM – chick" (or ONE – two, ONE – two), while the other group chants the poem (see below). The two will "fit" together. The addition of a drumbeat and a conductor will help keep things steady.

Many poems or song words are clearly either duple or triple meter. However, some texts can be fitted to either duple or triple meter, depending on one's viewpoint. Identifying which is which sometimes requires an expert. Here is *Blackbird* to use for duple meter:

> 2 Black - bird,   black - bird,   sittin' on a   rail   [rest]
>   BOOM-chick, BOOM-chick, BOOM chick, BOOM-chick
>
>   Pickin' his   teeth with the end of his   tail. [rest]
>   BOOM-chick, BOOM-chick,   BOOM - chick, BOOM-chick.

For triple meter, the "BOOM – chick" or "ONE — two" group will instead chant "OOM – pah – pah" or "ONE – two – three," while the other group tries to chant "Blackbird." Chaos will result, and the point is made that "Blackbird" is in duple meter, and won't fit into triple meter. The accents and rhythm of the words dictate the duple rhythm.

Now do the "OOM – pah – pah" chant with a poem in triple meter. Here is part of "Wheezles and Sneezles," from A. A. Milne's *When We Were Very Young*. (See Appendix A.) It fits into triple meter:

> 3   Chris – to – pher   Ro – bin had   whee – zles and   snee – zles. They
>   OOM-pah-pah,   OOM-pah-pah,   OOM-pah-pah,   OOM-pah-pah
>
>   Bun – dled – him   in –   to – his –   bed. [rest rest rest rest] They
>   OOM-pah-pah,   OOM-pah-pah,   OOM-pah-pah,   OOM-pah- pah
>
>   Gave him what   goes with a   cold in the   nose and some
>   OOM-pah-pah,   OOM-pah-pah,   OOM-pah-pah,   OOM-pah-pah
>
>   More for a   cold in   the   head [rest rest   rest rest]
>   OOM-pah-pah,   OOM-pah-pah,   OOM-pah-pah,   OOM-pah-pah

Now have the "OOM – pah–pah" or "ONE – two – three" group chant "BOOM – chick" or "ONE – two" while the other group tries to chant *Wheezles and Sneezles*. The resulting confusion will illustrate that *Wheezles and Sneezles* is in triple meter.

Conducting. Conducting is an experience that is valuable for any child. It combines structured, large-muscle movement with kinesthetic exploration of beat and meter. After a little experience, the fledgling conductor is aware not only of the beat and the meter which he or she is resolutely signaling with the arm, but of the rhythmic patterns which the group is distributing over this beat. Beat patterns for meters of two, three, and four are standardized, up to a point, across the spectrum of conductors from elementary school chorus and church choirs through professional choral organizations. Children can learn to draw them, to say the numbers of the beats or the words which indicate instructions for the beat, and to train the right arm to maintain these patterns without faltering. The verbal instructions (as for three, "Down, across, up") work for many children (and adults!), who first say them aloud while conducting, then just "think" them. For others, observing the demonstration and perhaps having the teacher physically put them through the motions (patterning) are the avenues for learning.

Conducting the beat is traditionally done with the right arm, whether the conductor is right-handed or not. Musical groups are accustomed to this. The left hand is used to indicate dynamics or other details; work with this hand can be done only after the right hand can conduct beat patterns automatically. Conductors can use their pencils or be equipped with a genuine baton. Here are the conducting patterns, with verbal instructions (Figure 5-3).

Playing games involving counting. The first suggestion for this is "Body machines" (see Chapter 3). In this game, the participants count "1 – rest – 2– rest," with one half of each two-person machine making its motion and sound on "1," the other on "2."

Another meter game is "Movement Tag." A group of about ten children is about right for this, depending on space allowed. All participants are "it." They scatter around into personal spaces around the room for the beginning. With the audible help of the rest of the class, they must count "ONE – two – three – four," over and over.

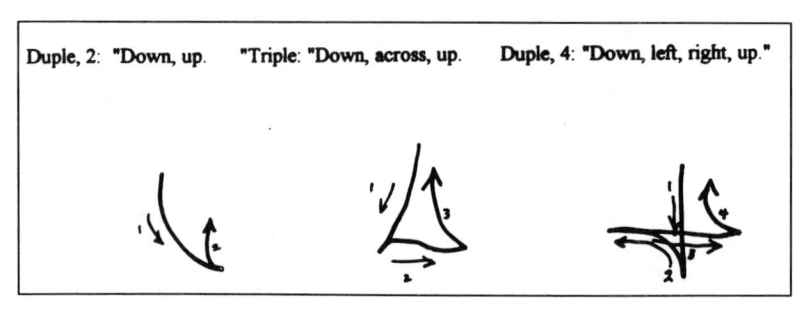

Duple, 2: "Down, up.   "Triple: "Down, across, up.   Duple, 4: "Down, left, right, up."

FIGURE 5-3: *Conducting patterns*

Each person may take one step on "ONE," and *only* on "ONE." If a participant takes more than one step or moves on a count other than one, that person is out. All players are vulnerable to being tagged, and all are determined to tag everyone else, because the object of the game is to be the last person standing. A drum may be used to prevent the beat from speeding up in the excitement.

Note: A game in which it is possible to fail—that is, to be "out"—is seen by many teachers as incompatible with child-centered learning. There are few such activities in this book; however, this one is a favorite with children. If all activities in which it is possible to be "out" are to be exorcised from a child's environment, that will include most sports activities, including baseball.

Pitch, Intervals, Melody

Another way of organizing music, besides duration, is by high and low sounds. The concept of high and low, up and down, can be confusing to a child. *High and low* sounds refer to *pitch*. However, if the child's mother feels that the television is too loud, she calls out, "Turn that TV *down*!". She is, of course, referring to *volume*, which is *loud and soft*. If she wants to hear the television more clearly, she may ask someone to "Turn the TV *up*." It is a good idea to include activities that clarify "up" and "down," "high" and "low," as these words relate to pitch.

Pitch

Pitch refers to *high and low sounds*. Some whole music approaches to the concept of pitch: involving exploring pitch through singing and movement are described in Chapter 4 under "Exploring the voice," and in Chapter 3 under "Make a low shape" and "Class sculpture."

Playing "follow the slide whistle." The teacher or other leader plays the slide whistle. Available at most music stores, the slide whistle has a metal slide which, when moved in or out, slides the pitch up and down. The children are asked to make a high shape with their bodies when the pitch slides up, a low shape when it goes to the bottom of its range, and medium shapes in between.

For an example of singing scale songs see *Ebeneezer Sneezer* (Appendix B). And don't neglect the all-time favorite song from *The Sound of Music*, "A Doe, a doe, a female deer . . .".

Raising and lowering the body according to pitch level. Most children can sing *Do Re Mi Fa Sol La Ti Do* and *Twinkle, Twinkle*. Have them sing that scale, starting in a sitting position on the first *Do*. On each subsequent syllable/pitch, they rise up from the chair a little more until they reach the high *Do*, at which point they are standing. Reverse the procedure going down. Songs can be sung the same way. For example, *Twinkle, Twinkle* works this way:

"Twinkle" (seated), "twinkle" (standing), "little" (tiptoe), "star" (standing),
"How I" (knees bent slightly) "wonder" (knees bent a little more)
"What you" (nearly sitting) "are" (seated).

Mary Had A Little Lamb goes:

Ma-(standing)-ry (knees bent) had (seated) a (rising, bent knees)
Lit-tle lamb (standing), little lamb (knees bent), lit-(standing)-tle lamb (hands held high),
Ma-(standing)-ry (knees bent) had (seated) a (rising, bent knees)
Little lamb, its (standing) fleece was (knees bent) white (standing) as (knees bent) snow (seated).

Acting out body scales. Scale degrees are assigned to parts of the body as follows (scale ascending):

Do – knees; *Re* – thighs; *Mi* – hips; *Fa* – waist; *Sol* – chest; *La* – shoulders; *Ti* – top of head; *Do* (high) – sky

These gestures can be used with *Ebeneezer Sneezer* (see Appendix B), giving an experience with the body scale ascending and descending as well as octaves (high *Do* to low *Do* and back again). After that the body scale can be used with other intervals.

Using Kodály hand signals for pitch, and/or "lining out." These signals are practiced until the children can use them while singing, associating the syllables and hand signals with relative pitches.

Intervals

An *interval* is the *distance between two pitches*. Intervals can be identified aurally or from notation. Intervals can be either *steps*, in which the adjoining notes are only one scale step higher or lower, or *skips*, in which one or more silent pitches separate the two pitches of the interval. (Skips are sometimes called *leaps*, but I prefer the alliteration of step and skip.) The most common interval in children's songs is a step, moving stepwise to the next note up or the next note down, such as *Mi* to *Re* (down) or *Sol* to *La* (up). *Mary Had a Little Lamb* consists largely of steps; that is, *Mi, Re, Do, Re, Mi, Mi, Mi*.

In the music of Western European tradition, there are two kinds of steps: *whole steps* and *half steps*. A whole step is a bigger step than a half step; the pitches are a tiny bit farther apart. The best example is the step from *Do* to *Re* or *Re* to *Mi*, as in *Mary*.

In a half step, the pitches are about as close together as you can get and still tell the difference. (Many other cultures have *quarter steps* and other micro-intervals, which sound to the Western ear like sliding or whining from one pitch to another.) To experience the difference between a whole and a half step, first sing *Do – Re*, a whole step. Then sing that same *Do* again, only this time, move your voice only a very small bit up, not all the way to *Re*. That is a half step. Sing *Do* again. This time, move your voice down only a very small bit, a half step. You will be singing the descending interval from *Do* to *Ti*. A common song that begins this way—moving a half step down—is *O, Little Town of Bethlehem*.

Moving to explore pitch. From the whole-body illustrations in this chapter, children learn to recognize steps or skips and to distinguish between large and small intervals. They can also learn to distinguish intervals aurally by listening and by using their voices.

Using Kodály hand signals. Singing while simultaneously using the hand signals internalizes the pitch relationships between any two syllables in the scale. Having begun with *Sol – Mi* (the calling tune), children can learn to sing *Do – Mi – Sol, Do – La, Do – Ti – Do*, and so forth. In the Kodály system, *Do* is moveable, meaning that it is not an exact letter pitch. (In a "fixed *Do*" system, *Do* is always C, *Re* is D, and so on) *Do* is set at random, with the other pitches relative to it. The teacher can say, "Give me a *Do*," and set the pitch from one of those hummed by the children.

Songs can be taught easily to children who have been trained this way. The leader might signal "*Do – Mi – Sol –* (rest) *Mi – Sol – La – Sol* . . ." with the children singing and signaling along. They have just sung the first line of *Michael, Row Your Boat Ashore*.

Exploiting interval "crutches." Intervals are customarily identified by how many notes apart the two pitches are. This is calculated by counting up or down the scale from the first pitch, numbered 1, to the next pitch. For example, to determine the interval between *Mi* and *Sol*, *Mi* is 1; the silent intervening pitch, *Fa*, is 2; *Sol* is 3. Therefore the interval between *Mi* and *Sol* is an *interval of a third*. Intervals of a step, whether a half step or a whole step, and *intervals of a second*.

Kodály referred to the process which enables one to "hear" music in one's head as *inner hearing*. Edwin Gordon (1980) called it *audiation*. Training in inner hearing accounts for the ability to recognize and sing intervals. There are some "crutches" that are a shortcut to recognizing intervals. By comparing an interval that one hears to the opening fragment of a familiar song which begins with that interval, the hearer can identify the interval.

Interval of a . . .

- Second (step) Up (whole step): Do re mi
  Up (half step): the refrain of *Dry Bones*
  Down (whole step): "Ma-ry had . . . ."
  Down (half step): *O Little Town [of Bethlehem]*
- Third Up: Do–mi or "Michael, Row . . ."
  Down (in children's music, usually a minor third when going down): Call, "Mo–om!" Answer, "I'm here."
- Fourth Up: "Here comes [the bride]" or first interval of *Taps*
  Down: "Old MacDonald . . ."
- Fifth Up: "Twinkle, Twinkle . . ."
  Down: (no common songs begin with this)
- Sixth Up: the NBC network identification jingle or *My Bon[nie lies over the ocean . . .]*
  Down: "No-bod[y knows the trouble I've seen . . ."]
- Seventh (So difficult to sing that it is practically nonexistent in folk music. For example, if you're curious, refer to *West Side Story*, by Leonard Bernstein.)
- Eighth (octave) Up: "Some-where [over the rainbow . . ."]
  Down: (More difficult than going up. No common examples.)

Melody

Melody is a *succession of pitches* or a *tune*. Musical competence, or internalized familiarity with the musical idiom of our own culture, includes programmed samples of characteristic melodies. From these samples, we have subliminally derived transformation rules, which enable us to learn other melodies from the musical idiom of our environment more easily. These rules also allow us to construct an infinite number of new but characteristic melodies that we have never heard before. The folk music of a culture is predictable to members of that population.

When adults of Western European background are presented with melodies of a different culture, such as those of India or China, effort and concentration are required for these listeners to follow and remember. We conduct an unconscious search for internalized samples with which to relate this new material. When there are none, the music does not "make sense" to us.

Children in the early grades of elementary school are still at a stage when their cognitive structures are programmed for language acquisition (and music acquisition). Unfamiliar utterances and sound patterns are immediately assimilated as new samples, which on the next repetition are familiar. Early childhood is a perfect time for storing samples, whether of the children's own musical culture or others.

In addition to singing melodies, children can play them on simple instruments, such as inexpensive xylophones, Orff mallet instruments, and recorders. The players can compose original melodies or "pick out" familiar tunes.

Inner Hearing

Inner hearing is the ability to "hear" music mentally. It is an integral part of making music, of perceiving music aurally or reading music from notation. Kodály constructed much of his music curriculum with the objective of developing inner hearing. Edwin Gordon (1980) uses the term *audiation*, which he defines as "hearing music through recall or creation and deriving musical meaning" (1980, 2). According to Gordon, meaningful listening, as well as meaningful music-reading, depends upon audiation for reference: the listener audiates what has just been heard as a basis for what will subsequently be heard. Efficient music readers "hear" music directly from notation before producing any sound.

You can test your inner hearing this way: Listen to a recording of a song, any song that is not too complicated. Turn off the recording. "Think" the song, concentrating on getting the starting pitch the same as on the recording. Sing a phrase of two of the song aloud, then listen to the recording again to see if you approximated what you heard. To the extent that you did, your inner hearing was functioning.

The ability to use inner hearing or audiation is acquired unconsciously through musical experience. However, there are activities that help focus consciously upon this skill. Here are some examples:

Pitches omitted, "thought," and signaled

Think of the sound of your mother's voice, or that of some other beloved person. You can possibly hear that voice, even though it may have been a long time since you last heard it with your ears. Think of your favorite song, or a musical commercial; you can "hear them in your head," from memory. Hearing mentally, in the absence of sound, is "inner hearing." It is a valuable skill in perceiving music. The following are exercises in inner hearing:

"Thinking" pitches in scales. Sing *Do – Re – Mi – Fa – Sol – La*. Then sing the same, but substitute silence for *Fa*. (The teacher can signal this with finger against lips.) If *Sol* was sung to the correct pitch, inner hearing was providing the pitch for *Fa*. If not, repeat the process until the objective is reached. (The resulting sequence of pitches—*Do Re Mi Sol La*—is a pentatonic scale.) Learn to do this with one or more other pitches omitted. Then proceed to the diatonic scale; that is, the eight-note major scale which includes *Fa* and *Ti*. The most difficult is omitting all the pitches between *Do* and *Ti*.

"Thinking" pitches in intervals. Sing intervals with solmization syllables; then repeat the intervals with one or more pitches silent. For example, *Do – Mi – Sol*, then *Do –* (silence) *– Sol*. If *Sol* is on the correct pitch, inner hearing was functioning.

"Thinking" pitches in songs. Sing songs from which words are progressively omitted during successive repetitions of the song, substituting silence and gestures for the missing pitches. Many songs will do, but there are songs that are traditionally sung this way. The best known of these is *Bingo*. Another example is *My Hat, It Has Three Corners* (see Appendix B). The singer must "hear" (mentally) the omitted pitch in order to continue with the correct pitch after the silence.

Dynamics and Tempo

As with most of the other concepts discussed in this chapter, dynamics and tempo are rarely studied in isolation. These aspects of music can be highlighted in most of the other activities in this book. Everything overlaps; most music consists of many of these elements combined.

Dynamics

Dynamics in music refers to *loud and soft sounds*.

Exploring "loud" and "soft" is very appealing to children. They love to invent their own dynamics games. To get them started, here are a few suggestions:

Adding dynamics to chants. The teacher or student conductor uses an agreed-upon signal to make the chanting louder or softer. The developing student conductor can learn to "turn on" the right arm, designating the beat, and simultaneously use the left hand to ask for softer or louder sound. A simple "soft" signal can be the left hand, palm out, "shushing" the group. A signal for "louder" can be a vertical "winding-up" movement of the left arm, indicating "crank it up." The scissors motion with the fingers to cut off the sound will remain necessary. The potential of student conductors, as well as the value of the experience, should not be underestimated. I have recently seen a fifth grade student conduct an audience of about seven hundred people at a festival featuring fifth graders from four schools. While the teachers taught the audience four different parts for a partner song, the student firmly conducted the whole thing, successfully keeping it all together.

Making a "loud and soft" bulletin board display. The students can bring pictures (drawn by themselves or cut from magazines) illustrating things that make loud or soft sounds. The teacher will have prepared the bulletin board with three headings: "Loud sounds," "Soft sounds," "Loud or soft sounds." This is a variation on a parallel activity for high and low sounds discussed in Chapter 4.

Singing "Where, O where has my little dog gone . . ." with a toy dog. A dynamics game that is a favorite with all ages involves the song *Where, Oh Where Has My Little Dog Gone?* (see "Dynamics" in Appendix B) and a toy stuffed dog. First, the class learns the song. Then a person who is "it" leaves the room while the class agrees on a hiding place for the toy dog. "It" is summoned, and the class indicates whether "it" is "warm" or "cold" in the search for the dog by singing louder for proximity and softer for distance. Children tend to end up shouting more than singing when "it" is on the verge of discovering the dog, but a little shouting never hurts. It is worth it for the enthusiasm.

Tempo

Tempo refers to a *fast or slow beat*. The rope-jumpers and ball-bouncers can be engaged as demonstrators again, showing a steady beat that increases or decreases in speed: steady-fast, steady-medium, steady-slow. After that, the possibilities are endless. And no one has ever improved on Dalcroze for illustrating tempo: the class matches the tempo of the music with the speed of their own body movements: running, walking, walking slowly, skipping, and so forth.

Timbre

Timbre and instruments

Timbre refers to *quality or kind of sound*. This is best experienced with various kinds of sound generators, from "found sounds" through home-made instruments and classroom rhythm instruments to the Orff instrumentarium and standard band and orchestra instruments.

Exploring "found sound." This involves the use of sound generators found in the classroom (the bottom of the wastebasket) or brought from home (spoons, a pan lid, an alarm clock, keys, or as one child in one of my classes brought in, a hair dryer). Each child demonstrates what he or she has brought, after which the teacher helps the group to classify the instruments into "families": clanging things, rattling things, jingling things, banging things, and so forth according to the objects represented. The teacher or a student leader can clap rhythmic patterns for the "families" to take turns imitating. This highlights the unique timbre of each of the families. Groups can be combined, or can share a rhythmic pattern. For example, in the familiar pattern of "Shave and a haircut, two bits," one family could do "shave and a," another "haircut," and everyone together, "two bits."

Associating timbre with colors. This experience can utilize found sounds, homemade instruments, or standard classroom instruments. Either the teacher or the class creates a story (for a class-generated story, see Chapter 9, "Whole Music Across the Curriculum") that involves as many colors as possible. (I include a story of my own, "A Colorful Story," in Appendix B.) The class is then asked to listen to the sound of each of the available sound families or classroom instruments. Then they are asked which one they think sounds like a green sound, or a red sound, and so forth, for the colors included in the story. (This is a problem with multiple possible solutions. There are no "right" answers.) The story is then read aloud (by teacher or student), with a pause after each color is read; at this point the family that represents that color makes a few seconds of sound.

Using timbre to illustrate a story, poem, or drama. Homemade instruments can be used as sound effects for a poem, story, or drama to dramatize events like storms or to represent the characters in the story. This is a variation of the story using timbre with colors. This time, each dramatic event or character of the story is represented by an instrument or a group of instruments of similar timbre. A story like the fable of "The Foolish, Timid Little Hare" (the little creature who panicked all the forest creatures into thinking that the earth was cracking) is good because of the variety of dramatic events and roles: hares (clarify with your students the meaning of "hare"), lion, elephant, tiger, deer, and so forth. The students get to decide on a timbre to characterize each of the creatures and elements suggesting sound effects.

Using timbre to emphasize beat. The identifying phrases for duple and triple meter, "BOOM – chick" for duple and "OOM – pah – pah" for triple, can be used for this "arrangement." The class can sing a song in duple meter (*Go, Tell Aunt Rhody*), with one timbre of instruments on "BOOM," another on "chick." Triple meter (*Happy Birth-*

day) is even more fun, with one timbre on "OOM," another hitting the "pah – pah."

Exploring timbre with home-made instruments. Making original instruments can be a project as incidental or as integral to the curriculum as the teacher wants. This activity may comprise part of a social studies or science unit (see Chapter 10) and/or a music or art project. It can be an individual project for a student who will profit especially from this kind of work. Most of all, these instruments are delightful tools for learning. They can be very simple, such as cans or plastic jugs filled with dried beans, or elaborate with cooperative work in a group or help from parents. (See Appendix A for a short bibliography of books about making instruments.) They can be a class project, with everyone making similar instruments and painting and decorating them.

A class project that sounds risky but is invariably successful is *light bulb maracas*. The teacher must alert all of his or her friends and relatives to save burned-out light bulbs. On the first day of the activity, the students coat the light bulbs with a layer of papier-mâché, and on succeeding days after the first coat has dried, add two more coats. When the papier-mâché is dry and rigid, the light bulbs are struck against something hard until the glass breaks inside, making the rattling sound. The children can then paint the light bulbs with designs. The favorite embellishment is to make each maraca a self-portrait, with painted face and yarn hair. The glass-breaking part sounds scary, but in all the years I have had children do this, the only mishaps have been a collapsed (not leaking) maraca as a result of striking it before the coating was dry or making the coating too thin.

When the instruments are completed, they can be used in activities described throughout this book and in other ways limited only by the imagination. The following are examples:

- Accompanying songs like *Oh, Susanna* or *She'll Be Comin' 'Round the Mountain*. Part of the group can provide singing; kazoos are a perfect timbre for the singing in this setting.
- Organizing a *jug band* or *skiffle band* ("skiffle" is an archaic word referring to a shuffle used in American folk dancing). To add to their other original instruments, students can construct a washtub bass and include such folk instruments as the jug, the washboard played with a thimble, and spoons. This can be a smash hit as a performance in the lunch room or for other classes.
- Providing sound effects representing colors, dramatic events, or characters in a story, poem, or drama
- Playing along with recordings

Exploring timbre with Orff instruments. Timbre was a key concept in Carl Orff's ideas about music. He believed that children should be able to explore sound on instruments of high quality in order to experience beautiful and rich sounds. To that end, he commissioned the manufacture of barred percussion instruments of various kinds as well as unpitched percussion instruments like drums, wood-blocks, and a large assortment of others that now constitute the *Orff instrumentarium*. Barred instruments, all available in at least three sizes, include the *xylophones*, with wooden bars, and two with metal bars, the bell-like *metallophones* and the jingling *glockenspiels*. All have removable bars in order to narrow options to only the notes desired (to increase the probability of satisfying sounds and success), to replace F with F sharp or B with B flat, or to alter the scale: pentatonic or diatonic. Mallets with different kinds of heads also offer varieties of timbre.

Orff instruction involves exploration of musical concepts with these instruments and creating ensemble compositions which feature their unique timbres. Group improvisations can feature the "woods" (various sizes of xylophones) and the "metals" (various sizes of metallophones and glockenspiels) in contrasting and descriptive ways.

Lucky are the teacher and students who have some of this beautiful equipment. However, Orff instruments are very expensive, and having them may require some creative fund-raising on the part of teacher or parents. Even very small children can learn how to respect and care for these instruments. And, as Carl Orff intended, anyone can make beautiful sounds on them.

Experiencing timbre through standard orchestral and band instruments. Music specialists who teach band and orchestra classes can sandwich in a little consciousness-raising about the expressive qualities of different kinds of sound: why a composer would choose the timbre of a trombone or a viola for a particular desired effect. When different solo instruments or sections are featured in a composition, the teacher can make the students aware of the composer's design and choice of instruments.

Few elementary classrooms come equipped with these instruments, and unless the teacher is an expert at both playing and maintaining them, it is an impractical idea anyway. The key to classroom experience with band and orchestra instruments, until the child is old enough for special classes (when available), is *demonstration*. If a picture is worth a thousand words, then a demonstration is worth a thousand pictures. Pictures give no idea of size or proportion, and—well, what is music, anyway? Organized sound. Pictures cannot make sounds. Recordings do, but except in a video, there is no visual image with which to relate the sound.

It would be very good to have demonstrations of different families of instruments, including strings, winds, percussion, and folk instruments of various kinds. Demonstrations can be provided by students; even if the efforts are elementary, the listeners get an idea of how the sound is produced and what the characteristic timbre is. Teachers are often able to play an instrument, and community members are usually obliging. Best of all, if a small musical ensemble already exists, such as a folk group or a string trio, the children can have a demonstration of how the timbres of the instruments are used in combination.

The teacher should prepare the class for a demonstration. The omnipresent television and other broadcast musical media in the environment—the grocery store, elevators, the dentist office, and even school corridors—have caused people to feel removed from the source of music. People talk over the music and go on with their lives, hearing it only subliminally. A veteran church organist friend has observed a steady increase in the noise from a church congregation. In the "old days," he notes, "people were reverently quiet in church. Now, playing the organ is just a signal to talk louder." The result of this is that when children and adults are in an audience to hear "live" musicians, it does not occur to them that if they talk, the musicians can hear them and be distracted or disturbed by it. It is important to explain this to children and to discuss standards of audience behavior *before* the visiting musicians arrive. The emphasis should be upon not only good manners and politeness, but on avoiding the result of hurting people's feelings or seeming ungrateful for their efforts. The expectations should be clear and firm, including good manners about applause: enthusiastic clapping, but no whistling and never booing. Offenders should be quietly but immediately removed from participation. Demonstrating musicians should be prepared to answer questions after the performance. If it is possible to have similar instruments for children to try after the question period, that is ideal, although not usually feasible.

In conjunction with these demonstrations, the children can discuss the various standard instrument "families," relating them to the "families" of their own sound generators: rattling sounds, jingling sounds, and so forth.

Timbre and voices

Experiencing overtones. A beginning classroom experience with vocal timbre can include having children take turns speaking at the back of the room while the other students close their eyes and try to guess whose voice it is. Since timbre is a function of overtones, this could lead to an acoustics lesson involving vibrations, fundamental pitches, overtones, and the Pythagorean and harmonic series. (This works for instruments, as well.)

Composing and conducting with hula hoops. A different exercise in timbre, conducting, and dynamics can be accomplished by very young children. Three or four hula hoops are placed in a triangular or square formation on the floor in an open space. A small group of children clusters around the outside edge of each of the hula hoops. Each group decides on a sound that the group will make. The student conductor stands in the space in the middle surrounded by hula hoops. By putting a hand or foot into one of the hoops, the conductor signals the players in a group to make their sound. The conductor can choose to combine two of the group sounds by stepping into two hoops simultaneously. He or she can combine three and four sounds by putting hands into the other two hoops. The length of time the conductor's foot remains in the hoop determines the duration of the sound. The final possibility is dynamics. While inserting a hand and/or foot into a hoop, the conductor can signal a dynamic level, either with a free hand or by whispering instructions ("Sshh" or "Louder!"). To stop the sound, the conductor need only step out of all the hoops.

Listening to singers. In providing experiences with timbre and voices, demonstrations are again the most valuable tool. However, with voices, a little more discretion on the teacher's part is required than with instruments, in which case just about anything goes. With voices, some cultural biases and vacuums resulting from previous experience will evoke embarrassment from children. When they are embarrassed for the performer, they will respond with derision or by covering their ears. This response invariably appears when a woman singer performs in a classically-trained voice, with considerable vibrato and more volume than the classroom space will accommodate. Since the objective in studying voice timbre is usually experience with various ranges of male and female voices (soprano, alto, tenor, bass), the ideal would be demonstrations by soloists in each of these classifications. However, the singers should be able to perform in a "folk-quality" voice, simply and with little vibrato or high drama. All these qualifications are a tall order, but an experience that is uncomfortable for both children and performer is worse than none. Perhaps the most practical and effective solution would be a performance by a group of singers: a madrigal group from the high school or a community barbershop quartet. This would be a perfect medium for the discussion of voice ranges and timbres. If such "live" demonstrations are not possible, a video is the next best option.

Form

Exploring form incorporates an important skill: distinguishing between same and different. The children work with smaller forms first, such as *Twinkle, Twinkle*, listening for musical phrases that are the same as or different from each other. The first phrase in the piece is labeled "A." If the next phrase is the same, it is another "A." If it is different, it is labeled "B." Subsequent sections differing from A or B are labeled "C," "D," and so on. In *Twinkle, Twinkle,*the opening "Twinkle, twinkle, little star" could be identified as "A." "How I wonder what you are" is a B section. Is the next section again a different tune? ("Up above the world so high . . .") Yes, so that is a "C." What about "Like a diamond in the sky"? The same tune as the previous one, so that is "C" again. The song ends with one more "A" section and one more "B." So the form of the song is ABCCAB. This serves as a good beginning model. After that, the group can work on other songs they have learned. A good way for the children to perceive and internalize differences is by inventing body motions for the rhythm of each section. These can be slapping of shoulders, knees, top of head, and hips; or they could be a little dance routine or combinations of the Orff sound gestures. For *Twinkle, Twinkle*, three small groups can be assigned, one each for "A," "B," and "C." Each group devises a special set of motions to accompany the words in their section. As the class sings the song, each group provides the special motions for its section, highlighting the same and different sections. For a section which is almost the same but not quite, a little prime number is added. If a section sounds like the B section but is just a little different, that would be designated B1. The motions of B1 will be likewise a little different from those of B, an interesting challenge for the B1 group.

The study of form can go as far as the teacher's objectives dictate, including such types as theme and variations (this will be an opportunity for A—the theme—and A1, A2, A3, and so forth); rondo (the recurring rondo tune will always have the same letter name); and other larger forms. A good example of a larger piece that inspires original motions is the "March" from the *Nutcracker Suite*, by Tchaikovsky.

Music specialists who teach band, orchestra, and choir classes are often too pressured with performance aspects of rehearsals to incorporate concepts such as form. However, with a little planning in advance, a brief discussion of the form of a piece being played or sung can improve musical understanding and aid in memorization.

Harmony

Harmony could be loosely described as *singing or playing two or more different pitches at the same time.* (The simplicity of this definition would probably give a music theory professor a heart attack. Nevertheless, it is adequate for a whole music approach to harmony.) In other words, harmony involves doing different things simultaneously, an excellent developmental task. One musician is singing or playing one set of pitches while another musician is singing or playing a different one. However, the two sets of pitches are such that they go together to enrich the sound.

Very young children can learn various types of harmony, but for anyone, this feat of concentration requires patient introduction and much practice. A sequence of experiences in harmony could be the following:

Chanting more than one rhythmic chant at the same time

A good introduction to the requisite concentration is simultaneous chants. This is an experience in doing different things at the same time, but it need not incorporate pitch at first. With a conductor and a drumbeat, two or three different groups produce a rhythmic composition, each using different words and rhythmic patterns but all keeping the same beat. Words can be children's names, food items, automobile brand names, weather conditions, or words associated with a unit of study. Dynamics can be incorporated.

Forming a chord

This is a good initiation into hanging on to one pitch while other people are singing different ones. The class could begin in two groups that make a chord of *Do – Mi*, one group holding a pitch for *Do*, the other for *Mi*. Progress is made to *Do – Mi – Sol*, and finally to *Do – Mi – Sol – Do*. Words or phrases can be substituted for the *Do – Mi – Sol* syllables. The words could be the ones used in the chants; alternately, phrases could be something like, "I am very hungry—" (*Do*), "When will lunchtime be—" (*Mi*), and "give me pizza now—" (*Sol*).

Singing a tune along with a chant

This has the advantage of getting just one foot wet in the ocean of harmony: one part is singing while another one is chanting. Here is a good example:

Group one sings, to the Ur-song:

Good night, sleep tight, don't let the bedbugs bite.
If they do, take your shoe, beat them 'til they're black and blue.

Group two chants:

Grass—hoppers, bed—bugs, beetles [short rest] and fleas, [rest]
Ants and mosquitoes [rest]—stay away from me!

An embellishment can be a group of six children who roam the room going through the motions of the six insects in the chant.

Rounds (canon)
Examples of rounds are myriad, easily located, and available for different skill levels. My example is *Scotland's Burning* (see Appendix B). A good sequence:

1. the round using only the words
2. the round using words and motions
3. finally, the round using words, motions, and tune

Partner songs
Children learn two different songs which fit together when sung simultaneously. The following partner songs are some examples (Appendix B):

1. *Land of the Silver Birch* sung with *Canoe Song*
2. *When the Saints Go Marchin' In* sung with *All Night, All Day* and *Swing Low*

Ostinato
Ostinato, a basic technique of Carl Orff's, is *an accompaniment consisting of a repeated melodic and/or rhythmic pattern*. The term derives from an Italian word meaning "stubborn or persistent"; the English cognate is "obstinate." Thus, an ostinato is a persistent accompaniment pattern that remains the same throughout. It can be an instrumental pattern played on a xylophone or metallophone, an unpitched percussion instrument, or a recorder. It can also be a vocal ostinato to a song. The song *Rain, Rain* (Appendix B) uses the pitches *Sol, Mi,* and *La*. An ostinato could be *Do Re Do Re Do Re Do*, using the words, "Pit-ter, pat-ter, pit-ter, pat."

Songs which incorporate two or more separate melodies (tunes)
For examples of this, see Appendix B for *One Bottle o' Pop* and *Orchestra Song*.

Accompaniment using instruments
This can be a piano, a guitar, an autoharp, or whatever instruments are played by the class members. If the instrument is a wind instru-

ment such as a recorder, a clarinet, or a trumpet, the teacher can devise an ostinato that will be successful but not too demanding.

Part songs

Part songs are the most advanced form of harmony in the classroom. One group sings the melody while another group sings a different tune that "harmonizes" with the melody. The harmony part usually is not another memorable "tune" and may therefore be difficult to remember and maintain. For an accessible example, see *Bill Grogan's Goat* in Appendix B. This song can be taught with an "echo" technique, in which the leader sings the first line ("Bill Grogan's goat"), echoed immediately and exactly by the group, followed by the second line ("was feeling fine"), echoed immediately by the group, and so on. After the song is learned in this way, the echo can be replaced by the simple notes of the second part (in smaller notes in my arrangement). Children love the "barbershop"-type ending.

How Firm a Foundation

This chapter has offered samples of activities designed to develop *competence—internalized schemata—*in every facet of music. These are whole music activities because they involve the whole body; they exploit as many as possible of the sensory and information-processing centers. These activities also begin with *whole, real music* from which to derive the "parts," such as dynamics and meter. Children bounce a ball, jump rope, devise motions, chant, sing, conduct, play active games, crouch on the floor, reach into the sky, run, skip and walk, make and play instruments, give demonstrations (and watch and listen to them), create sound sequences, provide sound effects to their own and other stories, poems and dramas, and learn to sing one tune while others are singing another. Through these avenues, they have internalized experiences with beat, rhythm, meter, pitch, intervals, melody, inner hearing, dynamics, tempo, timbre, and harmony. Meanwhile, they have had adventures which benefit them in other developmental ways.

If you are an elementary classroom teacher, proceed to Chapter 7.

If you are a music specialist, proceed to Chapter 6.

6

Whole Music Activities for Musical Understanding, Part 2

The material in this chapter consists of continuations of the steps in Chapter 5, but is geared for music specialists. The "whole" is still being mined for "parts," however, the concepts in this chapter comprise the more difficult ones for teachers to illuminate or for students to master. To ask these questions, much less understand the answers, students must have had a great deal of experience in music. The music specialist will use whatever methods with which he or she is most comfortable. My avenues are only suggestions, but represent ideas that I have developed after long experience.

From Kodály to Counting

Kodály rhythm symbols and syllables exist for complex rhythmic patterns. In addition to the quarter note (tah), paired eighth notes (ti-ti), and two tied quarter notes (tah-ah), there are the single eighth note (ti), paired sixteenth notes (ti-ri), dotted quarter plus eighth (tah-i-ti) or eighth plus dotted quarter (ti-tah-i), and triplet (triple-ti) (see Appendix B). However, it is my personal preference to use the syllables only until children can read the simple rhythmic patterns that require only tah's, ti-ti's, and quarter rests. Noteheads should be added very soon, before the staff is introduced. A song can then be introduced first with tah's and ti-ti's, then right away with the same piece on a staff, so that the developing note readers can see that the stems can be read the same way on "real music." A good piece with which to do this is *Billy Boy*. At the end, however, there is an eighth plus dotted quarter (ti tah-i).

FIGURE 6-1: *"Billy Boy"*

Then convert the syllables to "one-and-two-and" as follows, in whatever way you as a trained musician are most comfortable (Figure 6-2).

Meter

These items are a continuation of the section "Whole music activities for exploring meter," in Chapter 5.

Compound meter

A. A. Milne's *Sneezles* (Milne 1992, originally 1924) can be said to be in triple meter, or a count of ONE-two-three in each measure; this is the easiest way to understand it:

```
3 Chris–to– pher    Ro–  bin had    whee–zles and    snee–zles. They
  OOm–pah–pah,      OOm–pah–pah,    OOm–pah–pah,     OOm–pah–pah
  ONE–two–three,    ONE–two–three,  ONE–two–three,   One–two–three
```

It could also be said to be in *six* beats per measure:

```
3 Chris–to–pher    Ro–   bin had  whee–zles and    snee–zles. They
  ONE–two–three    FOUR–five–six, ONE–two–three    FOUR–five–six,
```

82···· WHOLE MUSIC

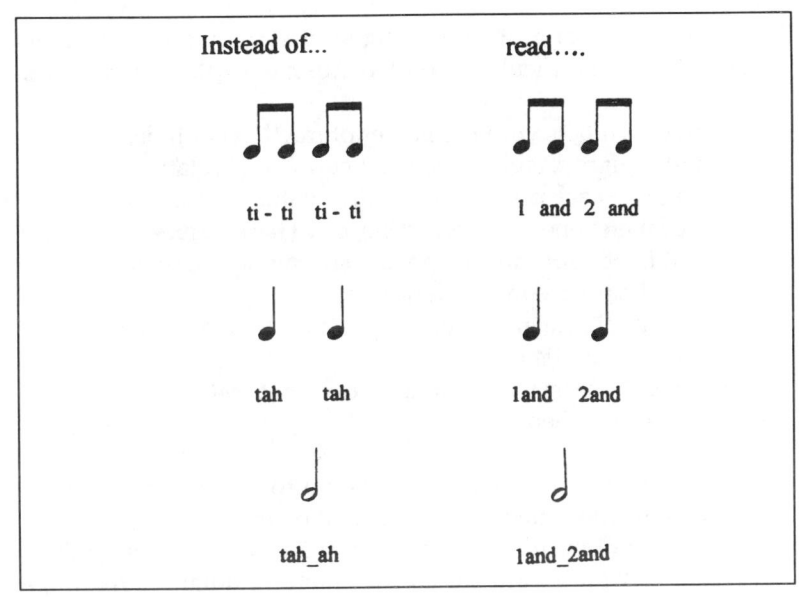

```
    Instead of...          read....

    ♫  ♫                   ♫  ♫

   ti-ti  ti-ti           1 and 2 and


    ♩   ♩                  ♩   ♩

    tah  tah              1and  2and


      ♩                     ♩

    tah_ah                1and_2and
```

FIGURE 6-2: *Kodály to counting*

It could also be thought of as two beats per measure, with three little pulses per beat, like this:

2 Chris–to–pher   Ro–bin had   whee–zles and   snee–zles. They
  One   Two   One   Two

This is an example of compound meter. It is also an example of how meter can be rearranged and thought of in different ways, depending on where the accent is placed.

The meter (time) signature

The top and bottom numbers are not a fraction (no line in between), but instead convey two different pieces of information; memorizing these phrases establishes a vital reference point:

- top number — how many beats per measure
- bottom number — what kind of note, in this piece, is worth one beat

The top number of the meter signature. Children grasp the idea of this one without much difficulty. On the floor, huge "measures" can be marked off with tape. Carpet squares inside each measure represent the number of beats. The students make Kodály stick notation with their bodies to fill the beats in each measure (see Figure 9-6).

The bottom number of the meter signature. In my experience, this is one of the most difficult symbols in music to explain. It involves:

1. note symbols with the names of fractions (whole, half, quarter, eighth, etc.) and equivalent relationships to each other, with relative values that are *other* numbers: one beat, two beats, etc. These values are not fixed, but can change, depending on the bottom number of the meter signature.
2. a symbol (the meter/time signature) that *looks* like a fraction, but isn't.
3. logic: If *this* is true, then it follows that *that* is true; given *this*, then *that*.

Making clear the meaning of the bottom number requires a carefully planned sequence. I offer the following:

Adding noteheads: transition from Kodály rhythm symbols and syllables ("tah's" and "ti-ti's") to standard notation. Although rhythm can be read with words (tah's and ti-ti's) for some time, the rhythm symbols should be equipped with noteheads as soon as possible and referred to by their standard names. At first, these are just names. With very young children, it is not necessary at first to explain the reference to fractions. Many musicians' children call those notes by name long before they have worked with the concept of wholes, halves, and fourths.

Understanding the relative values of the notes (whole, half, and so forth). A piece of cake: I make several cakes in ring pans, which is as close as I can get to whole notes. I also have pictures on separate poster board cards of a whole note, a half note, and so on up to sixteenth notes. After identifying the ring as a whole note, I then cut it into halves, fourths, and so forth, as small as sixteenths. As I make each subdivision, I talk about the fractional relationships and display the note of the same name. (It would be easier if quarter notes were called "fourth" notes.) I also plant a plastic fork upright in each piece, as a stem. After that, I serve pieces of cake to the class, with questions like, "Which is larger, an eighth or a sixteenth? Would you like an eighth of this cake, or a sixteenth?"

Inventions. Teachers and music merchants have invented all sorts of devices to make understanding this easier; for example, a huge whole note into which two half notes will fit, into which four quarter notes will fit, and so on. Since these relative sizes do not exist in standard notation, I doubt if this helps. However, whatever works is a good idea.

Decoding the bottom number:

If the bottom number is 8, it means that an eighth note gets one beat.

If the bottom number is 4, it means that a "fourth note" (actually called a quarter note; remember that a quarter is a fourth of a dollar—a dollar is worth four quarters) gets one beat.

If the bottom number is 2, it means that a half note gets one beat.

Kodály educators use a note standing in for the bottom number in the meter signature, that is, they introduce the kind of note that gets one beat by putting the note itself instead of the shorthand number for it:

$$\frac{4}{\quarternote}$$

However, this does not avoid the calculations ("If a quarter note gets one beat, then an eighth note gets one-half beat . . ."). It just delays explaining what that bottom four means.

This would be easier to understand if meter signatures were written like this:

$$\frac{6}{1/8} \qquad \frac{4}{1/4} \qquad \frac{2}{1/2}$$

However, they are not written that way, probably because that would have incorporated so many numbers for music engravers to engrave on metal plates by hand. So the bottom number of the meter signature is an abbreviation: 8 for a one-eighth note, 4 for a quarter (one-fourth) note, 2 for a one-half note.

Why can't there be a 3, or 6, or 9, or quite a few other numbers in the bottom number of a meter signature? Can those numbers be used in the top number of the meter signature?

The relationships of notes to each other:

- A half note is worth half as much as a whole note.
- A quarter (fourth) note is worth half as much as a half note.
- An eighth note is worth half as much as a half note.
- A sixteenth note is worth half as much as a half note.

We can turn that around and say:

- An eighth note is worth twice as much as a sixteenth note.
- A quarter note is worth twice as much as an eighth note.
- A half note is worth twice as much as a quarter note.
- A whole note is worth twice as much as a half note.

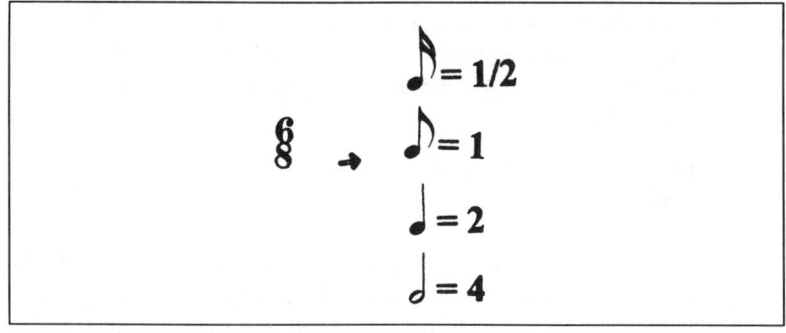

$$\begin{matrix} & & \eighthnote = 1/2 \\ \dfrac{6}{8} & \rightarrow & \eighthnote = 1 \\ & & \quarternote = 2 \\ & & \halfnote = 4 \end{matrix}$$

FIGURE 6-3: *Chart of values*

Logic: **"If *this* is true, then *that* is true."** If the bottom number of the meter signature says 8, it means that an eighth note gets a beat. We can write a chart that tells how many beats the other notes have, based on the relative worth of the notes, if an eighth note gets one beat (see Figure 6-3).

A movement exercise for the bottom number of the meter signature. Four children stand in front of the room holding cards that identify them respectively as a whole note, a half note, a quarter note, and an eighth note. A meter signature is written on the board. If there is an eight at the bottom, the eighth note gets one beat, the quarter note gets two, and so on. Each "note" will, when its name is called, make a number of motions equal to its number of beats in that meter signature. For example, if the bottom number is an eight, the eighth note will make one motion, the quarter two, and the half four. The motions should be something besides clapping, such as flapping an elbow, waggling a knee, or wiggling the hips.

Scales and Key Signatures

These subjects are equivalent to the bottom number of the meter signature as concepts that are difficult to explain. Here are sequences that I have developed:

Scales

A *scale* is composed of *successive pitches* that serve as melodic building blocks from which the pitches for melodies are chosen. We have already examined the *pentatonic* scale, which is *Do Re Mi Sol La*, and has no half steps. The other scales that apply to most Western European music are the *diatonic scales*, which can be *major* or *minor*. The starting point for exploring scales and key signatures is the *major* scale, the scale of most children's songs. A major scale (*Do Re Mi Fa Sol La Ti Do*) sounds the way it does (and almost every schoolchild can sing it) because it has both whole steps and half steps; the placement of the half steps gives the scale its characteristic sound. With that in mind, here is a sequence for teaching about major scales:

The musical alphabet. The musical alphabet runs from A through G, whereupon it repeats: A B C D E F G A B C D ... and so forth. There is no H in the musical alphabet (except in Germany, where B is B flat and H is B natural). The musical alphabet goes forward as the scale goes up and backward as the scale goes down. The children enjoy learning to say this alphabet backwards rapidly, since it is a new experience. They can sing the musical alphabet forwards, rising from their chairs as the pitch goes up; they then sing the descending scale with the alphabet backwards, lowering themselves back down as they sing.

Scales starting on any letter of the musical alphabet. A scale can begin on any letter of this alphabet. The teacher writes the musical alphabet in a circle and points out that a scale can start on C and go clockwise back to C again (a C scale) or start on F and go clockwise back to F again (an F scale) and so forth.

Seven children, each assigned a letter in the musical alphabet, can stand in a circle, as it is written on the board. A student stands in the middle and points to a person, who speaks his or her letter; the following letters each give their names in order until the scale ends with the starting letter. The person in the middle then points to another letter and the process is repeated. The process can then run backwards, for descending scales. Musicians are uncomfortable hearing the letters of scales without their key signatures, but this is not the point at this stage.

Key signatures

Whole steps and half steps in scales. Children can understand the difference in sound between a whole step and a half step, and how it "feels" to sing them. The class can sing (someone gives a starting pitch, first) *Do Re*, taking a big step forward as they do. That is a whole step. A whole step always sounds like *Do Re*. Students sing the same *Do* again, only this time they pull the *Do* pitch up a very little bit (the teacher can direct this by using hands and "body English") just enough to tell the difference, while taking a very small step forward. That is a half step. A whole step has two half steps in it. The group then practices singing whole steps and half steps up or down, taking large or very small steps forward or backward.

Half steps between *Mi-Fa* and *TI-Do*. Write the *Do Re Mi* ... scale on the chalkboard. A major scale sounds the way it does because it has half steps between *Mi-Fa* and *Ti-Do*. All the rest are whole steps. Make little roofs over the *Mi-Fa* and *Ti-Do* to indicate half steps (Figure 6-4). Have a group stand in a line in front of the room (in "follo-the-leader" formation) and sing the scale (from a given starting pitch), taking big steps between all the scale degrees except *Mi-Fa* and *Ti-Do*, when they will take very small steps.

Half steps between 3–4 and 7–8 ("telephone number"). Under the *Do Re Mi* syllables, number the scale degrees from 1 to 8. Which numbers are *Mi-Fa* and *Ti-Do*? [3–4, 7–8] There are half steps between 3–4 and 7–8. Put little roofs over 3–4 and 7–8 (see Figure 6-4). Repeat the follow-the-leader line, except singing the scale with the numbers, taking very small steps between 3–4 and 7–8, and large steps on the others. Have the children memorize this *telephone number* for where the half steps are in a major scale: 3–4, 7–8.

"Natural" half steps: E–F, B–C. It is important to memorize one more thing: when letter names are used for a scale, all the letter names of the scale are a whole step apart except: *E and F* and *B and C*, which are the *natural half steps*. Why? They just are. They developed that way in the course of music history, got frozen into the standard keyboard, and have been that way ever since. Demonstrate on a keyboard (or, in a pinch, on paper keyboards) that there are pairs of white keys on the piano with no black keys in between. Those are all E–F, B–C. There are no black keys in between these pairs because there is no *room* for them; E–F and B–C are already only a half step apart. The other notes (A–B, D–E, etc.) are all a whole step apart, so there is room between them for the black keys, which are sharps and flats. (Make sure that these concepts are all illustrated with *sound*, on a keyboard.)

Scales using letters from the musical alphabet. Now we'll do a scale with letter names. Write the *Do Re Mi* scale on the chalkboard, with the little roofs over *mi-fa* and *ti-do*. Underneath that, write the numbers, 1 through 8, with the half-step roofs over 3–4 and 7–8. Then write the C D E F . . . scale under that (see Figure 6-4). What pairs of letters are the natural half steps? E–F, B–C. Put half-step roofs over them, and point out that they came out in just the right place: the half steps in a major scale must be between 3–4 and 7–8 to *sound right*, and if you start on C, the E–F and B–C come out at 3–4 and 7–8. Perfect. Play the C scale on a keyboard or a xylophone to demonstrate that it "sounds right."

Scales starting on letters other than C. What if the scale starts on some other letter than C? Alterations must be made in some of the notes to put the half steps in the right place: between 3–4 and 7–8. In

		⌃			⌃
Do	Re	Mi-Fa	Sol	La	Ti-Do
		⌃			⌃
1	2	3-4	5	6	7-8
		⌃			⌃
C	D	E-F	G	A	B-C

FIGURE 6-4: *Halfsteps in a major scale*

order to move pitches around, there are symbols that make a pitch a half step higher or a half step lower. The symbol that makes a pitch *a half step higher* is the *sharp*, which looks like a little tic-tac-toe sign: ♯. The symbol that makes a pitch *a half step lower* is the *flat*, which looks like a lower-case b: ♭

The sharps or flats that were needed to put the half steps in the right place are called the *key signature* ("key" in this case meaning "scale").

A whole music exercise in key signatures. Using sheets of colored construction paper, write letters on each one. To demonstrate the simplest key signatures (and that's all that is necessary at this point), you will need the musical alphabet, plus an extra each for C, F, D, and G. Use a different color for each letter or pair of same letters; however, make all Es and Fs the same color. Make two cards with a sharp on each one (the same color paper) and a card with a flat. Before beginning, review:

- the function of a sharp and a flat
- the telephone number for half steps
- the fact that E–F and B–C are the only "natural" half steps
- the guideline that when students are standing in a row making a scale, they are in the configuration of a piano. If someone were facing them as a piano player, the low pitches are on the player's left, the high pitches on the player's right. A sharp will move a pitch up—to the player's (or the class members') right. A flat will move a pitch down—to the player's (or the class members') left.

Eight students stand in a line holding the letter names for the C major scale. E–F and B–C stand as pairs with linked arms. The class will count 1 through 8 to see that the natural half steps (E–F, B–C, all in the same color) came out on 3–4, 7–8. Play this on a keyboard or xylophone to demonstrate that it *sounds right*.

Now the students make a G major scale. (Give one of the C's a G card instead.) E–F and B–C still stand with linked arms. Have the class count. The B–C will come out on 3–4, but the E–F will come out on 6–7. *Play this* on a keyboard or a xylophone so that the class can hear that it *doesn't sound right*. The half steps must link arms, so 7–8 have to be close together. Who must move? Number 7, F, to get close to 8. Which direction? Up. To move a pitch a half step up, add a sharp. The F now holds an F and a sharp, moves away from the E and links arms with the G. What change had to be made to put the half steps in the right place? We changed F to F♯. Play this so that the listeners can hear that it now *sounds right*. The key signature (or alterations that had to be made) of a G Major scale is F♯.

The students make an F Major scale. (Give one of the G's an F instead.) The students line up from F to F, with E–F and B–C as pairs with linked arms. Have the class count to see that the E–F comes out on 7–8, but the B–C comes out on 5–6. Play this so that the hearers can tell that it *doesn't sound right*. To get the half steps to come out right, the 3–4 (A and B) must link arms. Who must move? The B. Which way? Down, to get close to the A. To move a pitch a half step down, a flat is needed. Give the B a flat; the B now holds both a B and a flat, moves away from the C, and links arms with the A. Play this so that the students can hear that it *sounds right*. What change had to be made to put the half steps in the right place? We changed B to B♭. The *key signature* of an F Major scale is B♭.

Go through the same procedure with D, which will need two sharps, F and C. You will then have demonstrated the scales of C, F, G, and D. That is far enough, since it covers the alterations of both flats and sharps, and shows the beginning of the process of multiple sharps (and by implication, multiple flats). I have discovered that proceeding to two flats is confusing because the scale begins with B flat. I would postpone that one.

When a piece is notated, the first notation on the staff after the clef in the beginning is the ♯s or ♭s used in the key (the scale from which the notes for the composition were chosen). The first sharp is always F♯; a ♯ is placed on the top line (F) of the treble staff, and means that whenever F's appear in the piece, F sharp should be played or sung, instead.

When there are two sharps, F is still there on the top line; C is the second sharp, and is placed on the third space from the bottom, indicating that all F's *and* C's are to have sharps. If there is one flat, it is always B flat; it is placed on the middle line (B) of the treble staff and means that all B's are B flat.

I have a set of blocks that I made, each painted white (like white piano keys), with the same letters as above. With these I made three blocks painted black (like black piano keys), two with sharps and one with a flat (painted on in a light color). Students can manipulate these blocks on the floor in the same way as the people are manipulated in the foregoing sequence, placing blocks with a space between them for a whole step and close together for a half step. The required sharp or flat block is placed above the note which is altered.

Memorizing key signatures. A good teacher helps children "discover," by manipulating objects, the meaning of multiplication tables. A child places three sets of five ice cream sticks on the rug and learns by counting them that three sets of five add up to fifteen. This process is vital for understanding "math facts." However, it is essential to go beyond this step, since multiplication would be unwieldy if we had to go through that for each computation. Instead, *after* the multiplication facts are explored, they are memorized, for efficiency: 3×5 is 15.

The same goes for key signatures. Music students must manipulate blocks or cards in order to understand why those sharps and flats are added. However, after that process, it is more efficient to memorize the key signatures for the most common keys (scales) in children's songs and folk music: C (no sharps or flats); G (F sharp); F (B flat); D (F sharp and C sharp).

Minor scales

If a scale begins on *La* instead of *Do*, the scale is *La Ti Do Re Mi Fa Sol La*. The half steps are still between *Mi-Fa* and *Ti-Do*. This means that the half steps are in a different place than in a major scale; instead of 3–4, 7–8, they are between 2–3 and 5–6. This scale, the *minor scale*, has a completely different sound and as a result a different mood—one which is often perceived as sad, in contrast to the "brighter" sound of the major scale.

Minor scales can be explored in all of the ways already described for major scales.

Every major scale (starting on *Do*) has a *relative minor* scale (starting on *La*). If the major scale *Do* is C, then *La* is A. The relative minor scale of C Major is A Minor, a scale that begins and ends on A but has exactly the same pitches as C Major. If the major scale *Do* is G, then *La* is E. The relative minor scale of G Major is E Minor, which begins and ends on E, but has exactly the same pitches as G Major, including an F sharp. Minor scales have the same key signatures (sharps or flats) as their relative major scales.

If there is an opportunity for the music specialist to go further into minor scales, the next step is the three different kinds of minor scales: the two in addition to the one already discussed (the *natural minor*) that evolved because of a desire for a *leading tone: an interval of a half step between the two last notes in the scale*. Major scales have leading tones: the half step between 7–8. Since the natural minor half steps are 2–3 and 5–6, leading tones (7–8) must be created by adding sharps and flats.

Harmony: Studying I, IV, V Chords

The harmony experiences in Chapter 5 are valuable enrichments for the understanding of music, even if that is as far as the students explore harmony. From this foundation, however, it is also possible to go on to the more academic study of harmony. The whole music experiences serve as internalized background on which to build the more detailed information: from whole to part. I would not recommend embarking on the study of I, IV, V triads unless the class has access at least to several barred or keyboard instruments. I have managed it with paper keyboards, but this is a charade, because music is—remember? Paper keyboards make no *sound*.

The following is a sequence for studying I, IV, V chords. This is not intended as a condescending tutorial for the readers of this book. If you have previous training in music theory, this is nevertheless not a section that you are supposed to omit. It is a carefully-constructed sequence—a kind of script—of how to teach this subject to beginners. It is a classroom-tested sequence that begins at the beginning, with each step leading to the next. If you have courageously embarked on this chapter with no musical background, this sequence may help you to launch some classroom exploration in which you and your students learn together.

Sequence for teaching I, IV, V chords

Chords: pitches that "sound good" together. All the harmony experiences in Chapter 5 (rounds, partner songs, etc.) "work" because the pitches have been manipulated to make *chords* when they coincide. Chords are two or more pitches which "sound good" together. They "sound good" because our culture has agreed that they do. (Leonard Bernstein and some other theorists have hypothesized that "sounding good" is related to the natural harmonic series. According to this theory, certain simultaneous pitches do not "sound good" because of their relative positions in the harmonic or overtone series; they are not "natural." I offer this only as an interesting idea.)

The three pitches from a scale that are most used to accompany melodies. There are eight different pitches in a scale. Melodies use all of these pitches, up and down. To accompany a melody, only three of these eight pitches are necessary. All could be used, but three are sufficient. That is because, with any of the notes in the scale, at least one of those three will make a pleasant sound. Number the degrees of the scale from 1 to 8; the three "accompanying" pitches are 1, 4, and 5, or the first, fourth, and fifth degrees of the scale. These are usually identified by Roman numerals: I, IV, V.

In the C Major scale, the first note in the scale is C, the fourth is F, and the fifth is G. A melody (tune) in the *key* of C Major (meaning that the pitches in the melody have been chosen from the C Major *scale*) will probably use all of the notes in the scale. However, the harmony or accompaniment part might use only C (I), F (IV), and G (V), whichever *sounds good* with the individual pitches in the melody.

For a composition in the key of F Major (the notes were chosen from an F Major scale), the I (first note in the scale) is F, the IV (fourth note in the scale) is B♭, and the V (fifth note in the scale) is C.

Chord symbols. On the sheet music of songs, these accompanying notes are often printed over the top of the staff. For an example, see *The Bus Song* in Appendix B. In this song, the I, IV, and V, B♭, F and C are indicated throughout. Incidentally, many children's songs are written in the key (scale) of F Major because it is a good range for children's voices. These accompanying note indications on sheet music are called *chord symbols*, because, although these indicated notes can be used singly for harmonic accompaniment—a string bass or electric bass does that—(a recording of country music can illustrate this), they are usually used as the *roots* on which to build *three-note chords* called *triads*.

Triads: three-note chords. A triad is built by using the I, IV, or V note as a starting point, then adding two other notes by playing every-other-note up, proceeding in intervals of a third.

Here again a keyboard that makes sounds is essential. But in terms of the reading of this book, a silent keyboard will have to suffice. If the accompanying note is F, like the first one in *The Bus Song*, the chord would be F–A–C. If the accompanying note is C, the chord would be C–E–G. These triads can be played on a keyboard instrument by putting the left hand on the piano, with the *root note* (the I, IV, or V note) under the little finger. The notes under the middle finger and the thumb are the other two notes of the triad. If the little finger is on C, the middle finger will be on E, the thumb on G. The triad is C–E–G. In this way, the accompaniment is played with I, IV, and V chords or triads.

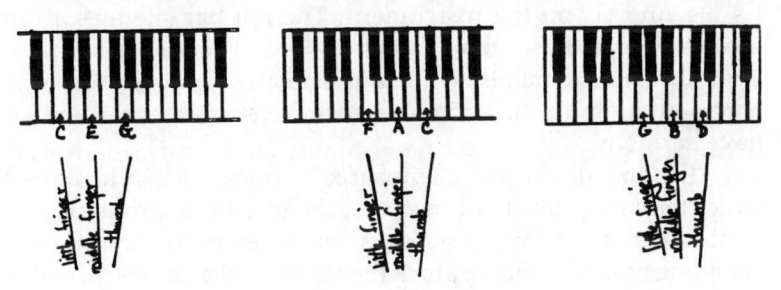

In constructing the triads, care must be taken to include the sharps or flats that appear in the beginning of the piece, in the key signature. In *The Bus Song*, there is a flat on the B line at the front of the piece. That indicates that instead of B, whenever B appears a B♭ (or black key one-half step below the B) must be substituted.

The explanation for a little "7" after a chord symbol (a *seventh* chord) is too advanced for this sequence, but effectively it means that the chord has four notes in it instead of three. If, for example, a chord symbol is G⁷, skip yet another note after the GBD and play an F sharp; the G⁷ chord is GBDF♯. However, the player[s] can substitute a plain G triad (GBD).

Playing harmony on instruments

Piano or electronic keyboard. Keyboard instruments present a very clear picture of how music "works:" scales, whole and half steps, sharps and flats, key signatures, and triads. Although usually limited to individual work, a keyboard can accommodate two or three people simultaneously to explore harmony.

Xylophones or Orff instruments. Barred percussion instruments are excellent for playing triads as accompaniment. Two players can cooperate on the same instrument, and several instruments can be used at once.

Resonator bells. A resonator bell is an individual little sound-box with a metal bar like a xylophone bar, played with a little mallet. A set of resonator bells has two or three octaves of these, including sharps (or flats) painted black, each engraved with its letter name. These are excellent for demonstrating and using triads.

Autoharp. An autoharp is a handy instrument because a player can play the chord symbols indicated in the music without knowing *any* of that stuff I just went through about harmony. The autoharp is a stringed instrument with buttons labeled with letters (C, E, G, etc.). Each button is attached to a bar with a felt strip under it. The felt strip is notched. When the player pushes down the C button, for example, the notches in that felt bar coincide with the Cs, Es, and Gs on the instrument. The felt bar silences all the strings except those in a C triad: C–E–G. The autoharp player reads the chord symbols on the music notation and just pushes the corresponding button, strums across the strings, and there you have harmony.

The only drawback to autoharps is tuning them. The notes to which the strings must be tuned are printed in the appropriate place on the instrument. With practice, a person learns to play the corresponding note on a piano, pluck the string on the autoharp, and listen for any difference, higher or lower. The string is tightened or loosened with a tuning wrench that fits on the pins to which the strings are attached, as in a piano.

Guitar. Guitarists learn to play strummed chords, which are identified by letter names and learned by rote from other players or from finger positions on a chart. Players learn an "A" chord or a "D" chord. The names of the other notes in the chords are seldom referred to consciously. Guitarists who strum just read the symbols and play the chords by letter name, as with the autoharp. Many self-tutoring books are available, with fingering charts for chords.

Handchimes. Handchimes are a practical adaptation of the more elegant and fragile handbells. In addition to being sturdier than handbells, they are less expensive. Their beautiful tone makes them a glorious asset to any classroom or music group. Among their many uses, they are perfect for exploring harmony.

Improvising harmony

Many musicians play chord accompaniments without either reading chord symbols or understanding I, IV, V chords. They simply play by ear, improvising what "sounds good." Almost anyone who is interested enough to do a great deal of listening and experimenting can become fluent with this skill. Vocalists as well as instrumentalists learn to improvise harmony, although, of course, singers doing harmony can sing only one note at a time from the I, IV, or V chords. (If you can sing a chord, I'll be your manager, and we'll take you on the road.) The chord results from two or more singers each singing a single note; together they form a chord.

Harmonic and melodic instruments

Instruments on which two or more pitches can be played simultaneously are classified as *harmonic instruments*. These include the keyboard instruments, the guitar, autoharp, and banjo, the harp, the harmonica or mouth harp, and any other instrument which can play two or more pitches at once. Harmonic instruments are so called because they have self-contained harmony. *Instruments which can produce only one pitch at a time* are called *melodic instruments*. The most common of these is the voice. (Remember my promise to take you on tour if you can sing more than a single pitch at once.) The term *melodic* is used because a *melody*, or a tune, is *a succession of single pitches*. Most wind instruments are melodic instruments. Players of instruments of the violin family can produce chords, which in the context of these instruments are called *double stops*. However, for the most part these instruments play a single line of pitches.

Notation

The notation activities in Chapter 8 and Chapter 9 provide the whole: a broad foundation of understanding musical concepts that must precede the "parts," such as notation details. This is the role of whole music; by the time we have arrived at the notation details which follow the whole music sequence of exploring notation (see a brief sequence outline at the end of Chapter 9) whole music has fulfilled its role. The "parts" will fit into the prepared schema. The music specialist—the probable guide, at this point—will employ whatever methods are comfortable to him or her to familiarize students with such items as accidentals, naturals, repeat signs, sixteenth notes and smaller, rests beyond the quarter rest, first and second endings, markings for dynamics and tempo, metronome markings, and so forth. The imagination of the teacher can devise whole music approaches to these components.

For example, a traditional way to differentiate the half rest ▬ and the whole rest ▬ , which both look like little hats, is: if the hat is only half full (half rest), it will remain upright ▬. If it is full (whole rest), it will fall over ▬. Or, a half gentleman leaves his hat on his head in the presence of a lady; a whole gentleman lifts his hat .

Another whole music approach to notation details in reading notes by direction and intervals, rather than note names. "Is this a step, or a skip?" "Which direction does it go, up or down?" "How many pitches do we skip from this note to the next?" The letter name of the note is important only for the starting pitch, or when the reader gets "stuck" because of a wide interval or unpredicted interval or direction.

7

Listening

Listening—really listening—is a rare and precious skill. As the word "skill" implies, listening is a capacity that can be learned. It entails a difficult task for young people: turning one's attention out of the self and onto someone or something else. It involves selection of stimuli, concentration, and focus. *Every* musical undertaking both requires listening and teaches listening.

Listening Throughout the Sequence of Whole Music Activities

Body machines
This activity, described in Chapter 3, is a good introduction to the art of listening. After the machines get going with their motions and sounds, they are asked to watch each other out of the corner of the eye for the combined visual effect and to *listen* to the composition that the class has made with the combined sounds. This is reinforced by a tape recording to listen to later.

Rhythmic organization
When children are chanting different names together to a beat for the combined effect, strumming a string to the beat of recorded music, playing the beat and rhythmic patterns on instruments, or listening to the beat on a drum to keep together, they are *listening*. Identifying the accents of a poem to decide if it is in duple or triple meter is *listening*.

Pitch and melody

Distinguishing between high and low sounds, learning to match a pitch, recognizing and singing intervals, learning a song—all involve *listening*.

Timbre

The children who invent group sounds that they produce at the signal of the student conductor are listening to the effect of this impromptu group composition. Arranging a composition or accompaniment with homemade instruments, improvising an accompaniment on an autoharp, deciding what sound could represent a lion or the color green, and recognizing the sound of an oboe or a banjo, or the voice of a classmate—all are listening activities.

Harmony

Harmony is the point at which the fine-tuning of listening begins: when the child is singing or playing with someone who is singing or playing something different. This includes holding different pitches to make a chord and singing ostinatos, rounds, partner songs, and part songs as well as playing harmony parts and chords on instruments.

Creating

Listening is an intrinsic part of improvising a melody, putting a tune to a poem, creating a composition from different kinds of sounds or with an instrument, or inventing sound effects for a story or drama. When a person is organizing sound in any way for any kind of composition, an intrinsic part of the process is listening to the effect as the work progresses. Creating means starting with something and building on it; it means having an idea or a vision and working to make it a reality. Much of the listening in a creative effort takes place in inner hearing.

Listening to classmates making music

Throughout all these musical experiences, opportunities are present to participate in music as an expressive medium, as a communicative art. Expression and communication are interactive processes between the performer and the listener; as creating and performing are artistic endeavors, so also is active listening. Skill in listening begins with the basic acts of being courteous and quiet, and applauding without whistling or booing. There is an old saying that "Music is a picture painted on a background of silence." Learning to provide that silence so that music can take place is a major part of learning to listen.

Some Examples of Other Listening Activities

A listening "field trip"

The students go outside and position themselves silently around the playground. The assigned task is to listen for a sound there, memorize it, and bring it quietly, mentally, back to the classroom. No one is to speak until all have returned to the room, standing in a circle. The children then take turns, each reproducing the sound that he or she had heard. There is usually a variety that includes automobile sounds, birds, and many other environmental sounds of which we are often unaware. The process of repeating the sounds around the circle can be speeded up until it is almost continuous; then all sounds can be made at once. A student conductor can indicate dynamics or solos. A tape recording can be made of the composition.

Listening to recorded music

Drawing or working puzzles to music. Any time that children—and sometimes adults—are asked simply to sit and *listen*, when there is nothing to *do* or to *watch* at the same time, in all probability the lesson will be a failure. They do not know where to look; as soon as they exchange glances with each other, concentration is lost. Since they are not skilled enough to "lose themselves" in the music, they are very self-conscious about how they must look just sitting there. They do not know what to do with their hands and feet; children will *find* something to do with them, and the teacher won't like it!

The solution to this problem, if the lesson requires the use of a recording (which has nothing to watch), is to incorporate something to *do* at the same time. This can be drawing to music, or it can be a music-oriented picture to color, or a word-game or a crossword puzzle involving musical words. An effective way to handle this is for each student to have a folder including copies of these word games and puzzles. When there is a recording to listen to, the folders are distributed and each child selects something from it on which to work. Doing something else while listening does not mean that the children do not hear the music. Quite the contrary, they are much more likely to hear it when their hands are busy.

Knowing what to listen for: preparation. Obviously in a lesson that involves listening to a recording, the teacher has an objective in mind. The goal may be simply letting the motion and mood of the music dictate the motion of the crayons, as in drawing to music. If the objective is to attend to something specific in the music, then the following guidelines apply; the key word is *preparation*.

Just asking children—or adults—to listen to a Mozart piece because it is pretty and because Mozart wrote it when he was only twelve just will not accomplish anything. As with other experiences in civility, such listening experiences must be properly introduced.

What concepts the students are prepared to listen for depends on the objectives of the lesson. This can include meter ("Is this a march? See which fits: ONE – two THREE – four, or ONE – two – three"), phrases or form, kinds of instruments, the "surprise" chord in Haydn's *Surprise Symphony*, exploitation of dynamics and tempo, the significance of words in a song, or the musical expression of mood or motion.

Program music is music which is intended to tell *a story without words*. The "program" is the intended scene or event that the music is portraying. Of course, if we do not know the program in advance, we will probably not discern it solely from the music itself. If the children are prepared by hearing the story first, a recording can be part of a lively lesson. Being introduced to the instruments or musical themes that portray the characters and events makes the music familiar instead of impenetrable. The repertoire of such program music is large (see Appendix C); examples include *The Sorcerer's Apprentice* (Dukas), *The Moldau* (Smetana), and "The Hall of the Mountain King" from the *Peer Gynt Suite* (Grieg).

Children enjoy making an illustration of the music in a series of cartoon drawings, like the comics in the newspaper. With a step-by-step demonstration by the teacher, they can fold a large piece of newsprint into six or eight sections, making a drawing of an event from the story in each section. A work such as *Peter and the Wolf* (Prokofiev) or *The Sorcerer's Apprentice* is especially inspiring for this.

Listening to "live" music

In this case, preparation must be not only for what to listen for in the music but how to be courteous to real performers. Although musicians on television cannot hear us, "live" performers can. If there is noise and disruptive behavior, the musicians' feelings will be hurt, and the performance will be spoiled for everyone. After an advance discussion of this, no discourteous behavior should be tolerated.

It is important to get information from the performers in advance about the music they will be playing so that the children can be prepared. When the performers are there in person, one of the accessible things to listen for is the timbre of the different instruments. There is also the aspect of what to *watch* for, such as the technique of playing the instruments.

Listening When You Cannot Hear

Music *requires* listening? Well, it is possible, although difficult, for someone whose hearing is profoundly impaired to enjoy music. A teacher of a hearing-impaired child can help the child reinforce a musical experience by substituting seeing and/or feeling vibrations for listening. Depending on the range of hearing loss, a child can play and "feel" beat and rhythm with drums and other percussion instruments. He/she can watch a conductor—and be one. Movement and dance activities can be followed by watching what everyone else is doing. A metronome that has a visual feature, such as a flashing light or a little swinging baton, like the more old-fashioned wind-up models, is a great help in maintaining a steady beat. The "string string bass" activity (see Appendix B) is excellent, since the child can internalize the beat through vibrations carried directly to the head. In this case, it is usually better to hold the free end of the string against the bone behind or in front of the ear instead of into the ear.

Hearing loss can be limited to certain ranges, which, if identified, can suggest an appropriate instrument. I have taught 'cello to a boy who heard only a limited low range, and I have observed a young violinist who hears only higher frequencies that do not include some frequencies of the human voice. He played in a high school orchestra with an aide provided to sign the conductor's instructions for him.

There are many very moving performances by choirs all of whose members are hearing-impaired; those who can hear well enough to sing together on pitch provide the choral music while the others sign the words.

I once taught a girl with profound hearing loss to play the clarinet in my junior high school band class. All that she could "hear" from her clarinet came to her through vibrations of the reed and the body of the clarinet. She and I developed her tone through a system of trials on her part and signaled responses on mine. She learned to match fingerings to the printed notes (*not* a whole music technique, but the only one available in this case) and to watch me, the conductor, with intense concentration. From the beat of the baton, she could tell the first and last beat of a measure ("one" is always down; the last beat is up), and if she lost her way for a measure or two, I would sign the next upcoming score rehearsal number or letter and cue her entrance there. Intonation was always haphazard, since even on a one-to-one basis it could be adjusted only by my instructions to do some physical thing, the results of which she could not hear.

Why did she want to go through all of this? To be one of the group and participate, even though the audible effect of the whole was lost to her. She practiced hard enough to become fluent with matching fingerings and notes while constantly watching the conductor. In fact, to do this she had to have much of her part nearly memorized, an astonishing feat, since she could not hear it. She did all of this well enough to eventually play in her high school band, to wear a uniform, and to march. For four years, she emphatically resisted being publicly praised for her accomplishment. At graduation, however, her special award and public recognition—a standing ovation—made her blush with pleasure. Although that was the end of her musical ventures, I'm certain that she kept with her both the social rewards and the knowledge that she had achieved something that is usually so dependent upon the very faculty of which she had been deprived.

8

Creating

Allocating a special chapter to "creating" is largely for emphasis on the importance of invention and experimentation in a whole music approach. Every section of this book incorporates creative activities. This chapter will contribute an outline of possibilities and some additional exercises.

Spontaneous Improvisation

There should be many opportunities for spontaneous improvisation. Examples have already been included in Chapters 1 to 6, and opportunities are limited only by the imagination of the teacher. Even in such a structured activity as a recorder class, students can improvise. After the students can play the recorder with both hands, they can improvise from a pentatonic scale, CDEGA; any combination of notes from a pentatonic scale has a pleasing, floating quality. Alternating ensemble improvisation with solo improvisations, children can create music together in the same way that jazz players do.

Original Composition

This implies a more deliberate approach to composition than spontaneous improvisation. Again, there are examples throughout this book, such as composing a tune for a poem or inventing tone poems with non-traditional sound sources.

Ways to Make Children's Compositions "Permanent," with or Without the Ability to Read and Write Standard Music Notation

It is satisfying for children to compose something with an existence of its own, something to keep. That means writing down or otherwise making permanent a composition that can be performed the same way later, maybe even by different people. The process of doing this not only makes a tangible entity of the composition, but demonstrates to children why and how standard notation developed.

Invented notation

The musical equivalent of invented spellings is invented notation. Anyone who has spent time with children knows that they are fluent at making sounds: motors, explosions, guns, and an infinite range of other descriptive noises. They also have learned from television and cartoons how a sound *looks*:

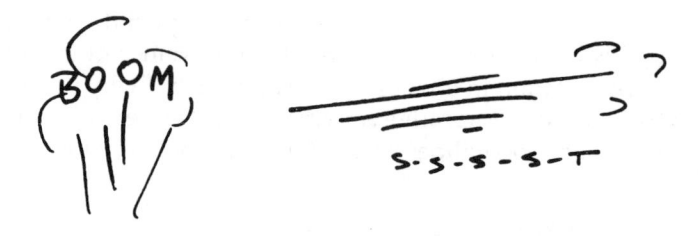

This facility gives children great originality about making *symbols for sound*, which is what *notation* is. The following are two examples of class activities that get the children started with invented notation. After this orientation, individual students can write their own stories with sound notation.

The class-generated story. The teacher suggests an opening line for a story. In the example (see Appendix B, "Class Story"), the opening line was, "One dark Halloween night...." Class members take turns each adding a line to the story that builds on the one before. If the class is too large, a smaller group might be designated as storytellers. In any event, before the story starts, the teacher chooses an "ending committee." When the story is about to get unwieldy, if time is running out, or when the class is getting restless, the teacher puts the ending committee to work creating an ending to the story. Guidelines to the ending might limit it to a certain number of sentences or require that it incorporate all of the characters or situations that have been introduced. In some classes, the teacher may need to establish in advance some guidelines about content, such as no gory violence. As the story is composed, the teacher is writing it on the chalkboard; a designated scribe is also writing it on paper for later reference by the teacher. When the story is finished, the students suggest various sound effects and symbols to cue them. The symbols are drawn in. If there is room on the chalkboard, a "legend" is shown, with the symbols and the sounds to which they refer. The story is then read aloud, with pauses for sound effects. Before the next class, the teacher makes copies of the story from the scribe's transcription, including the symbols and the legend. A reader (or the entire class) reads the story from their "scores," providing the sound effects according to the symbols.

"Composition for Laughter." This exercise in composition has been successfully used by several high school teachers I know, but is equally effective for elementary classes. Necessary participants are a conductor, at least two soloists, and a chorus (the class). The two soloists rehearse and demonstrate their characteristic laughs, then the "chorus" rehearses group laughter. The class decides on possibilities, the order of the composition, and symbols with which these can be notated. Some very effective musical tools include dynamics, sudden cutoffs, silence, and laughter continuing for a set number of beats. Musical vocabulary ("tutti," "crescendo," "dynamics") can be incorporated. Figure 8-1 shows a sample of student group composition.

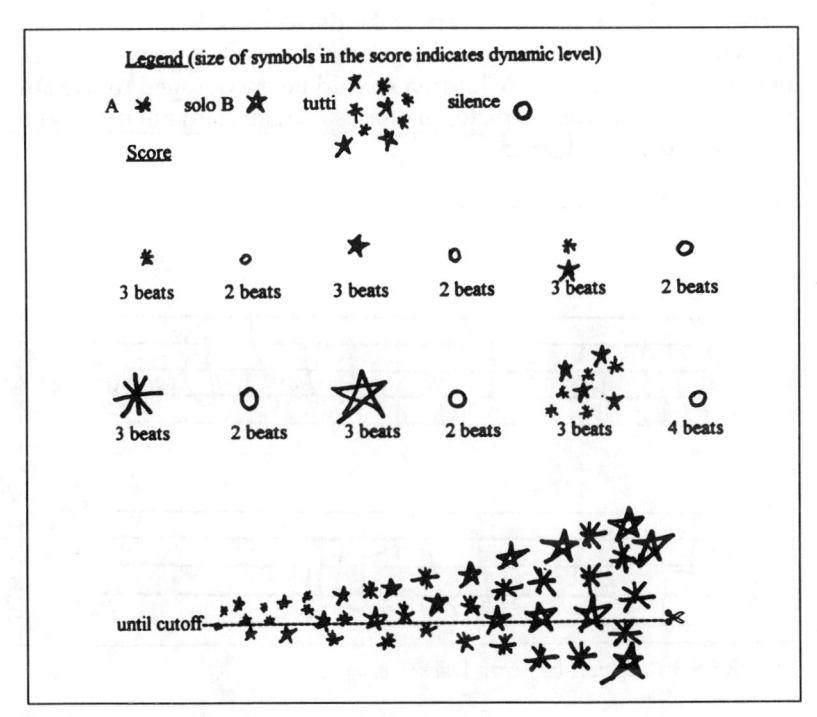

FIGURE 8-1: *"Composition for Laughter"*

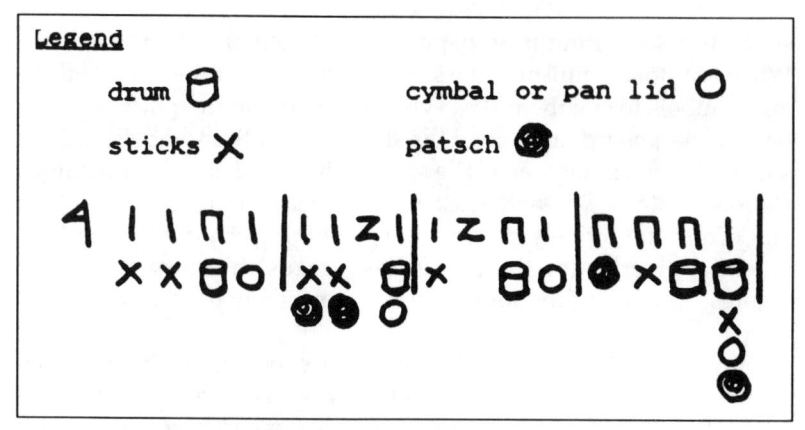

FIGURE 8-2: *Invented notation*

An instrumental score with invented notation. Working in groups, children can devise percussion compositions with scores which show, in the children's invented notation, which instrument does what and when. This is best initiated by working with the whole class the first time, composing the score on the chalkboard. The score might look like Figure 8-2.

Other forms of children's notation can be used as novices to notation begin to get the idea of creating their own symbols for sound and experiment with various kinds of symbols, including pictures representing the song words, verbal instructions, and pictures of how the sound looks. Children should be encouraged to use abstract symbols as well as pictorial ones, since standard notation—the eventual goal—is abstract.

FIGURE 8-3: *"Music," by Sierra Valentine, age 6*

Free exploration of standard notation. From the time the staff and notes are first introduced (see Chapter 9), children enjoy simply drawing all of those symbols: staves, notes, and whatever they choose. At the beginning, the placement is random and often quite prolific (see Figure 8-3). However, as a genuine experience in notating a musical idea, this one usually means that the "composers" have misunderstood the process. They believe that in writing the symbols, they have created the musical idea, which will magically appear when someone plays their notes. Whether or not children have a definite mental sound image of their pieces, they are usually disturbed that when someone plays their work, it doesn't sound like music, or what they had in mind.

Therefore, as a deliberate activity, this exercise has limited value, except to motivate children to learn how standard notation works. If there is a piano or a xylophone in the room, the teacher might "play" each child's composition, saying, "Your piece sounds sort of like this . . ." In playing the compositions, the teacher points out the relationship between the notes on the staff going up or down and the rise and fall of the pitch. The teacher can gently explain that the class will be learning more about the notation system so that the score can really "say" what the composer is thinking. With more experience, children begin to assume real ownership of the standard notation system (Figures 8-4 and 8-5).

Other ways to "keep it":

- If barred percussion instruments are being used in composition, the letter names of the notes in the piece (engraved on the bars) can be written down in order.
- If the composers can use solfège—*Do Re Mi* syllables—they can use these to write down their sequence of pitches.
- The composition may be recorded with a tape cassette recorder.
- A person knowledgeable about standard notation can be invited to class (or can borrow the tape recording) to help write down the compositions.

Original, nontraditional organization of sound

As discussed throughout this book, children should be encouraged to organize sound in original ways using non-traditional sound sources: "found" sound, recorded environmental sounds, unusual vocal sounds, and whatever else they can invent or adopt.

An interesting approach to composition, especially for older students, is appropriated from techniques of innovative twentieth-

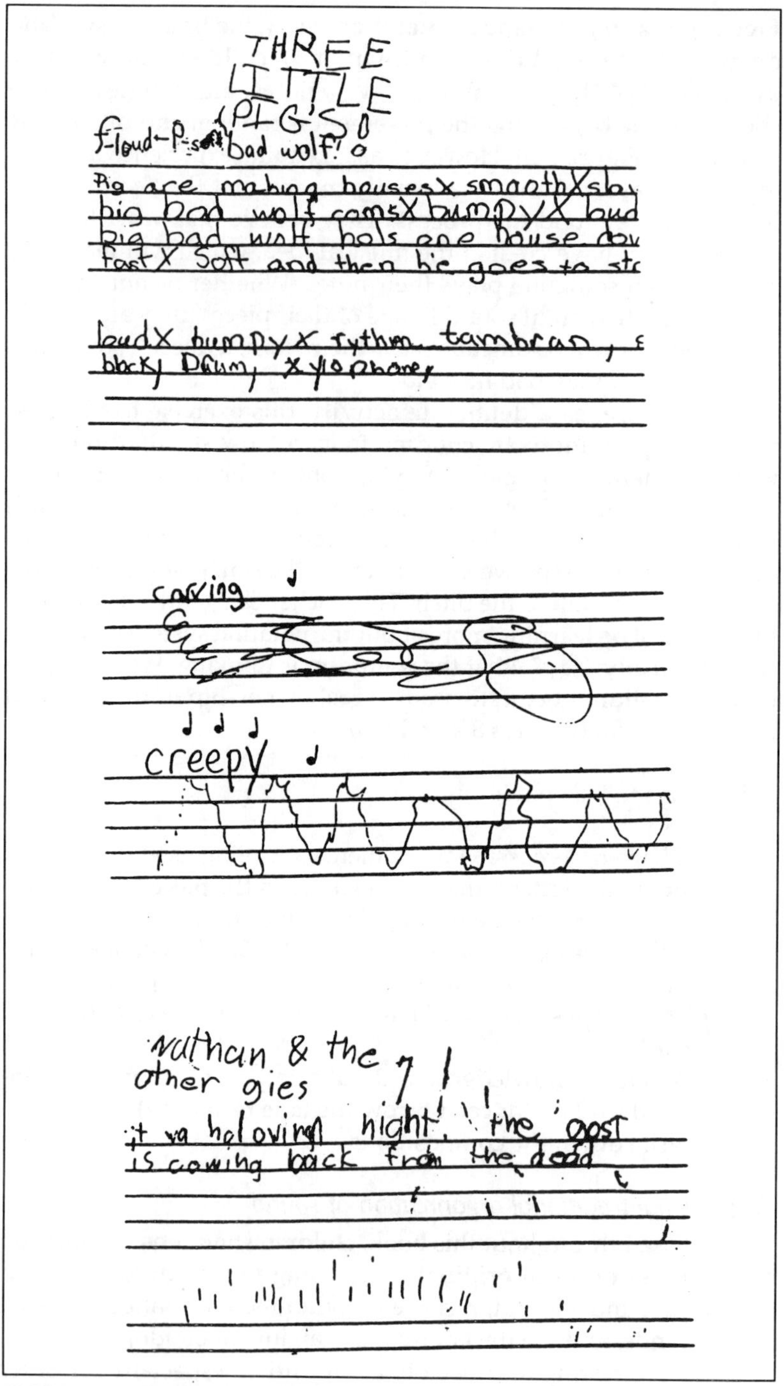

FIGURE 8-4: *Children's notation*

FIGURE 8-5: *Children's notation*

century composers. Sound pieces are composed using such sound generators as the gurgling of a straw at the bottom of a nearly-empty glass, the slamming of a door, or a recording of a dog's barking. Non-traditional instruments, such as stones and brake drums as mallet percussion, can also be incorporated. The student writes a score, usually with invented notation, and performs the piece, either "live" or as a recording. Professional twentieth-century composers have developed a substantial glossary of innovative notational symbols to represent new uses of sound.

Compositions in the Western European tradition

From birth, and possibly before, children are surrounded by their "mother music" as well as their mother tongue. Howard Gardner has found (1981) that children, much like baby birds, go through several developmental stages in learning to sing, including periods of babbling and of experimenting with snatches of adult song. Ultimately, they are "programmed" with the music of their culture. Creating music that resembles that cultural model is very satisfying and is an avenue of expression and communication with other people. In the case of most public school children, particularly with the homogenization of music through exposure to television, that model is the music of Western Europe.

Free exploration of sound and original notation are ends in themselves, but are also the foundation for composing music of a traditional model. Here are some examples:

Writing a song: A tune for a poem. Using original or other poems, children can compose tunes for them using a xylophone, a keyboard instrument, or just by humming into a tape recorder. The technique is to chant the words, a line at a time, mentally reviewing possible tunes that would fit. If the teacher can strum I, IV, V chords on the autoharp or the guitar in the background, this is very effective in suggesting snatches of melody. The initial experience can include the entire class composing the poem, then chanting the lines. The tunes that children suggest are usually bits and pieces of other songs, which is just fine as a first step. It has been said that there are no truly original tunes. Here is a poem written by a fifth grade class; it was a communal effort, with class members suggesting, rejecting, and confirming parts of it while the teacher wrote on the chalkboard, erased, and rewrote until they had this:

> Homework is the pits.
> It wastes all my time.
> If there is a paper with an A on it, then
> It probably isn't mine.

FIGURE 8-6: *"Homework"*

Figure 8-6 shows the tune that was composed by the same group effort.

Tunes can be composed to existing poems, such as A.A. Milne's "Happiness," from *When We Were Very Young* (see Appendix A). The words are in rhythmic patterns which can be expressed in Kodály rhythm symbols; these in turn will suggest a tune.

John had Great Big	❙ ❙ ❙ ❙
Waterproof Boots on,	⊓ ❙ ❙ ❙
John had a Great Big	❙ ⊓ ❙ ❙
Waterproof Hat.	⊓ ❙ ❙ Z
John had a Great Big	❙ ⊓ ❙ ❙
Waterproof macintosh,* and	⊓ ❙ ⊓ ⊓
That (said John) is that.	❙ ❙ ❙ ❙ ❙

(*Clarify for the class that this macintosh is not a brand of computer.)

The tunes expressed by very young children are often slight variations of the Ur-song. That will do very well, since it is then within the capability of everyone in the class to sing it.

Tunes can be composed for repeated phrases in favorite stories, such as in Dr. Seuss's *Horton Hatches the Egg*: "I meant what I said, and I said what I meant. An elephant's faithful, one hundred percent." This is in triple meter (OOM – pah – pah, OOM – pah – pah) and makes a very good song. In a different vein is *I'll Love You Forever*, by Robert Munsch (see Appendix A). The recurrent quatrain, which undergoes slight variation at the end of the story, is deeply touching. (I am unable to read that book aloud without choking up.) Children will spontaneously fit it to simple, sad little tunes. I find it interesting that the tunes occasionally emerge in a minor key. The association of the minor scale with sadness is a cultural manifestation that is prevalent in North American folk music; however, this is not the case in other cultures and was not always so even in Western European music. (Bach wrote some arias with joyous words set to minor modes.) Munsch's little refrain goes like this:

> I'll love you forever,
> I'll like you for always.
> As long as I'm living
> Your Mommy I'll be.

This can be a wistful little song in triple meter.

Although catalogues full of musicals written for children exist, children are quite capable of writing their own. The sequence of tasks for the class is: (1) choose a favorite story, (2) write a script of the story, transforming it into a play, (3) pick out key phrases or events from the story and make little poems of these, (4) compose tunes for the poems, (5) perform the play, with the songs in appropriate places. This is a lengthy sequence and can best be accomplished in smaller groups. For example, in the musical described below, written by sixth graders in Santa Fe, New Mexico from the book *The Shrinking of Treehorn*, by Florence Parry Heide (see Appendix A), a group was appointed to be responsible for each chapter of the book. The group wrote the play script for that chapter, chose two phrases for songs, wrote the poems, and composed the music.

The Shrinking of Treehorn is about a little boy who finds himself shrinking, but cannot get anyone, including his parents, to concentrate on him long enough to notice. His father says only, "Sit up, Treehorn," to which he sadly replies, "I *am* sitting up." His mother is preoccupied with her cake in the oven. The school principal, not really listening, only jovially tells him, "We're a team here" and sends him out the door with a pat on the back. Three of the songs written for the musical were "I'm shrinking," "I *am* sitting up," and "We're a team."

Children are eager to create, and they can produce artistic work that ranges from interesting to breathtaking. However, the environment and motivation must be provided by the teacher. The teacher must present the idea, one about which he/she is enthusiastic and confident. The teacher must plan the sequence of tasks involved in reaching this goal, demonstrate each step in turn, generally serve as cheerleader, and be prepared to see it through. Different classes have different collective strengths and limitations, which will require flexibility and resourcefulness on the teacher's part. But original composition from individuals or the group is a memorable accomplishment for everyone concerned.

9

Standard Notation and Music Reading

Music notation represents *symbols for sound*. Notation is not music. Notation is just a map, a chart, of how the composer wanted the music to sound. In the same way that written and spoken language are related but not the same, so music and music notation are related but not the same. For some reason, the idea of "learning music" usually seems to imply learning to *read* music. Musicians themselves perpetuate this misconception by referring to notated music as the "music." ("Did you remember to bring your music?")

The advanced position of standard notation in the sequence of this book is intentional. All the foregoing activities have been with the objective of learning *music*. Only now have we arrived at the point of exploring notation. This is analogous to the fact that we do not attempt to teach an infant to read because an infant has had insufficient experience with language. Only at the age of five or six has the child internalized enough experience with language (Chomsky's *language competence*) to be prepared for the introduction of a new symbol system related to it.

Whole language researchers have analyzed the strategies used by efficient readers, with the objective of orienting novice readers that way from the beginning. These strategies correspond directly to those utilized by efficient music readers. The whole music approach to music reading involves introducing music reading through those strategies from the beginning. This approach is based on musical paraphrases of seven psycholinguistic principles, particularly as they are advanced by Kenneth Goodman (1982) and Frank Smith (1982). A listing of these principles follows. Each will later be considered in turn in detail:

Principle I. Receptive and Generative Aspects of Language and Music. Both language and music have *receptive* and *generative* modes. Speaking and writing are generative aspects of language; listening and reading are receptive. Playing/singing and composing/writing are generative aspects of music; listening and reading are receptive. In both whole language and whole music instruction, these two modes have equal emphasis from the beginning.

Principle II. Reading and Experience. Reading written language is interaction between the reader and the author through print. Language is ambiguous; *meaning* is constructed by the reader according to the *experience* that he or she brings to the text. Reading music is interaction between the reader and the composer through notation. Music is ambiguous; *meaning* is constructed by the reader according to the *experience* that he or she brings to the score. Whole music provides experience with music.

Principle III. Whole to Part. In both whole language and whole music, initial instruction is in context rather than through introduction of symbols in isolation, with the goal of assembling them later. Written language is introduced through whole real language that is relevant to the child's experiences. The reader learns to perceive *groups of words*, units of meaning. Notation is introduced through whole, real music that is familiar to the students. Children learn initially to perceive patterns, *groups of notes* rather than individual notes one at a time.

Principle IV. A Straight Line to Meaning. Efficient music readers arrive at meaning (sound) directly, without recourse to names of notes, solfège (*Do, Re, Mi* . . .), numbers, or any other secondary identification. This is analogous to the strategies of whole language readers, who arrive at meaning directly, without recourse to spoken words.

Principle V. The Graphic "System." The type of "notation system" is not a factor in learning to read music. Children approach all notation systems in the same way, as units of meaning. One is no "easier" than another, nor does introducing one system first make another one "easier to learn." Since the most practical goal is reading standard notation, it makes sense to start with that. This is analogous to "writing systems"; the type of writing system—alphabetic, ideographic, or any other—is not a factor. Children perceive all writing systems in the same way, as units of meaning. One is no "easier" than another. However, there are aspects of standard notation that are more accessible than others. These constitute good vehicles for beginning instruction.

Principle VI. The Goodman Model of the Reading Process. The music-reading process corresponds point for point with Kenneth Goodman's model of the language-reading process: *Sampling, Predicting,* and *Correcting* or *Confirming,* in a continuing cycle that Goodman refers to as a "psycholinguistic guessing game" (1982). This process can be observed, in both music and language, through *miscue analysis.*

Principle VII. The Freedom to Take Risks. Efficient reading, in both language and music, can be promoted by an environment that encourages novice readers to take risks and to depend on their own intuition. The antithesis of this is the teacher's repeated interruption of the reader to "correct" a "mistake."

Principle I. Receptive and Generative Aspects of Language and Music

Reading and listening are receptive modes of language; writing and speaking are generative modes. In a more traditional approach, emphasis is put on *reading*, with special attention to word recognition. Any attention given to writing is concentrated on formation of letters and writing words. No time is usually given to creative writing until the teacher is confident that the child "knows" enough words and can spell them. Whole language, on the other hand, begins early with exploration of writing stories, journals, and poetry and with being a storyteller. The child is encouraged to create text, using invented spellings when necessary.

Reading and listening are receptive aspects of music; writing/composing and playing/singing are generative aspects. Almost without exception, music students in both classrooms and private studios spend most of the time working on note-reading. Very seldom are they given the opportunity to *generate* music: to write their own music or even copy notes onto a staff.

A whole music approach incorporates composing and writing as well as reading. The preceding chapters have many examples. Invented notation—the child's own notation—is the musical equivalent of invented spellings.

Principle II. Reading and Experience

Reading of written language is an interaction or transaction between the reader and the author through the text. Reading of notated music is an interaction or transaction between the reader and the composer through the score. The reader *constructs* meaning according to the experience (schemata; competence) that he or she brings to the printed page. The ambiguities of both language and music combine with the individuality of each reader's experience to make each reader's construction a unique one. Preschool experiences with language in the United States tend to range from adequate to profound; as in most human societies, language is a high priority skill. Music development, on the other hand, does not have a high priority rating with most North American families.

Most human families are methodical to some degree about giving infants and children experience with language. Family members make a point of talking to the child and encouraging him or her to repeat sounds and words. Parents are delighted with the process of language development in their children. However, much of a child's exposure to language is simply interaction with the environment: utterances overheard from other people or from radio and television. Indeed, most parents underestimate how much an infant or young child absorbs of overheard conversations.

Young children are assimilating written language systems as well. Yetta Goodman (1981) has observed from her "kid-watching" that children are reading long before any formal instruction in reading. They know the meaning of road signs, print on food packages, commercials on television, and signs for fast-food restaurants. "Knowing the meaning" of written symbols means *reading*. Moreover, a child who is read to by a real person (not a cassette tape) knows what each page "says." Adults are often amused by this, commenting that the child has "only memorized" the action on the page. Memory is recognition. Recognizing what print "says" is reading. In fact, understanding that the page "says something" is reading behavior. It is true that the child's recognition is cued by the illustrations, but the child assimilates the entire contents of the page; he or she does not automatically take in only the pictures. The neophyte reader internalizes the configuration of the *whole*. Without being able to identify individual letters or words and without separating the different kinds of symbols (print and pictures), the child knows what it "says." That is reading. When the child comes to school, he or she brings a level of language competence to the focused study of reading.

Just as a child brings all previous experience with language to school, so also does he or she bring internalized music experiences.

As with language, most of these schemata were assimilated unconsciously from the environment. In addition to the "wallpaper music" omnipresent in the community, there has been some kind of music in the home, if only on television and the radio. However, in most households there are no musical stimuli comparable to the concentrated attention given to language development by most parents.

When there *is* extra home emphasis of any kind on music, the musical development of the child is infinitely more advanced than that of the average preschooler. If the family listens to recordings, the child is "programmed" with that style of music, whatever it is: classical, country and Western, jazz, rock, gospel, or "easy listening." Any musical experiences are good; Beethoven is not a requirement. Composer Igor Stravinsky said that there are only two kinds of music: good music and bad music. In other words, in some ways, music is music. All musical forms have things in common, and there are good and poor examples in every musical style. Good examples of rock or country and Western music are good musical experiences. If a parent has sung lullabies to the child, if the family sings in the car, if family members sing or play instruments in the house, if there are musical toys or a piano available to the child—all these things have contributed to the development of musical competence.

There is evidence that the development of musical competence has more general developmental advantages than simply for music. A study by Frances Rauscher (1994), reported at the 1994 conference of the American Psychological Association, relates music study by pre-schoolers to increased spatial reasoning and resulting higher performance levels in reading, math, and puzzle-solving. Harry Chugani, a neuroscientist at Children's Hospital, University of Michigan, says, "By enrolling a child in music lessons, you've changed the fine anatomy of the brain" (1994, B7).

Children arrive at school with some level of language competence and some level of musical competence. Effective classroom instruction in both language and music will provide experiences to which the child can apply what he or she already "knows" as a path to further learning.

Reading both written language and notated music involves learning systems of printed symbols. Primary school children are able to operate on a symbolic level. Piaget (1966) observed a period of "concrete operations," including symbolic competence, at approximately between ages seven to eleven. Jerome Bruner (1967) believed children capable of symbolic representation between the ages of five and seven. However, in order to learn symbols for something, experience with the thing to which the symbol refers is a prerequisite. In the case of language, most preschool children have had sufficient experience to learn a relevant symbol system. In the case of music, additional development of musical schemata is usually necessary before the introduction of the relevant symbol system: notation. If, during the preschool years, attention to musical development were given the focused attention that language development receives, and if, in the society, individual involvement with music were equal to that of language, the cognitive database would be comparable. Since neither of these is the case, only teachers are in a position to compensate for the disparity. (Alas—yet another breach that teachers are expect to fill.) All the foregoing chapters of this book have outlined kinds of whole music learning that are designed to close the gap. They can both precede *and* accompany the study of notation/music-reading.

Principle III. Whole to Part

A fly on the wall at a first piano lesson might observe the following: The teacher places the method book, opened to the first page, on the music rack. The child's sweaty little thumb is placed on middle C while the teacher points to the corresponding note on the staff. "This," says the teacher, as if bestowing a great gift, "is middle C. Whenever you see *this* note, you press *that* key." At the first band class in many elementary schools, the students have their books ready, on the first day, opened to the first page. The teacher explains how to play B♭, and the class honks an approximation. The book presents a page of B♭s in quarter notes, followed by pages of B♭s in half notes and whole notes.

To this sort of instruction, I believe we can attribute the substantial number of adults who confess that they "took piano" or "took band" (a verb which may be all too descriptive), but never learned to read the notes. They just memorized their parts from the teacher's demonstration or the person sitting next to them. A person who can *do* that has musical intelligence. That makes their departure from the program (either mentally or actually) especially regrettable.

But what's *wrong* with that? Piano and beginning band have "always" been taught that way. And what can we expect from a band teacher with thirty excited, squirming children making an incredible din on six or eight different kinds of wind instruments? We can expect the teacher to give the children some *music*.

Three flaws in the start-at-page-one approach:

1. The notes are being introduced with absolutely no *context*. Just as there is no information in an isolated letter or word, there is no information in an isolated note. Flash cards as an introduction to music-reading are no more appropriate than in language reading. Frank

Smith (1982, 5) quotes Ronald Wardhaugh's description of reading isolated words as "barking at print." The musical equivalent, identifying one note at a time by letter name, is barking at notes. I have heard music students who could toot a whole notated line, one note at a time, and not recognize the very familiar tune they were playing. A sentence is more than a string of words; it is a unit of meaning. The whole is greater than the sum of its parts. A musical phrase is more than a string of notes; it is a unit of meaning (sound patterns). The whole is greater than the sum of its parts.

2. Embarking on music-reading simultaneously with making the first sounds on the instrument is analogous to trying to teach an infant to read. At least a lesson or two of just making sounds with the instrument, then playing some kind of *tune*, by rote, should precede note-reading, even with a stressful public-school schedule. The students will then be *making music*, which is what they wanted to do in the first place. They will be concentrating on making sounds with this new device without simultaneously trying to learn a printed symbol system. The approach of Shinichi Suzuki, who originated an instructional sequence for string instruments that is now used worldwide, begins with a long period of rote playing that eventually includes technically advanced pieces. Music-reading is not an issue until the student has internalized a great deal of *whole, real music* and is both comfortable and fluent on the instrument—sometimes as long as two or three years after the first lesson.

   Public school band instructors do not have the luxury of postponing music-reading. In fact, they sometimes begin in September with an administrative edict to introduce notation by November. But the first two or three lessons can effectively consist of a simple rote tune or two. The first can be as simple as this, involving only two pitches and a rest.

   The second can be faithful, old *Mary*, using only three pitches (skipping the high one, for now).

3. The concept of quarter notes, half notes, and whole notes involves *fractions*. With young children, it is

better to introduce long and short tones first. With the tune of three pitches (shown below), children can chant (after playing it by rote), "short–short–long—short–short–long—short–short–short–short–long—long—."

Mary can be chanted like this:

short–short–short–short–short–short–long—short–short–long—short–short–long—
Mar—y   had   a   lit— tle   lamb lit— tle   lamb lit— tle   lamb—

Students can then chant the shorts and longs again, clapping on the "shorts" and on the "longs," making an arc in the air with palms together to emphasize "long." The quarter note can then be introduced as the "short" note and the half note as the "long" note, with the gestures accompanying the reading of "short" and "long" from the notation.

It is inevitable that almost immediately thereafter, the teacher must tell children that a quarter note "gets" one beat, a half note "gets" two beats, etc. That is the way the method book is written, and besides, to do it any other way is to have to explain that bottom number of the meter signature and fractions. Later, however, a music teacher will have to confess to the children that they were given a truth that is true only part of the time. The values attributed to the quarter note, half note, and so on, are not fixed, but instead are determined by the bottom number of the meter signature.

The idea of "holding" a note for two or four beats is not so obvious to children as it seems to adults. A way to illustrate the meaning of "holding a note" for a certain number of beats is to have the students take part in a contest to see who can hold a tone the longest, without breaking it, while the teacher counts. After declaring the winner ("She held that note for *twenty* counts"), the teacher can point out that all of the class held the note for at least ten counts. "Now let's hold a note, all together, for four counts, then stop." That is identified as the whole note. The same thing is repeated with two counts, for the half note.

One final suggestion: postpone trying to get children to tap their feet to the beat while playing. After they are comfortable with the instrument and notation, that is excellent kinesthetic reinforcement. However, as a part of beginning lessons, which it often is, it is asking the beginner to concentrate on too many things at once.

Principle IV. A Straight Line to Meaning

In the vocabulary of Noam Chomsky (1965, 1969), *meaning* is the *deep structure* of a communication, derived from a *surface structure*, which is either speech or printed symbols. Reading is a meaning-seeking activity. It involves constructing a deep structure, meaning, from a surface structure, printed text. Efficient readers of written language arrive at meaning directly, without recourse to spoken words. The reader samples only as much of the graphic display on the page as is necessary to arrive at meaning (see "Sampling" in the Goodman model of the reading process, later in this chapter). It is the *print* that has cued the construction of meaning, not a decoding of the print into spoken words. Reading is not a process of recognizing the next word. Identification of words *follows* assignment of meaning. Reading by translating the print to spoken words is constructing a deep structure (meaning) from a surface structure (text), then re-encoding the deep structure into *another* surface structure (spoken words). A reader who is decoding the print into spoken words, identifiable by lips moving during reading, is slow and inefficient. Assignment of meaning from print is lightning-fast compared to speaking the words.

Reading of music notation is a meaning-seeking activity. What is meaning in music? Sound. Patterns of sound. What is the deeper meaning? What does the sound mean? It means, as the Queen of Hearts told Alice, what we say it means. Even more than language, music is ambiguous. Music, with changes in tempo, dynamics, timbre, pitch, and rhythmic organization, is an analogue of motion, of the pace of life, of human grief or joy. Philosopher Susanne Langer wrote (1953, 27) that "Music is a tonal analogue of emotive life." The meaning derived from music is filtered through each individual's emotive life.

Efficient readers of music notation arrive at meaning—sound patterns—directly, without recourse to names of notes, solfège (*Do, Re, Mi*), numbers, or any other secondary identification. This skill depends upon the phenomenon of *inner hearing*, or in Edwin Gordon's term, *audiation*. The music reader samples only as much of the notation as is necessary to arrive at meaning. A good music reader hears the sound mentally for a split second before producing it with voice or instrument. Identification of notes *follows* assignment of meaning. A music reader who is decoding the notes into letter names, solfège, numbers, or any other secondary (the sound is primary) identification is engaging in "double-think." He or she is taking time to construct deep structure (meaning, sound) from one surface structure (notation), then translate it to *another* surface structure (words). This lengthy process is slow and inefficient. For various reasons, music students in ear-training/sight-singing classes are usually required to read music with this "double-think" process. In the real world of sight-reading music, however, this step must be discarded.

Principle V. The Graphic "System"

Composer Roger Sessions (1965, 68) describes the Western musical notation system as "a remarkable cultural achievement" through which composers have learned "to convey to those capable of reading it the finest subtleties of pitch, of rhythm, of tempos, of articulation, etc., so that an accomplished player can, within the limits of his own technique, reproduce these things at sight, with a startlingly close approximation to what the composer first heard in his imagination." That is quite a testimonial.

Other composers have been less positive. Arthur Honegger (1966, 50–53) referred to the "anomalies, the incoherences, and the antiquated practices" of music notation, and compiled a list of these. One of his pet annoyances was the use of key signatures for music that modulates (changes key) frequently, anyway. Honegger complained that the obsolete signatures "remain there clinging like so many abandoned sausages." He also quoted the satirical observation of composer Erik Satie that the complexities of standard notation are "to drive off the stupid."

Varieties of music notation

Musicians and others have been criticizing standardized music notation for as long as it has existed, and a compilation of the suggestions for improvement would fill another book. What is more relevant here is a brief review of the attempts of educators to simplify the introduction of notation to beginners.

Pictures. A chart of pictures is used to illustrate the relative duration of notes in a familiar song. Pitch level is not incorporated, since the melody is assumed to have been memorized. Several well-known music educators have done this. To avoid offending anyone, I offer my own drawings as an illustration of this approach:

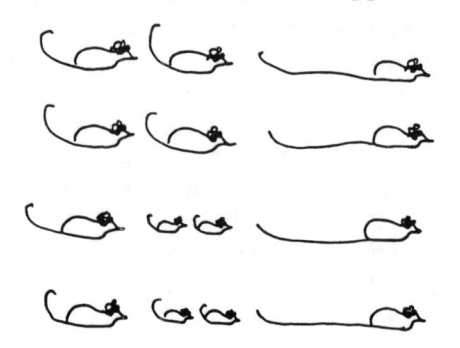

Short or elongated note-heads or pitch letter names:

F♯ E D
F♯ E D
A G F♯

Colors. Manufacturers of children's musical toys, junior instruments, and even beginning piano books have demonstrated a conviction that assigning different colors to each pitch, particularly if the color matches the corresponding key or tone bar of the notated pitch on the instrument, makes it "easier."

Shape notes. Shape notes (or shaped notes) have been an integral part of indigenous American musical culture since the seventeenth century. During the eighteenth century, at the instigation of the New England clergy, community singing schools were established with the objective of improving the quality of congregational singing. The chosen system of instruction was usually a four-syllable shape note system, "fasola," which originated in Elizabethan England. Syllables in the major scale were *Fa, Sol, La, Fa, Sol, La, Mi, Fa*. The notation was orthodox in designation of duration; the difference was only in the noteheads, which were shaped to correspond with the four syllables to indicate relative pitch level (Figure 9-1).

Competing systems were devised, but they were largely rejected by shape-note practitioners. Later revisions of the earliest shape-note tune books are still in use. "Fasola" singing is still a way of life for its many passionate devotees, especially in the Southeastern United States, where five-hour singing sessions and conventions

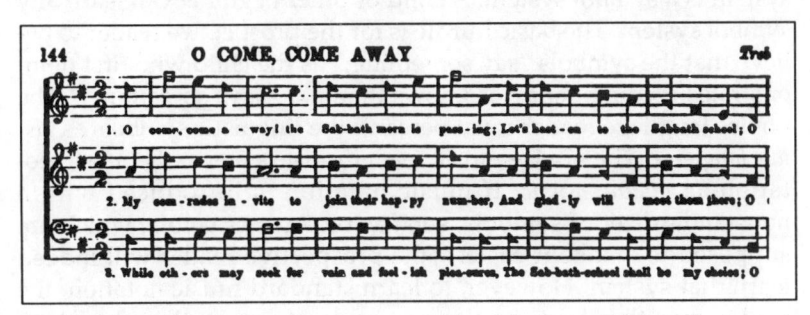

FIGURE 9-1: *Shape notes*

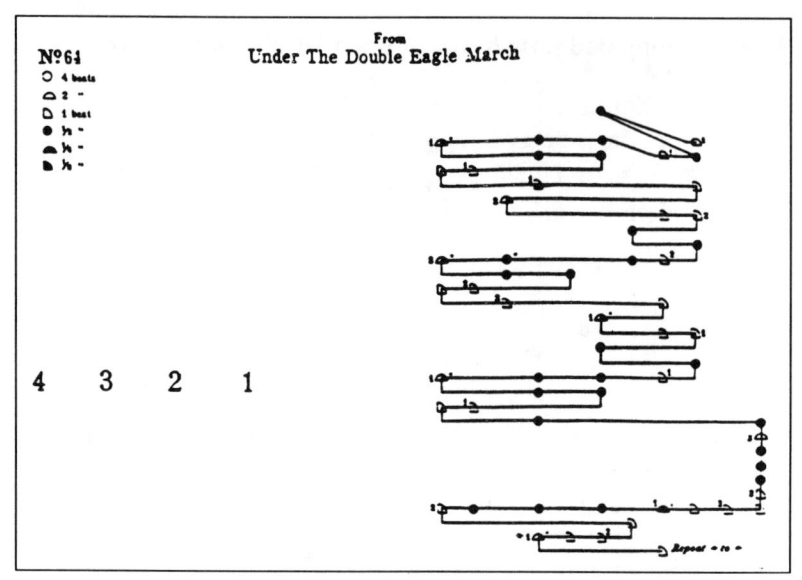

FIGURE 9-2: *"Under the Double Eagle"*

are still regularly held. This system has been proven effective in teaching efficient sight-singing.

Shape notes have been used in the folk tradition to represent duration as well as pitch. I have a nineteenth century American "farmer zither" (which looks like an autoharp without chord bars). It came to me with a set of yellowed diagrams that are to be positioned under the strings. The player follows the lines and plucks the string that is under each note. The legend in the upper left denotes the durational value of the shapes (Figure 9-2).

It doesn't make any difference!

All these notation systems have been devised to "make it easier," or at least to simplify the system for beginners. Do they work as music notation? Yes, in varying degrees. Are they easier? No. A symbol system is a symbol system. A child or other beginner can learn any symbol system. The basic hurdle is for the prospective reader to believe that the symbols "say something," as the child who first demonstrates reading behavior knows that text "says something." The novice language reader must perceive the linguistic symbols as *visible language*. The novice music reader must perceive the music notation as *visible music*. If music notation is introduced with a nonstandard set of symbols, such as pictures or colors, which are supposed to "make it easier," the prospective reader will indeed learn that system. However, to learn standard music notation, the reader must then learn *another* system. Is one easier than the other?

The truth is, *it doesn't make any difference.* The first one did not make the second one any easier; in fact, the situation is probably the opposite, since the first system must be discarded and another system learned. The student may as well begin with the standard system in the first place. Colors and pictures will not get him or her very far in the high school band or the church choir.

Direct and indirect symbols

A *symbol is a representation of an idea or object separate from the idea or object itself.* The degree to which a symbol corresponds to its referent can be described as somewhere on a continuum between pictorial/analogue, in which a recognizable picture is intended, to abstract, in which meaning exists only because meaning has been assigned and agreed upon. Symbols at the pictorial end of the continuum are sometimes called *direct* symbols. Symbols which are more abstract are classified as *indirect* symbols.

Certain direct symbols have been adopted internationally as part of a code that can be understood regardless of the native language of the reader. As with all symbols, experience of some kind with the referent is required for understanding. The message of the following is clear if the reader knows what a bicycle is and has learned the negative implication of the circle with a diagonal bar (Figure 9-3).

Researchers in information processing have described the process as one of *visual, verbal,* or *topical* coding. A picture of a dove is a direct symbol. If the picture is accurate and the viewer knows what a dove looks like, meaning is accessible without recourse to language. Cognitive coding, in this instance is visual, or analogue. However, the viewer might process the picture of the dove verbally, encoding and storing the visual information in the form of the *word* for "dove" in his or her native language. Alternatively, given more context, or the personal, individual aspect of the reading process, the viewer might encode a general idea or topic: something like "peace" or "drab bird" or "gourmet dinner" instead. In any case, a direct symbol is accessible without language. Thought can take place without words.

FIGURE 9-3: *International sign for "no bicycles"*

The *word* "dove" is an abstract symbol; its meaning derives from the assignment of that meaning with the concurrence of other users of that language. A word is an indirect symbol in the sense that only users of that language are privy to that information. It is an exclusive code. Again, the reader of the word may encode the verbal information in a visual code, mentally storing it as a *picture* of a dove—or as the topic of "drab bird," "peace," or "gourmet dinner" instead. But meaning was arrived at through experience with language. Whether symbols are direct or indirect, both context and experience (with life, or pictures, or language) are prerequisites to the assignment of meaning. Direct symbols require experience with symbols and life. Indirect symbols require experience with symbols, life *and* language.

Some written languages, such as Chinese, have pictorial components. Through usage, convention, and stylization, the relationship of the symbol to its referent may become less apparent; the symbol becomes more abstract, less direct. For example, Chinese characters were affected by the development of the calligraphy brush, which is better adapted to drawing rectangular forms than curved ones. That brought about transformations in the original pictographs, but many of the origins are still visible (Figure 9-4).

Chinese characters are composed of evolved pictograms combined with phonograms (symbols for speech sounds) and classifiers. Classification characters can also be pictorial. A character that looks like drops of water is a component not only in more obvious combinations that refer to something liquid, but also in symbols for harbor, leak, deep, and shallow. Using this type of association, anyone can invent a fairly accurate list of Chinese words in which the character for "mouth" appears. See Figure 9-5 for two examples. It is quite possible to read Chinese at some level with no experience with the spoken language.

The symbols of some written languages were designed to represent the sounds of the spoken language. The relationship between a symbol and a sound is by nature indirect or abstract because it is

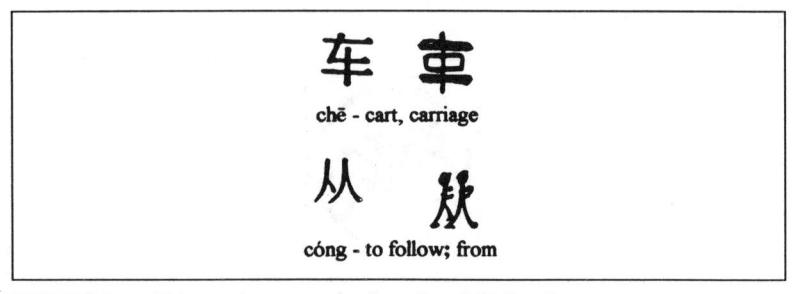

车 車
chē - cart, carriage

从 從
cóng - to follow; from

FIGURE 9-4: *Chinese characters for "cart" and "follow"*

吐

tǔ - to spit out
tù - to vomit

歌

gē - song

FIGURE 9-5: *Chinese characters*

difficult to imagine a picture of a sound. One of the categories of such languages is an alphabetic language: one composed of letters or combinations of letters, each of which represents a sound. English is an alphabetic language.

If someone shows you a flash card of the letter "A," you can identify it because someone, parent or teacher, told you long ago that it is an "A." If asked to "pronounce" it, you can assign sounds to it according to your training in the language(s) you speak. By itself, it has no meaning. It is not a picture of an apple or an ax. It becomes a symbol of these only when combined with other indirect symbols (other letters) that have no meaning in themselves and which, combined, form still other indirect symbols (words) to which have been ascribed a wide range of meanings, elucidated (to some extent) only by context. Alphabetic written languages consist of indirect symbols. Readers of alphabetic languages demonstrate a remarkable tolerance for alternate forms of these symbols: upper and lower case, cursive writing, different kinds of type, and so on.

Mathematics consists largely of indirect symbols. However, a few cardinal digits are direct, that is, actually countable; they are a picture of what they mean. That includes Roman numerals I, II, and III. Indirect numerals are those after 1 or written alphabetic words for cardinal and ordinal numbers.

Sooner or later, a study of the reading process as it relates to various forms of written language begets discussion about whether it is easier to learn to read a language like Chinese that has pictorial components than an alphabetic language like English. The studies that have been done on this have resulted in conflicting conclusions. If there is a "truth" to be inferred from that, it is probably that, like all of those ideas for "easier" music notation, *it does not matter*. The symbols used in all writing systems are arbitrary. There is evidence that readers read the same way, regardless of the system. The very nature of the reading process is one of reading *units* of meaning. Even in an alphabetic system, that is what good readers are doing. They do not decode symbols to sound; they are not identifying individual words. Instead, they perform grouping tasks and read for meaning in the same way that readers of Chinese do.

Kolers described the reading process as one of perceiving relationships among symbols. "The reading of English and the reading of Chinese have more in common than would first appear" (Levin and Williams 1970, 118). Tseng and Hung observed that skilled readers read alphabetic languages as ideographic signs: children perceive alphabetic text as "pictures, ideas, wordness" (Tseng and Singer 1981, 244).

If, for beginning readers, it does not matter what kind of symbols comprise the symbol system, why did I bring all of this up? Because it *may* matter what aspects of the symbol system, whatever it is, are chosen for the *orientation* to reading. Processing of any symbols requires previous experience. Direct/analogue symbols require experience with life. Alphabetic symbols require experience with life *and* language. I am able to read at least the pictorial aspects of Chinese on an elementary level. However, I am totally unable either to speak or to understand spoken Chinese.

Comparative reading is a field of research that seeks, through studying reading behaviors in different cultures and varying languages, to understand reading processes and how they are learned. John Downing, in his review of some of these studies (1973) concluded that it may not be the type of system, alphabetic or pictorial, that signifies difficulty in learning to read. Instead, it is the particular symbols that are chosen for the *orientation*. For beginning readers, the symbols should be the most accessible and representative of the language, and they should be limited in number at first. Downing's example for English was to limit, at first, the alternative written forms (different types of print, cursive writing) and to postpone as long as possible large doses of alternate spellings of the same sound.

In the case of orienting new music readers to music notation, I believe that it matters which symbols are chosen for the *orientation*. Music notation has a few relatively direct/analogue aspects that can be used for the initiation process. If there were any pictorial aspects of written English, I am sure that we would use them to introduce children to reading in the same way that I have introduced you to reading Chinese.

Kodály's [direct] symbols for rhythmic organization

A *direct symbol* is one which, like international road signs or the Roman numerals I, II, and III, *looks like what it means*. Zoltan Kodály developed a system to introduce children to music notation that exploits one of the few aspects of music notation that looks like what it means. Suppose you were to beat on a drum a pattern of four slow beats and to ask a musically-untrained listener to invent some way to write that. Chances are that person would write something like this: | | | |. Suppose you were then to beat a pattern of one slow beat, two fast ones, and two more slow ones. There is a strong likelihood that the listener would write something like this: | || | |. You can, in fact, test that hypothesis by asking a group of musically-untrained children to take part in this exercise. I have tried it many times, and the results are usually very much like the above. In Kodály's approach, children are introduced to notation of rhythmic patterns through symbols that represent a pair of short notes and a single longer note. For the rhythmic pattern above, Kodály's rhythm symbols look like this:

| ⊓ | |

The choice of these symbols for orientation to music notation is appropriate for at least three reasons: (1) These symbols are direct symbols; they *look like what they mean*. They are almost identical to the notation that musically-untrained people invent spontaneously. (2) These symbols are not an attempt to introduce standard notation through still another symbol system that is supposed to "make it easier." Kodály's rhythm symbols are *a component of standard notation*: the stems of notes. These are the stems of quarter notes and paired eighth notes: ♩ ♫ ♩ ♩ (3) Kodály related each of these symbols to a *speech pattern*, which is at the same time the origin of most rhythm patterns in music and the most natural way for people to apprehend them. The symbol representing the long note (a quarter note, though it is not so identified at first) is called a "tah." The symbol representing the two short notes (paired eighth notes) is called "ti-ti" (pronounced "tee-tee"). The pattern above is read aloud thus:

| ⊓ | |
tah ti-ti tah tah

This system, sometimes called "stick notation," was adapted by Kodály from one devised by a French physician, E. Chevé (1804–1864). It makes possible the reading of rhythms from notation by *saying words*. Beginners don't as yet have to count, or deal with fractions (whole, half, quarter, and eighth notes, and worse) or meter signatures. They just say the words associated with the symbols and the rhythmic pattern is clear. There are a whole set of words to go with the various rhythmic notation patterns. A triplet ⊓ is "tri-o-la" (called "triple-ti" by English speakers). Four sixteenth notes ⊞ are "Ti-ri-ti-ri." Therefore an eye-crossing rhythmic sequence like

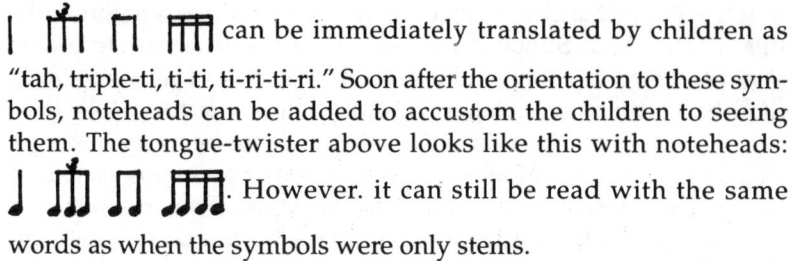

| ♩ ᴍ ♫ ♬ can be immediately translated by children as "tah, triple-ti, ti-ti, ti-ri-ti-ri." Soon after the orientation to these symbols, noteheads can be added to accustom the children to seeing them. The tongue-twister above looks like this with noteheads:

♩ ᴍ ♫ ♬. However. it can still be read with the same words as when the symbols were only stems.

Kodály introduced quarter rests right away, using a symbol like an upper-case "Z," because the printed form of a quarter rest is difficult to approximate by hand. The response to the rest is silence as well as a gesture of the hands thrown out to the side, palms up. This ensures that the rest will receive due consideration:

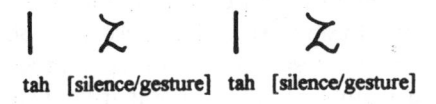

| 𝄾 | 𝄾

tah [silence/gesture] tah [silence/gesture]

One further benefit of Kodály's rhythm symbols: A symbol representing a note twice as long in duration as a "tah" (| ♩) is a "tah-ah": ⌢| or ♩⌢♩. This is a relatively direct symbol; two tah's tied together. In fact, the curved line that joins them is called a tie. Thus, a note twice as long as a quarter note is two quarter notes tied together. Later—*much* later—the very abstract/indirect symbol, the half note, ♩ is introduced as a shorter way to write ♩⌢♩. Children who have learned rhythmic values this way do not make the common error of cheating the half note. They know it as "tah-ah," which automatically makes it twice as long as "tah," the quarter note. Another symbol at the abstract/indirect end of the continuum is the whole note: ○. Does that look to you like what it means? This is also a very abstract *concept* for children: "holding" one note for four beats. In the Kodály approach, a whole note is introduced as four tah's (four quarter notes tied together): ⌢|||⌢. Later, when the whole note is introduced, it is still identified as "tah-ah-ah-ah." This tends to result in the whole note being held for its full value, an intent in which many musicians fall short.

The Kodály approach to rhythm can be described as whole music because new symbols are always introduced *in context*: first four "tah's," with the children saying and clapping the pattern. The ti-ti is then included, followed by the rest, each time in various patterns with repetition of clapping and saying the patterns. A new symbol is introduced in a pattern, casually, pulling the students along. Only after it is used is there any particular attention called to it.

Some adventures for experiencing Kodály's "stick notation." *Popsicle sticks and pipe cleaners*. Children can construct rhythmic patterns with ta's and ti-ti's made from popsicle sticks. Their patterns can be dictated by rhythms clapped or played to them or by the rhythms in a poem or song they are learning. As soon as possible, however, they should be working with notes with noteheads and standard names (quarter note, etc.). For this, black pipe cleaners are ideal. The end of the pipe cleaner can be rolled into a tight spiral for a quarter note or made into a loop for a half note, and so forth. They still read the rhythmic patterns with words (tah, ti-ti) until they are led from Kodály to counting.

Gossip. Two groups of children take part. One person from each group stands at the chalkboard with his or her "team" lined up behind. The teacher gives each of the last persons in each line a card with an identical rhythm pattern on it. At the signal to start, that person silently taps the rhythm pattern on the back of the next person. The pattern is passed to the person at the front of the line, who writes it on the board. The winner is either the one who writes it correctly or the one who writes it correctly first.

Beats in a measure. The top number of the meter signature, which shows how many beats are present in each measure, is much easier to illustrate than the bottom number. Large spaces on the floor can be designated as measures, with measure lines indicated with tape. Carpet squares represent the beats. If there are three beats in each measure, three carpet squares are placed in each measure. The class composes rhythmic patterns by designating whether a quarter note, two eighths, or a quarter rest go in each beat. Children form these entities with their bodies, after which the class claps the rhythm (Figure 9-6). (For more on Kodály, see Choksy 1981, 1988, and 1991, and Wheeler and Raebeck 1985, in the Reference List.)

FIGURE 9-6: *Whole body Kodály rhythm symbols*

Pitch notation: direct, accessible symbols

Beyond Kodály's adaptation of note stems, only one other aspect of music notation is somewhat pictorial or direct: the positioning of noteheads at varying relative heights to represent rise and fall of pitch. My suggestion for the next step is what I call "road maps."

"Road maps." After the rhythm symbols (stems) are introduced in the context of rhythmic patterns, the noteheads (without stems) are introduced in the context of melodic patterns, showing direction of the melodic line. This has the advantage of being complementary to the Kodály note stems. Like them, the direct symbols of the noteheads going up and down according to pitch level are a component of standard notation.

Using the chalkboard and the students' participation, develop a "road map" of *Mary Had a Little Lamb*. Make a beginning notehead for the opening pitch. The class then sings, "Ma—ry." Have the class point to show the direction of the pitch. Down. Write another notehead at a slightly lower level. Then the class sings "Ma—ry had." Which way did it go? Down. Write another notehead a little lower than the last. "Ma—ry had a." Which way? Up. The next notehead is higher than the last. "Ma—ry had a lit—." The next notehead is up. What do we know about "Lit—tle lamb?" All three notes are the same. The students will be able to say what is different about the last note ("lamb"): it's longer. Make that notehead an "empty" one, like a half note. When you're finished with the line, it looks like this:

Make a chart of that pattern for the class to identify the next day.

The next road map can be of "Twinkle." After the first notehead for the opening pitch, the class sings, "Twink—le." What do we know about the first two pitches? They're the same. Put the next notehead on the same level as the first. Then sing, "Twinkle, Twinkle." Is this a little step, like the ones in "Mary?" No, it is a skip. It skips some pitches on the way up. So the third pitch is some distance from the first two. Then sing, "Twinkle, Twinkle, Little." Which way does it go? Up. What do we know about the pitches of those two notes on "Little?" They're the same. Sing, "Twinkle, twinkle, little, star." "Star" goes down. The class then helps with the stepwise descent of the rest of the line. The road map will look like this:

132···· WHOLE MUSIC

Make a chart of that road map for the class to identify later. Then develop two more of these. *Old McDonald* is a good one, because it shows a skip down. *Jingle Bells* demonstrates seven pitches that are all the same, with the noteheads all in a row. It also incorporates long notes, so the half-note head can be used

Now the class has four charts of road maps that it has developed. The students learn to recognize which is which on sight. What is happening here? The children are learning to recognize the *whole shape* of each of those melodic phrases. They are reading a *group of notes*. This is the way efficient language readers read; they read *groups of words*.

The staff. The use of "road maps" retraces a stage in the early development of Western musical notation. One form of medieval notation was a series of dots or lozenge shapes over the text, indicating the relative pitch levels of the melody:

A-scendit De-us in ju-bi-la-ti-o-ne, Do-mi-nus in vo-ce tu-bae, al-le-lu-lia.

The limitations of this were the same as that of "road maps"; persons unfamiliar with the melody cannot duplicate it from the dots because, although direction is indicated, the *size* of the interval is a mystery. These inexact early symbols developed into *neumes*, notes in square or lozenge shapes with variations that could indicate single notes as well as groups of two, three or more tones. This notation was so sophisticated and subtle that it could be used to indicate duration, certain performance practices, and intervals, even without lines.

However, lines did come into common use, at first with one, two, or four lines. At one point, a red line indicated "f," a yellow line "c." Some manuscripts had as many as six lines. Eventually the staff became standardized at five lines. Liturgical music retained an earlier 4-line staff and the square shapes of early neumes.

After the students have worked with the "road maps," they can easily be made aware of the road maps' limitations: the noteheads show us when to go up or down, but not how far. If we put lines as reference points, then we can tell what the intervals are. This is again re-tracing the course of the historical development of notation. Some whole music ways of introducing the staff:

The floor staff. A giant staff is drawn on the floor using masking tape. The lines should be far enough apart so that children can stand on the lines and on the spaces to represent notes. At first, no clefs are used, and no exact pitches. Children stand on the staff, duplicating the patterns of their road maps. A group of children can each represent a pitch and form the whole pattern. Alternately, one child can "walk through" the melodic line, from line to space to line. This makes an excellent exercise of notating intervals. For the second "Twinkle" in *Twinkle, Twinkle,* the class can help the student walk to the right pitch by "humming up" along the scale from the low pitch until the target pitch is reached. The same technique is used to find the low note in *Old McDonald.* If you feel the need of leger lines, they can be introduced.

Individual staves and notes. The students can make their own staves on poster board or construction paper. All that is needed at this point are five lines, six quarter notes, and two half notes (*Jingle Bells* requires two). The students reconstruct the road maps of the four songs, with special attention to "humming up" or "humming down" on the skips in *Twinkle, Twinkle* and *Old McDonald.* Don't worry about specific starting pitch, sharps and flats, or keys. At this stage, the important element is the *shape* of the melody, the *whole,* and the concept of steps and skips on the staff.

A Suggested Sequence for Exploring Standard Notation

The order in which the activities in this book are presented constitutes a suggested sequence. Students explore musical concepts with whole music activities that include movement. They devise their own notation. They work with rhythm patterns, stick notation, noteheads and note names, measures, and the top number of the meter signature.

The next step is exact pitches and the names of the lines and spaces. Clefs are introduced as the "key" (in the sense of opening a door: giving a clue or reference point. "Clef" means "key"—a door key—in French.). A good associative device is pointing out that the treble or G clef is an old-fashioned G; the bass clef is an old-fashioned F. Names written with the clefs as initial letters, 𝄞eorge and 𝄢rank, will help. Except for those reference points, music-readers must learn to recognize a note simply by looking at it, as language readers recognize letters and words. Crutches like "Every Good Boy Does Fine" are "doublethink" and take too long. Playing recorder is an excellent way for children to learn to recognize notes simply by looking at them rather than counting lines and spaces.

In demonstrating how a staff "works," the teacher can point out that it is a "magic ladder"; notes can walk up and down on the rungs as well as on the spaces in between. I have a little ceramic turtle whose back is about the size and shape of a notehead. I have the children walk him up and down a felt-board staff to demonstrate high and low pitches. The best demonstration is a big floor staff (tape or chalk lines) upon which the children themselves become the notes.

Beyond that, the details—the "parts"—are more in the realm of the music specialist. Since they are "parts," the role of whole music has been fulfilled by the time we get to them: by giving the student a broad base of internalized musical understanding so that the details fit into place. Here is a brief reiteration of a suggested sequence for exploring standard notation:

1. Movement and other activities for the exploration of beat, rhythm, meter, pitch (located throughout this book)
2. Invented notation (the children's own notation)
3. Kodály rhythm symbols ("tahs" and "ti-ti's"), which are stems of notes
4. "Road maps" (noteheads without staff, mapping the shape of a pitch sequence)
5. Putting the stems and noteheads together; true names of notes (whole, half, etc.) but still reading them with words ("tah's" and "ti-ti's")
6. The staff: pitches going up and down
7. Meter: measure lines; top number of meter signature; filling measures with Kodály rhythm symbols (with noteheads attached)
8. Letter names of notes; musical alphabet
9. Exact pitches of notes: clefs; names of lines and spaces
10. (For music specialists) Other notation concepts and details, including the bottom number of the meter signature and counting.

Principle VI. The Goodman Model of the Reading Process

A great many researchers have studied parallels between language and music. My interest and studies have been the parallels between language-reading and music-reading. I have concluded, among other things, that Kenneth Goodman's model of the process of reading written language (1982) is adaptable almost point for point to a model of the process of reading notated music.

Goodman derived his model in part from his studies of people reading aloud. In his "miscue analysis," deviations from the text were transcribed and analyzed for understanding of why readers do what they do. Some of Goodman's conclusions were as follows:

- Readers only sample the text, using the least amount of available information necessary to arrive at meaning.
- Nothing readers do is random; all responses result from the reading process. A reader's "errors" are not mistakes (hence the term "miscues") but applications of the same reading strategies that can also bring more "accurate" results.

For example, the reader, in scanning the page, may inadvertently pick up a word from an adjoining line. A reader sometimes substitutes a *synonym* for the actual printed word. He/she may unconsciously alter the text so that it will make sense in his/her frame of reference. The reader may fail to correct a miscue that makes sense or is grammatically correct.

Experienced language readers unconsciously correct misprints or correctly identify incorrectly spelled words. This phenomenon, known as "proofreader's error," is actually a result of efficient reading strategies. I have a newspaper clipping (*Courier-Journal*, Louisville, Kentucky. By-line, William Mootz) given to me years ago and carried around in my wallet for so long that it is limp. I have shown this to many adult readers, asking them to find the error. Since all of my experimental group have been musicians, they grasp the context right away and have, therefore, certain expectations. Most of them read it as the writer intended, overlook the error in the headline, and begin searching the text. Only a reader who is consciously focusing on form to the exclusion of content will catch the error in the headline right away (Figure 9-7).

Goodman, on the basis of his miscue analysis research, constructed a model of the reading process, a description of what language readers do. Goodman calls the process a "psycholinguistic guessing game."

> *Elena Nikolaidi Gives Distinguished Rectal*
>
> By WILLIAM MOOTZ
> Courier-Journal Music Editor
>
> Elena Nikolaidi, the brilliant Greek contralto who burst upon the New York concert scene several years ago when

FIGURE 9-7: *Newspaper clipping with proofreader's error*

Sampling

Fluent readers do not read every word. Instead, they select minimal graphic cues and, on the basis of these, make guesses. Selection of cues and of guesses based on what "makes sense" are both determined by the background of the reader.

Predicting

From the information already constructed, readers, equipped with internalized grammars, are able to make predictions about probable continuations. Prediction is make possible by two characteristics of language:

1. Sequential constraint: internalized grammars limit the possible order of elements. Given the construction, "The dog looks . . .," a plausible or acceptable completion might be, "The dog looks fierce." An unacceptable one might be, "The dog looks barking." (Chomsky 1965, 76).
2. Redundancy: the repetition or reinforcement of information. In the sentence, "Rain was pelting down and the sidewalk was flooded," precipitation is cued three times. The reader can arrive at "wet" by sampling, without even reading all three cues.

Confirming

If predictions are confirmed and meaning is constructed (if it "makes sense"), the cycle of sampling and predicting is continued. Because of the ambiguity of language, every reader constructs a unique version of the message according to his or her experience.

Here is a simple illustration of Goodman's psycholinguistic guessing game that I have used for prospective teachers. I display to the group a card on which is printed "The frog . . . ." I have prepared (and concealed) three other cards, each with one of the following words:

        croaked   hopped   jumped

When I ask the group for a likely continuation of "the frog . . .," invariably the predictions are one of the above. I then produce the card for that word, to demonstrate just how probable that prediction is. Second and third guesses usually produce the other two. The popular conception of the narrow range of activities of frogs results in these associations. In a complete reading situation, once expectations are confirmed, the reader samples another chunk of text, and the cycle continues.

Correcting

But suppose that instead of one of the predictable words, the actual printed word is (and I produce a card): lectured. Since this is not a likely scenario, the reader *re-reads* to confirm the unexpected word. Having done so (and perhaps having formed a mental picture of a frog standing at a lectern), the reader plunges on, now anticipating a fantasy frog in a professorial, humanoid role. Interruption of the cycle took place because predictions were not confirmed and the result did not make immediate sense.

    Another snag could occur if sequential constraint is violated, that is, if the syntax or sentence structure seems unlikely. Suppose the reader reads, "The frog . . ." and having predicted "croaked," "hopped," or "jumped," encounters "leaning." "The frog *leaning*?" After re-reading to confirm that "leaning" is indeed the word, the reader continues: "The frog leaning on the desk was a professor at the Lily Pad Conservatory." Now it comes together. The reader samples more text and continues the cycle, with anticipations altered. The reader might have mis-read the word as "learning." When that was awkward with the sentence, the reader might have backed up, corrected, and then continued. Alternately, "learning," a word not out of place in that setting, is close enough to the context of the sentence that the reader might not have corrected the miscue. The sentence still makes sense, more or less.

A Musical Paraphrase of the Goodman Model of Reading

British psychologist John Sloboda conducted extensive experiments in the area of analysis of "errors" by music readers (1985). Among other things, he has concluded that:

1. Fluent music readers do not read every note, but sample just enough of the notation to enable them to construct a probable continuation.
2. "Meaning" in music has to do with an abstract, intuitive grasp of musical structures which are "likely" or appropriate within a certain musical idiom.
3. These meanings are assigned before exact notes are identified.
4. Some "errors" were acceptable musical alternatives to the printed score.

"Proofreader's error" occurs also in music-reading. A famous example is the Goldovsky Experiment (Sloboda 1985). A professional pianist/teacher, Boris Goldovsky, had a student whom he described as a poor music reader. The girl had prepared for her lesson the *Capriccio*, Opus 75, no. 2, by Brahms. On the first beat of the bar 47 measures from the end, she played a chord that was musically inappropriate. When Goldovsky moved to correct her, he discovered that she had played the chord exactly as it was written; it was a misprint. Better music readers before her had unconsciously "corrected" the chord by simply playing the predictable notes. Apparently, generations of pianists have overlooked the misprint; it still appears in standard editions of the work. Goldovsky later experimented by placing the piece in front of skilled music readers, asking them to play through it and find the error. None of them found it.

Inspired by all this, I constructed my own *miscue analysis*. Performance from notation was used as the musical equivalent of the oral reading by Goodman's subjects. For this small qualitative study, I transcribed a forgettable melody typical of the eighteenth century idiom by an obscure composer. I altered one note in a place where the musical configuration is almost a cliché in this idiom, predictable to the point that my note did not "fit." My subjects were five cellists and five flautists, all juniors and seniors in high school and all at a level of proficiency that could be called "high intermediate" in both technique and music-reading. I taped the sight-reading performances of my subjects, and, while listening to them later, wrote my observations of the players' deviations from the notation.

The types of "miscues" came straight from Goodman's list. One musician skipped a line, playing a measure from an adjoining line before correcting it. Four students played at least one note that made perfectly good sense musically, although it was not the note as printed. These were not corrected. As for the "wrong note" that I had inserted, two of the students played the note as it should have been, stopped, and "corrected" it to the note I had written. One student played the written note, stopped, peered at it, and played it again as written. The other four players played the note exactly as written, without pausing or "correcting" it. My only disappointment in the results was that only one of the students played the note as it should have been, without noticing the actual printed note and "correcting."

Goodman's psycholinguistic guessing game in its musical mode is as follows:

Sampling

Fluent music readers do not read every note. Instead, they select minimal cues and on the basis of these, make guesses. Selection of cues and guesses based on what "makes sense" are both determined by the music reader.

Predicting

From the information already constructed, music readers, equipped with internalized grammars, are able to make predictions about probable continuations. Irwin Edman (1948, 114) described music as "nine-tenths memory or premonition." Prediction is possible because of two characteristics shared by both language and music:

1. Sequential constraint: internalized grammars limit the possible order of elements. Any listener who has become familiar with a given musical idiom, say, Irish folk song, Protestant hymns, or eighteenth-century classical symphony, can predict likely continuations after a certain point. Unlikely continuations can be very humorous, a phenomenon exploited by musical comedians such as Victor Borge or Peter Schickele ("P.D.Q. Bach").
2. Redundancy: A musical signal, like a language utterance, is characterized by redundancy. A musical point can be made in several ways at the same time: melodically, harmonically, and/or rhythmically. For example, closure can be expressed melodically by falling pitch, harmonically by harmonic resolution, and rhythmically by lengthening note values.

Confirming

If predictions are confirmed and the music "makes sense," the cycle of sampling and predicting continues. Because of the ambiguity of music, every reader constructs a unique version of the message, according to his or her experience.

Correcting

If expectations are not confirmed (and if it does not "make sense"), the reader re-reads for additional clues.

I have explored these phenomena with a small musical experiment. I play or display on a card the following musical phrase for a group of musically "competent" (in the Chomskyian sense and in the Western European idiom) listeners or music readers:

When the musicians are asked to hum or write a predictable musical continuation, it is invariably one of five possibilities shown in Figure 9-8.

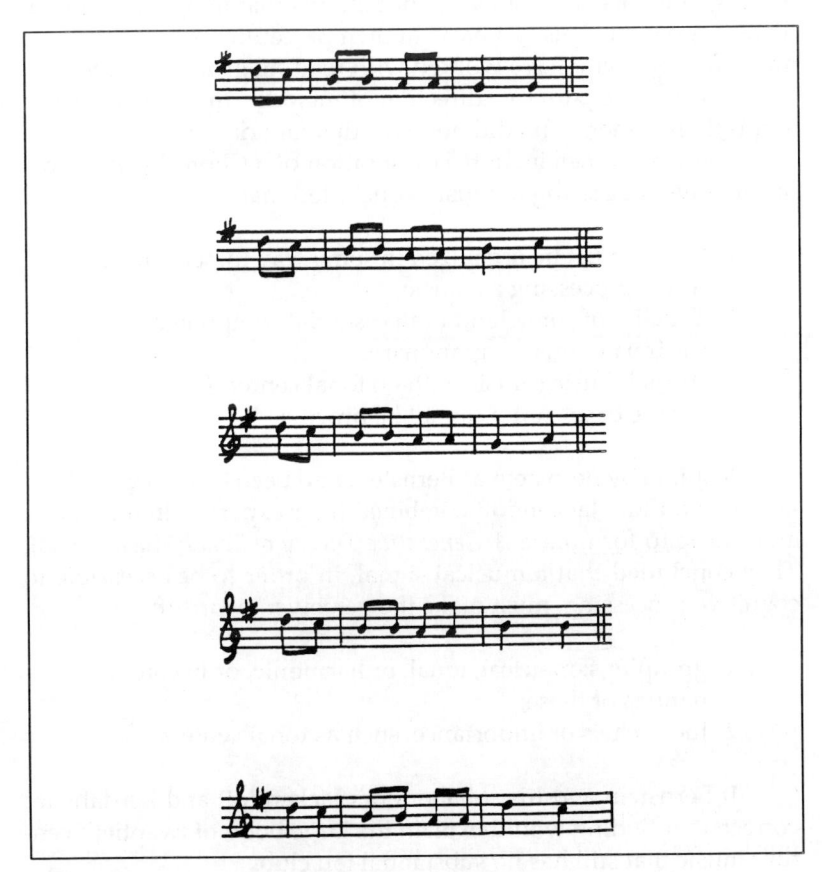

FIGURE 9-8: *Five possible completions of a fragment*

But what if it is unpredictable?

A good sight reader of music will probably predict one of these five continuations because these sequences are congruent with the Western European musical idiom. But suppose the actual score is:

This does not fit expectations (derived from experience with Western European music) which the score, up to that D#, led the reader to assume. After re-reading (correcting) to determine that the notes really *are* D# and G#, the whole music reader will correct and continue reading, this time with altered expectations. He/she will refocus from prediction following a standard Western mode to reading intervals and searching for patterns that may not be immediately apparent. This is a basic human perception strategy. Whole music readers, who have worked with reading groups of notes (intervals, rhythmic patterns, direction of melodic line) are just better at this than readers who did not have this foundation.

Leonard Bernstein, in his exploration of a Chomskyian model of cognitive processing of music, concluded that:

1. Sound must be organized in some way to permit cognitive processing as music;
2. Tonality of some kind is an essential component of the innate musical grammars;
3. Atonal music (music with no tonal center: *Do* or other "home base" note) cannot be processed.

Inspired by Bernstein as Bernstein had been by Chomsky, Fred Lerdahl and Ray Jackendoff combined their expertise in linguistics and music to formulate *A Generative Theory of Tonal Music* (1983). They concluded that a musical signal, in order to be accessible to cognitive processing, must make the perceiver aware of:

1. groupings: metrical, tonal, or harmonic, or in combinations of these;
2. hierarchies of importance, such as tonal centers.

If Bernstein and his collaborators Jackendoff and Lerdahl are correct, that finding would explain the large body of twentieth century music that still has no substantial fan club.

However, composer Roger Sessions (1970) attributed to the

human ear the ability to discover some kind of pattern in *any* musical signal. Musicians who have been trained to perceive units (whole music) rather than isolated details are often able to do this.

Principle VII. The Freedom to Take Risks

Successful reading strategies in both language and music depend on adventuresome confidence: a willingness to take risks. Instructors who insist upon word-for-word or note-for-note accuracy discourage risk-taking. Students become dependent on correction and will anticipate being interrupted. Playing a psycholinguistic guessing game means guessing and making predictions, which involves taking a risk. Sampling the text or the score in a search for meaning rather than laboriously reading one word or one note at a time means risking a "mistake": misreading or substituting a synonym. Whole language and whole music classrooms are places in which it is safe to explore.

Beethoven had something to say about risk-taking: "Do not interrupt [the student's] playing because of small mistakes, but point these out only when he has finished the piece. I have always followed this method, for it soon makes musicians" (Morgenstern 1961).

10

Whole Music Across the Curriculum

Whole music is an approach to learning that musters the whole body with all of its avenues for receiving and processing stimuli. The desired outcomes of this process are learning and growth. Music educators can effectively incorporate whole music into all facets of music instruction, in the private studio as well as in the classroom. However, whole music can be a vital tool across the curriculum. Whole music, like whole language, implies a scope that reaches out to the widest domains relevant to the child. This includes language/dialect, cultural background and origins, neighborhood, school and family, the native idioms of morals, myth, and music. It includes the skills needed in daily living. Thus, whole music suggests a partnership with language arts, social studies, science, mathematics, and art, as well as with some cross-curricular skills. In an ideal learning environment, children would experience each unit of study with a visual artist, a potter/sculptor, a dance/movement teacher, a music teacher, and innovative academic teachers who provide visual, kinesthetic, manipulative, and three-dimensional learning experiences. Maybe this crew could even include a chef.

Please note that it is possible to devise associations that are so contrived as to be absurd rather than illustrative. An example of that is a lesson I observed in which *I Know an Old Lady* [*who swallowed a fly . . .*] was used as a serious introduction to a study of the food chain!

Language Arts

The many parallels between language and music, explored and documented by linguists, music theorists, and psychologists, suggest a productive partnership between whole language and whole music. Both have aural and graphic modes; both have syntactic and semantic systems. *Competency*, in Noam Chomsky's sense of the term, is developed in both systems through experience. The processes of reading text and notation efficiently are more identical than analogous. The aural modes of both exist in time. However, these aspects of similarity, covered earlier in this book, are the theoretical rationale for linking the two. The following are actual manifestations of this theory, and practical ways to use this association in language arts study.

Music and language as communication through sound

This involves an exploration of the ways in which both spoken language and aural music make use of the characteristics of sound. A particular advantage of this is the examination by the students of oral communication, an aspect of language that often is neglected in the pursuit of reading and writing.

Various short utterances can be used as points of reference; an example is a sentence such as, "Oh—you're here to stay." Students take turns saying this, concentrating on giving different meanings to it each time by making it a question, an exclamation, an expression of joy or disappointment or disgust. The speaker might invent a situation in which his or her interpretation of the sentence might take place. Discussion is centered on how these meanings can be embedded by changes in sound. The following characteristics of sound can be covered:

Intonation: changes in pitch; the "tunes" or song qualities of a language
Tempo (fast, slow)
Duration: pauses (rests), lengthened words; phrases and sentences: the expression of a complete thought
Accents: stress
Dynamics (loud and soft)
Rhythms and word stream (linguistic opposites of the way robots speak in cartoons)

Subsequent lessons can incorporate: sound pieces composed by students exploiting various characteristics of sound, and various pieces of recorded music used as examples of the way music simulates human emotions (joy, anger, sadness, irony) through the use of the characteristics of sound.

Exploring and writing poems

Beat, rhythm, meter. Language and music share the components of beat, rhythm, and meter. Poems and musical compositions demonstrate this shared rhythmical organization. Students can find the *beat* of a poem and clap or stamp the beat, incorporating instruments and a conductor. The class then reads the poem, thus superimposing the *rhythm* over the beat. Analysis can then be made of the *accents* by exaggerating them while reading. From this the *meter, duple or triple,* can be deduced. It is important to introduce some poems that may incorporate the innate rhythm of language without necessarily a steady beat. Perceiving the absence of beat is as valuable as identifying its presence. Bird songs have rhythmic patterns but rarely adhere to a steady beat. Bird songs are, even in the absence of beat, music to the ears of most human as well as avian listeners.

After experience with another author's poetry, the children can write their own, first as a class with the teacher's guidance and example, then in groups and individually. Again, it can be emphasized that poems do not have to rhyme or have a steady beat. (However, most children enjoy creating rhythmical lines that rhyme.)

High school students can learn to "scan" poetry by working with the accents and underlying beat of the poetic lines. Their literary vocabulary can be expanded to include the words "iambic," "trochaic," and so forth.

If overt associations with music are part of the teacher's objectives, the transition to music can be made through analysis of song words, leading to the songs in context with their melodies, followed by study of the same sound characteristics in music with no words. The next step can be inventing melodies (tunes) for poems.

Form. If the poem or song words have repeated words or phrases, or stanzas and a refrain, this is an opportunity to explore *form*. (This is an experience in identifying same and different, a skill that crosses all disciplines.) The first stanza is labeled "A." The refrain is labeled "B." Since each stanza is different and each refrain is the same, the diagram of the form is ABCBDBEB—with B representing each recurrence of the refrain. Musical examples of this are songs with stanzas and refrains, and the rondo form, in which an identifiable melody keeps reappearing in between other musical events. The rondo melody is usually introduced first, so that the diagram of the form is ABACADAE.

Another example of form in poetry could be the limerick. The limerick begins with two rhythmically identical lines that are followed by two shorter lines with matching rhythm different from the first, ending with a single line in the rhythm of the opening two lines. Here is an example:

There was a young girl from McBride
Who ate some green apples and died.

The cider fermented
Within the lamented
Making cider inside her insides.

Both the rhythmic patterns and the form are characteristic of the limerick; a poem that does not have both is not a limerick. Children love to write limericks. Their efforts are often "corny," but give them great amusement. Before they attempt to create limericks, however, they must internalize the characteristic patterns and form. Movement and instruments can help accomplish this. Since this is a triple meter, one group could accompany chanting of the poem by bending at the knees on "one" and slapping the thighs (a sound gesture identified by Carl Orff as "patsch" [singular] or "patschen" [plural]) on "two" and "three." Another group could strike drums on "one" and stamp their feet on "two" and "three."

There are several simple tunes associated with limericks. However, the form easily suggests original tunes. The children can then sing their limerick creations, accompanying themselves with motions and/or percussion instruments.

Onomatopoeia. Another linguistic tool is *onomatopoeia*, the use of words to imitate sounds. Children are experts at this. (Some parents are convinced that little boys spring from the womb making noises to represent motors and explosions.) These can be incorporated into original poems, with accompanying sound effects cued by invented notation. Many musical examples of this—sound effects incorporated into the music—exist, such as the church bells and cannons in Tchaikovsky's *1812 Overture,* and recorded whale sounds in Honegger's *And God Created Great Whales.*

Alliteration, consonants, and rhyming words. These involve the concept of same/different again and are integral components of poetry, song words, and music. Alliteration is repetition of the same initial consonant or sound group, as in "the silly, sneaky, sissy snake." Alliteration is a valuable exploration of either written or spoken language and is very effective in poems and song words. It can be expressed musically by a repetitious consonant sound, such as "tah — tah — tah" on a wind instrument or a repetitious thwack (onomatopoeia) on a percussion instrument.

Rhyming words are also an important language experience and component of poetry and song lyrics. Children should be assured, through good examples by other poets, that rhyming words are not a requisite for poetry. However, just as they like to create rhythmic lines with an obvious beat, children love to write lines that rhyme. A musical manifestation of rhyming words is musical lines which share the same melodic ending. In *Amazing Grace,* there are both rhyming words ("... how sweet the sound," and "... but now I'm found") and the musical equivalent: identical melody.

Vowels. The song *Apples and Bananas* incorporates replacing the original vowel sounds in these words with one of the other vowel sounds each time the song is repeated. (See Appendix B.)

Mood: evocation of human emotions. In language, emotions are cued by key words. A characteristic of language is redundancy, the embedding of meaning in several ways. Consider a sentence such as, "The boy shuffled slowly down the street, his head lowered, his shoulders drooping." Without reading every word, the reader deduces sadness and melancholy, which are cued by direction ("down," "lowered," "drooping") and gait ("shuffled" and "slowly"). In reading and writing poetry and song words, children can experiment with expressing mood and emotions with words. This can include working with synonyms and descriptive verbs, adjectives and adverbs. For example, children can be asked to list words that come to mind with the word "night," or "anger," or "peace." In a poetry-writing exercise, the author can list words that come to mind relating to his or her subject for the poem.

In an analysis of mood created or emotions evoked in music, students can describe the musical tools used to create the effect. (See "Music and language as communication through sound" at the beginning of this chapter.)

Spelling

Very young children enjoy forming letters with their bodies to spell short words. This exploits large-muscle movement and muscle memory in the interest of forming letters and words. For older children, even as old as junior high school, spelling can very effectively be taught with musical components: beat, rhythm, and melody. Children are divided into groups, each responsible for illustrating the spelling of a word. Their mission is to "act like cheerleaders," devising a rhythmic cheer with motions that will help them and others remember how to spell the word. The teacher can walk the students through an example, which could be the word "rhythm." Eight students stand in a line in front of the class. Two of the students have large cards with H on them. The first student says "R" while clapping rapidly twice ("ti-ti"). The first H shouts "H!" while jumping up. The third student says "Y" while raising both arms to make the letter Y. The fourth student throws hands to the side, palms up, in the silent quarter rest gesture. The fifth student says "T" while clapping rapidly twice ("ti-ti"). The second H shouts "H!"

and jumps up. The seventh student says "M," followed by the eighth student, who makes the silent quarter rest gesture. The aspect of the word that is usually misspelled is the *two* H's; students holding the H cards, jumping up and shouting, emphasize the two H's. The chant could be notated like this:

♩ ♩ ♩ 𝄽 ♩ ♩ ♩ 𝄽
R H Y   T H M

Muscle memory from the motions combined with the rhythmic chant help internalize the spelling. When the students devise their own "cheerleader" chants for spelling, the teacher helps them to identify the specific trouble spot(s) with the spelling of that particular word. One group to whom I assigned the word "separate" put the troublesome "ARA" (the word is usually misspelled as "seperate") in large print on a card. At the end of the chanted spelling, the group shouted "separate!" The person holding the "ARA" card then "separated" from the others to stand in front. Instruments can be added for variety and effect. Children often come up with a tune for the "spelling chant."

Language "facts"

The best-known example of learning language "facts" through musical experience is the "ABC" song. Grammar can be emphasized through folk songs that illustrate grammatical "errors," such as, *I Wish I Was a Bumbly Bumbly Bee* (instead of: "I wish I *were* . . .") and *It Ain't Gonna Rain No More*. What if these grammatical "mistakes" were "corrected?" Would the song be as effective? Why or why not? A discussion of poetic license would fit in here.

Writing stories and other literature

An original story with sound effects and invented notation is often useful to involve the entire class.

Autobiography. A good launching point for an autobiographical sketch is to have each student list some sounds remembered from his or her childhood, followed by the other memories that the sound evokes. Children have remembered such sounds as father knocking out his pipe (bedtime) and the sound of chopping wood (wrapping Christmas presents). These remembered sounds and associations can be expanded into an autobiographical sketch.

Essays. The children sing, along with a recording if necessary, "My Favorite Things" from *The Sound of Music*. They then write short essays about their own "favorite things."

Reading stories

Sound effects. Sound effects cued with invented notation can be incorporated into reading of stories. Sound generators can be "found sound" (objects in the classroom, such as the bottom of a wastebasket, or objects brought from home, like pan lids and plastic boxes), classroom or homemade instruments, sound gestures like clapping and stamping, or vocal sounds. Children can incorporate sound effects into their own original stories. Sound effects are especially effective if they appear in rhythmic patterns. If King Lion is represented by a drum (or beats from the bottom of the waste basket), the rhythmic pattern of his "theme sound" could be: ♩ ♫ ♫ ♩. The "theme sound" of a deer could be soft taps on a tambourine with a shy, hesitant rhythmic pattern: ♫ 𝄽 ♫ 𝄽.

When invented notation is used for the sound in conjunction with rhythmic notation for the rhythmic pattern, both forms of notation can appear with the story:

". . . and all of the other animals listened to the words of King Lion . . ."

♩ ♫ ♫ ♩
O oo oo O

Songs. Recurrent phrases in favorite stories can be put to music. Examples in the chapter on "Creating" are from Dr. Suess's *Horton Hatches the Egg*: "I meant what I said and I said what I meant . . ." and from Robert Munsch's *I'll Love You Forever*: "I'll Love you forever, I'll like you for always."

Entire stories or books can be made into dramas, with songs for special characters or special events. This is the class musical, which can be performed with costumes and props.

Social Studies

The musical resources for enrichment of social studies units are vast. For almost any aspect of social studies there are appropriate songs, recordings, and music videos. Since this is such a broad area, I will use largely examples from United States history. Appropriate songs abound, since our forebears were more inclined to be singers than we are and used songs as a medium for commemoration and commentary.

Songs About the United States

The states. Virtually every state has a state song. Some of them are difficult to remember and/or sing (because they are not very good songs) or are rather silly. They are still useful in the classroom if the teacher can teach the songs or if there is a recording to sing along to. There is also the song *Fifty Nifty United States*, by Ray Charles.

Patriotic songs. *The Star Spangled Banner* is regrettably difficult to sing. However, we also have songs like *America the Beautiful; God Bless America;* and *My Country, 'Tis of Thee*. Children should know these, and there are history and geography embedded in them.

Rivers and mountains. Examples of these in songs are numerous. River songs include *Roll On, Columbia* and *Shenandoah*. Mountain songs include *Rocky Mountain High* and *Take Me Home, Country Roads*. There are songs about lakes, too, including *The Wreck of the Edwin Fitzgerald* (about Lake Superior).

War. In chronological order, some songs from our country's wars include *Yankee Doodle, 'Round Her Neck She Wore a Yellow Ribbon, When Johnny Comes Marching Home, Over There,* and *White Cliffs of Dover*. Since wars are fundamental to our history, songs from wars are countless and can be a study in themselves.

Antiwar. This category includes *Johnny, I Hardly Knew Ya*, which predates the period usually associated with an antiwar context, and *Where Have All the Flowers Gone?*

Transportation. There are songs about sailing ships (*Blow, Boys, Blow*) and sailors' work songs (*What Shall We Do with The Drunken Sailor*), Railroads (a multitude of songs beginning with the one everyone knows, *I've Been Workin' on the Railroad* and including the ballad of *John Henry*), automobiles (Woody Guthrie's *Riding in My Car*), buses (*The Bus Song*), and airplanes (*Leavin' on a Jet Plane*).

Westward expansion. This can include miners (*My Darlin' Clementine*), wagon trains (*Sweet Betsy from Pike*), homesteading (*Starvin' to Death on My Government Claim*), and cowboys (*The Streets of Laredo*), as well as songs of Native Americans. (See *Navajo Happy Song* in Appendix B.)

Social movements and conditions: Slavery. Included in this category are the many songs classified as African American negro spirituals. (Three well-known ones works as partner songs, sung simultaneously: *Swing Low; All Night, All Day;* and *When the Saints Come Marchin' In.*) Another interesting category includes slave songs about trains (*Get on Board, Little Chillun*), which are references to the abolitionist underground railroad. In a category by itself is *Follow the Drinking Gourd*, which incorporates instructions for navigating by the stars on the long and perilous journey to escape to the North. The "drinking gourd" is the Big Dipper, and the instructions, given by "the old man who is waiting to carry you to freedom," are geographically accurate.

Civil rights. The best known in this group of songs are *We Shall Overcome* and *Lift Every Voice and Sing* (written by J. Rosamond Johnson and James Weldon Johnson; known as the "Negro National Anthem").

Industrial Revolution. *Way Down in the Mines* and *Joe Hill* (about union organizing) are examples of this.

Songs for study of other countries: A multicultural perspective

Songs from other countries are a must in material included in these units. Whenever possible they should be sung in the original language—from a recording, if necessary. There is no shortage of repertoire or resources appropriate to any unit. Children especially enjoy lullabies, animal songs (I include *Mi Chacra*, a Hispanic equivalent of *Old McDonald*, in Appendix B), and translations of songs they already know in English (see Spanish version of *Eensy Weensy Spider* in Appendix B). Children enjoy *Sur Le Pont d'Avignon* in French. *The Lion Sleeps Tonight* makes a good stand-in for African music, but songs from specific African countries in the native language are also available.

There are songs that the class can learn that are related to the history and social movements of other countries. Examples in this category include *The Peat Bog Soldiers* and the *Skye Boat Song*. There are also national anthems of other countries.

In the whole language tradition, not only music but costumes, food, folk tales, architecture, art (both authentic and originated by children), dance, and drama should be included in social studies units.

As the classrooms of the United States grow more ethnically mixed, it is ever more important to solicit contributions from the children and their parents of songs, poems, and folk tales from their respective backgrounds. This can be a rich source of lullabies, ballads, children's songs, and fables for the class to share. Such was the theme used by Susan Payne for a project for her master's degree in the College of Education at the University of Idaho. She sent notes home to parents explaining that the children were being asked to share these things with the class and that parents were invited to visit the class or to borrow the class cassette recorder to make a tape of a song, poem, or story. The response from the families of the children was enthusiastic, and children brought to the class songs to sing and poems to read in the original language. These were collected into a big book for the class and individual smaller books for the children, with each poem, song, or story illustrated by the student who had contributed it. At a program for parents and at an assembly for the school, the students, many dressed in ethnic costumes, read and sang from their books, with accompaniment provided by Ms. Payne on guitar. This profound and exciting project contributed to the individual self-esteem of the children and emphasized the importance of all the groups represented in the class. The idea is not to build the kind of group esteem that encourages children of a single ethnic group to cling together, pulling apart from the others. Instead, the emphasis is on the valuable contributions that each child can make as a member of the class and as a citizen of the city and the country.

Recordings, videos, and other musical resources

There are recordings and videos that enrich the study of United States culture and history. Some examples are Aaron Copland's *Billy the Kid*, musicals like *Oklahoma*, and Bernstein's *West Side Story* (with all-too-clear parallels in current gang culture).

Videos and recordings of authentic music of other cultures are valuable resources for social studies units. Some examples of this are Chinese opera, the gamelan of Southeast Asia, African drumming, music and dance from Central and South America, and the music of India. Examples of musical instruments from other cultures are also excellent; sometimes parents or other teachers can bring these to show to the class.

There are examples of classical music repertoire that have historical and social connotations. *The Moldau*, by Bedrich Smetana, became a nationalistic symbol in Czechoslovakia during periods in that country's history when the people could not openly express their patriotism. Audiences at concerts would stand for the playing of *The Moldau*, a programmatic tone poem depicting one of the country's great rivers. Tchaikovsky's *1812 Overture* vividly describes Napoleon's retreat from Russia.

Activities for social studies "facts"

Social studies "facts" that must be memorized can be incorporated into "cheerleading chants" with large-muscle motions that utilize "muscle memory" in the same way as the spelling chants in the preceding section on Language Arts. For example, the state capitals can be learned in chants like this:

Montgomery, Alabama, and Phoenix, Arizona
Are capitals of "A" states, most of which are hot.

That goes for Arkansas, whose capital is Little Rock,
But Juneau, Alaska — hot it's *not!*

"I" states, like Idaho, whose capital is Boise,
And Springfield, Illinois, call for something noisy! [cymbal crash]
Indianapolis, Indiana, Iowa (Des Moines)
Call for something rattle-y, like dried beans or coins. [jingling and rattling]

Students can invent these chants (and chances are, their efforts will be better than mine!). They can invent tunes for them, accompany them with instruments, or march around the room chanting them to a recording of a Sousa march. This parade might also feature flags bearing the names of states.

Mathematics; logic

These two areas are linked by Howard Gardner as one of the seven intelligences in his theory of Multiple Intelligences. This seems more plausible to me than the oversimplified "Right Brain-Left Brain" theories, in which mathematics is housed unequivocally in the left hemisphere of the brain, the alleged headquarters for analysis, details, and cold facts. That probably depends on which kind of mathematics we are talking about. I remember a mathematician friend who would cover the chalkboard with equations, then stand back with a dreamy look in his eye and murmur, "Now that's *beautiful.*" Although all of it was totally incomprehensible to me, I believe that he had some very large, right-brain concept in mind that was larger than the sum of its left-brain parts. A whole learning approach to mathematics can offer a creative approach to the necessary left-brain parts, the "math facts." Below are some concepts involved in mathematics which can benefit from whole music.

Counting; measuring; numbers

There are countless (no pun intended) counting chants and songs that tally up monkeys, ducks, Indians (that one is demeaning and should be omitted, but the tune will accommodate other entities to be counted), pumpkins, and whatever other objects appropriate to a unit that the teacher might devise. An example of a counting song is *The Inchworm* (see Appendix B).

Order, sequence

Songs with words. An excellent path to skill in perception of order and sequence is singing cumulative songs. Some examples of these are *The Twelve Days of Christmas, I Know an Old Lady* (she can introduce sequence much more appropriately than the food chain!), and *I Love My Rooster*. Singing cumulative songs involves accumulating (hence the term "cumulative") a new idea in each verse, then reviewing it all in reverse order.

There is also order and sequence in songs with stanzas followed by a recurrent refrain.

Music without words. A more subtle observation of sequence and order can be experienced through such musical forms as a rondo, which features a melody that reappears after each of a series of other musical events; a canon (like a round) or a fugue (parts enter at various times, each presenting an imitation of—but not necessarily exactly the same thing as—the previous entry); and an ostinato, which is a repetitious (from the Italian word and cognate of the English word "obstinate," meaning "persistent") rhythmic or melodic accompaniment figure.

Larger musical forms. Order and sequence can be perceived through study of larger two-part (AB) and three-part (ABA) forms, sonata-allegro form, and other musical forms for which a model became prescribed through custom.

Math computation and drill

Obligatory memorization of such background material as multiplication tables can be accomplished with the help of the rhythms, repetition, and movement of the "cheerleader chants," embellished with signs, instruments, hats, or whatever; these are described under "spelling" in the Language Arts section. Tunes can be added.

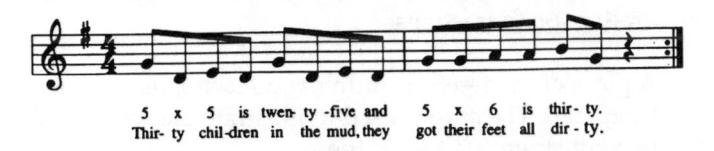

> 5 x 5 is twen- ty -five and 5 x 6 is thir- ty.
> Thir- ty chil-dren in the mud, they got their feet all dir - ty.

"Multiplication March." The children march, first in place beside their seats, then around the room, to a recording of a march, such as John Philip Sousa's *Stars and Stripes Forever*. Some can wave flags, crepe paper streamers or paper plates; some can wear funny hats; and one group carries rhythm sticks, which they tap to the beat. A drum and cymbals would increase the festivity. Words like the following can be chanted, according to the "math facts" being memorized:

> [Marching in place, with rhythm sticks tapping the beat:]
> 5 × 5 is 25. I am glad to be alive.
> 6 × 6 is 36. This is what I do for kicks.

3 × 7 is 21. This is really lots of fun.
4 × 7 is 28. Walk too slowly, you'll be late.

[Marching around the room, with sticks, drum, cymbals, and waving flags:]

4 × 6 is 24. March your way across the floor.
5 × 7 is 35. I am glad to be alive.
6 × 8 is 48. Walk too slowly, you'll be late.
4 × 8 is 32. I would SHOUT, IF I WERE YOU!
4 × 9 is 36. Stop for rhythm with the sticks [Everyone stops while the sticks play a rhythm pattern.]:

♩♩ ♩♩ ♩♩ ♩

6 × 9 is 54. March your way across the floor.
5 × 9 is 45. I am glad to be alive.
9 × 9 is 81. This is really lots of fun.
6 × 7 is 42. I would SHOUT, IF I WERE YOU!
7 × 8 is 56. Stop for rhythm with the sticks:

♩♩ ♩♩ ♩♩ ♩

Shapes and space

Children can form geometric shapes with their bodies against a wall or on the floor. Some shapes require group cooperation. Manipulatives are important for understanding three-dimensional objects such as cubes and pyramids.

Duration: Fractions, musical math

Relative values unrelated to meter signatures. The values of different notes in relation to each other (but with no assigned value) can be an introduction to fractions:

- A piece of cake — See cutting and serving the cake in Chapter 6. The cake is used to illustrate the concept of "in this note there are two of these..."
- "Musical Math," as shown here.

Background music for math

Studies have shown that certain kinds of music played before and/or during problem-solving activities result in greater concentration and increased efficiency in reasoning and analysis. The "certain kinds of music" have usually been examples of music from the Classical Period, characterized by balance, clarity, and moderation. Researchers conclude that this phenomenon is somehow a result of a mental organization brought about by cognitive processing of this kind of music, the qualities of which imitate the characteristics of logical thinking. Background music, then, although it has long suffered bad press, can muster the forces of the brain into organized configurations. It can do this *if* it is music characterized by balance, clarity, and moderation, like the music of Mozart. Muzak does not qualify. A bonus side effect is that the music is making traces in the brain simultaneously with the mathematics.

Profound intersections between music and mathematics

Persons who are more knowledgeable than I about mathematics have emphasized that music and mathematics intersect in infinitely more profound ways than the examples I have developed. An example given to me was with respect to form: retrograde in music corresponds to reflection in mathematical terms. I am awed by this line of thinking, and feel that it supports my convictions about interdisciplinary connections. However, I shall leave that book for a mathematician to write.

Logic: Values related to meter signatures

Values prescribed by the bottom number of the meter signature require the application of logic: if this is so, it follows that this other thing is so. Given this, then that . . . If the bottom number of the meter signature is 2, that means a half note gets one beat. That means that a whole note gets two beats, a quarter note gets one-half beat and an eighth note gets one-fourth of a beat. If the bottom number is 4, a quarter note is worth one beat. Therefore, a whole note gets four, a half note gets two, and an eighth note gets one-half. If the bottom number is 8, an eighth note is worth one beat, so a sixteenth note gets one-half beat, a quarter note is two, a half note is four, and a whole note is eight beats. This is a complex road through logic, and it helps to make charts of the "Given this, then that . . ."

Science

There are ways in which whole music can address scientific concepts.

Songs related to units

For younger children, songs and recorded music can be incorporated when they are appropriate to science units or concepts: animals (*Grizzly Bear*), birds (*Mockin'bird Hill*), insects (*La Cucaracha*), seasons (*Good King Wenceslas*—it describes winter well enough to bring on frostbite), rainbows (*The Rainbow Song*), gardens (*Plant My Garden* in Appendix B), and environmental studies (*Baby Beluga* and *Garbage, Garbage*). There are many excellent sources. Two books by Ruth Crawford Seeger are rich in authentic North American Folk Songs and include many animal songs: *American Folk Songs for Children* and *Animal Folk Songs for Children*. For newer songs, Raffi's *Songs to Read* books are very good (Appendix A).

Physiology

A study of the ear, its parts, and its functions, and the role of the brain in perception of sound and processing of information can be included in a study of acoustics (see later in this chapter). Similarly, a study of the physiology of voice production can include breath control, tone production, and using the voice in ways that avoid strain and damage.

Order and hierarchies

Study of the relative values of notes and the logic required for "Given this, then that . . ." is related to order and hierarchies as well as to mathematics. The study of musical form and sequence also involves order and hierarchies.

Space

Gustav Holst's descriptive program music *The Planets* provides an excellent backdrop for drawing or painting pictures of our galaxy.

Movement and dance can be used to illustrate orbits of planets around the sun. Children can make models of the planets to carry in their orbits around the sun. (A big one-dimensional sun is customary for this activity, since the size of the sun relative to the planets is too big for a feasible model.)

Earth science

Rocks: sedimentary, igneous, metamorphic. Children can write a script describing how each of these rock types is formed. Sound effects can be added, using voice sounds and/or instruments. If listening to recorded music is part of the curricular objectives, appropriate "sound bites" of recorded music can be tape recorded as sound effects. For example, something slow, quiet and peaceful like *Clair de Lune* would be appropriate for sedimentary rock. Music that is more dramatic and turbulent, such as Stravinsky's *Rite of Spring*, would be effective for igneous and metamorphic rock. Movement (or lack thereof, for sedimentary rock) and dance are appropriate.

The water cycle; storms. Using instruments with timbre suggestive of water in various forms, children can write a script with sound effects describing the water cycle: first a sound representing tiny evaporating particles, then sounds for gathering clouds, condensation into drops, then all of the components of a storm (cymbal crashes for lightning, drums for thunder, rattles for rain). The script can be in the form of a poem, to which a melody might be written.

There are recordings of program music related to water and storms. An example is the storm sequence in Ferde Grofé's *Grand Canyon Suite*. This subject, also, lends itself to movement and dance.

Acoustics: the science of sound

Sound and silence, in language and music. Activities can be examples of the use of pauses in speech, commas in written language, and rests in music.

Vibrations and the ear. Activities can include:

1. Manipulatives in the form of three-dimensional models of the parts of the ear
2. A dish of water and a drum or other significant sound source: the experimenter strikes the drum and observes the sympathetic vibrations on the surface of the water. This illustrates the way vibrations activate the eardrum.

Vibrations: frequency (pitch), duration (beat, rhythm, meter), and intensity (dynamics). Activities suggested to learn about vibrations could include:

1. An acoustic string bass, on which the vibration of the large strings is observable
2. the "string string bass" (see Appendix B)

Timbre: overtones; the harmonic series; and Pythagoras and the "music of the spheres." Activities: Visiting musicians demonstrate the use of overtones on an instrument: the technique of causing only one part of a string or column of air to vibrate. The entire harmonic series can be demonstrated visually as well as aurally on a 'cello.

Vibrations and the vibrating source. My experience suggests the following activities:

1. A monochord, made by mounting one guitar or 'cello string between two screw eyes on a board. Tightening the string with a screw eye can demonstrate the relationship between tension and pitch.
2. Demonstrations of violins, 'cellos, and string basses; all of these have strings with easily observable differences in diameter (fat ones and thin ones). This can demonstrate the relationship between size of the vibrating source and pitch.
3. Tumblers filled to progressive levels with water; the more water vibrating in the glass, the lower the pitch. Achieving a major scale will take some experimentation with different sizes of tumblers. The "player" gently strikes the glass with a spoon. Another technique is to wet the index finger in detergent water and run the finger smoothly and rapidly around the rim of the tumbler. When the player gets the hang of it, an ethereal tone results. (This can lead to research on the glass harmonica, a now extinct instrument consisting of various sizes of glass disks mounted on a rod. Powered by a footpedal, the disks were rotated through a trough of water and "played" with the fingertips in the same way the rim of a glass is "played." Mozart composed music especially for this instrument.) Either way, a player of glasses can learn to play melodies. I once had a sixth grade class that played Christmas songs on glasses for a program. Note: avoid filling the tumblers too far in advance. Glass is porous and becomes "water-logged," resulting in an unpitched "clunk" instead of the usual melodious sound.
4. Bottles filled to various levels with water in the same way the glasses were, except that the bottles are "played" by blowing. After a major scale is achieved the first time, a tape line may be put on each bottle so that the next playing session can begin without trial and error about the water level. Players can also strike the bottles with a spoon or hard mallet.
5. "Buzzing" a plastic drinking straw: a "mouthpiece" is formed by flattening the end of the straw and snipping off the corners. After the "buzzing" is mastered, begin snipping off the other end of the straw a little at a time. Each time it is blown, the pitch will be higher. This demonstrates the relationship between the pitch and the length of the column of vibrating air.

Visual Art

Visual art and music have much in common, even though visual art exists in space, whereas music exists in time. There are many ways that associations can be made between the two; in fact, the discipline referred to as "allied arts" explores relationships between the various art forms.

Some simple activities combining art and music

Drawing to music. Children are given crayons and large sheets of newsprint. They are instructed to listen to the recorded music and to draw designs that the music makes them think of: "Let the music move your crayons." Some children will draw representative pictures, but most will draw patterns that reflect the tempo, speed, and other characteristics of the music. Meanwhile, a side benefit is that the children are subliminally absorbing the music.

If the teacher's objectives involve listening to a piece of program music and mentally fitting the program (the story that the composer is illustrating with the music) to the music, the children can draw pictures of events or characters in the story. One activity that children enjoy is making a kind of comic strip of the story. For example, in a story like *The Sorcerer's Apprentice*, the class develops a condensed list of six or eight main events in the story. Each child folds his/her large piece of paper into six or eight sections and while listening to the recording, draws a cartoon-like picture of each event in one of the rectangles formed by the folds.

Music and visual art in historical periods

Parallels between the visual arts and the music of any given historical period are striking, because the forces that shaped visual artists affected the musicians of the time as well. The awakenings of that aptly-named period of the Renaissance stirred all the arts as well as the sciences. Baroque music reflects stylistic characteristics similar to those evident in the visual arts and architecture of the period. Of course, no bell signals the beginning and ending of any period in history, art, or music. However, for the most part, generalizations about historical periods are justifiable, and associations and comparisons between visual arts and music are pertinent.

Music and visual arts: characteristics and components

Exploration in allied arts focuses on parallels between the following components and characteristics shared by all of the arts:

- **Color** in the visual arts corresponds to timbre and tone color in music. The word chromatic in music refers to a se-

ries of half steps (intervals of a minor second) often used for dramatic effect: to add color.
- **Form**, the essence of the visual arts, has its counterpart in musical forms. Elements such as repetition, same and different, positive and negative spaces, angular and rounded shapes, darkness and light, and contrasts in intensity, size, and elevation are evident in both visual art and music.
- **Texture:** in both visual art and music, texture can be spare or dense, smooth or rough, "busy" or relaxed.
- **Pattern, shape, line, and direction** are all components of both the visual arts and music.
- **Motion:** both the visual arts and music are analogues of motion. Motion is achieved visually either by actual pictorial representation of objects in motion or by line and other elements of composition which imply motion. In music, motion is achieved by rhythmic patterns and variations of tempo.
- **Intensity** is achieved in visual arts through using color, texture, contrast, and size. Intensity is achieved in music with timbre, texture, pitch, and loudness.
- **Mood, emotion:** the visual arts as well as music are, as Susanne Langer expressed it, analogues of emotive life. The effects of mood and emotion are achieved in the arts by all the means just described.

11

Summing It Up

During children's preschool years, they make sense of the world by absorbing information using all of the senses, with the whole body, testing new information against what they already know. Children are surrounded with various manifestations of language, as well as with nonlinguistic information and nonlinguistic symbols. In the way natural to all human beings, children have stored visual information along with memories of sounds and smells, taste and touch.

A child entering school crosses a threshold into a world in which all conscious emphasis is upon linguistic symbols. Information is conveyed through linguistic symbols, and it is expected that it will be cognitively stored in this same manner. There is usually a little music of some kind, and there are some opportunities to manipulate artistic symbols by drawing or finger painting. However, whatever new discoveries may have been revealed by and to educators about differing learning styles or multiple intelligences, the focus of schools is still "readin', ritin', and 'rithmetic" taught through spoken instructions and print. The learning potential of nonlinguistic avenues of perception and nonlinguistic symbols is virtually untapped. A child whose intelligences are spatial, bodily/kinesthetic, or musical is suddenly on the outside trying to look in, as surely as a new student who speaks no English might be. Before the child boarded the school bus, he or she was absorbing signals from all directions. In school, the custom is to immobilize the body as much as possible, except for the eyes, ears, and writing hand. After all, there are so many children. We cannot have them milling about. There must be order and structure. Stay in your seat. Spell these words. Work these problems. And be quiet.

The benign revolution of whole language has done a great deal to change this situation. In addition to working with whole, real language that is relevant to children, whole language teachers aim to create a safe environment for exploration and inventiveness. A tenet of whole language is that the child's interests, background, and abilities are at the center of the process. Children develop their own questions and then use their own best aptitudes in searching for the answers.

I am proposing whole music: music that involves the whole body, that relates to what is relevant to the whole world of the child. Whole music gives children experience with whole, real music: music heard, felt, and/or created by the children. These experiences provide an environment that encourages children to ask their own questions; the teacher guides them in finding the answers. In this way children deduce music knowledge, music "facts," the details about musical structure and notation. Learning is from whole to part.

Whole language exploits the actuality that people not only learn language but learn *through* language. Whole music also exploits this property: people not only learn music but learn *through* music. Music, in a whole music manifestation, is a medium for learning in many areas. Music, an analogue of motion and human emotion, and its close relative, movement, can be the teaching tools they have always been through many eons and many cultures in human history. Music and movement are nonlinguistic symbols which can convey meanings and cultural messages of all kinds.

Movement employs muscle memory, kinesthetic reinforcement. A concept experienced through the whole body has been cognitively processed through multiple avenues. Many other aspects of music can be learning tools, pathways to perception. Human beings perceive and process signals by organizing them. Information placed in a rhythmic framework or a melodic framework is already organized; it is predigested, ready for absorption. This is applicable to many different kinds of information.

Music is related to many different disciplines. Meter signatures and note values involve arithmetic and fractions. Meter signatures invoke reasoning and logic: "given this, then that." Music is sound and hence is vibrations and all that is involved in acoustics, the science of sound. Sound involves the physiology of the ear and the voice. Music is social studies: it is intimately connected with the history, beliefs, customs, languages, physical environments, and even clothing and foods of all peoples. Music and visual art share many characteristics: form, intensity, color, shape, and direction.

Music is a nonlinguistic mode of expression. Its very power lies in its ambiguity. Where words leave off, the music begins. Music can be a medium of expression for anyone, but especially for people whose abilities are extra-linguistic. These individuals, even more than others, not only learn music but learn *through* it.

So closely related are music and language that they could well be classified as the two strongest "wiring systems" in the human mind-body complex. There is evidence that human beings are born with cognitive structures programmed for the acquisition of musical forms, just as they have such structures for the acquisition of language. The close relationship of movement with music brings kinesthetic perception into the equation, making a triumvirate of avenues for information-processing.

I propose whole music as a pathway to learning, as a non-linguistic symbol of powerful and historic significance, as a mode of personal expression, as a natural partner to whole language, and as a teaching tool with a wealth of untapped potential. If you can talk, you can sing. If you can walk, you can dance.

Bibliography

Bernstein, Leonard. 1976. *The Unanswered Question: Six Talks at Harvard.* Cambridge, MA: Harvard University Press.
Bruner, Jerome S. 1973. *Beyond the Information Given: Studies in the Psychology of Knowing.* Ed. Jeremy M. Anglin. New York: W.W. Norton.
———. 1967. *Toward a Theory of Instruction.* Cambridge, MA: Belknap Press of Harvard University Press.
Choksy, Lois. 1981. *The Kodály Concept.* Englewood Cliffs, NJ: Prentice Hall.
———. 1988. *The Kodály Method.* Englewood Cliffs, NJ: Prentice Hall.
———. 1991. *Teaching Music Effectively in the Elementary School.* Englewood Cliffs, NJ: Prentice Hall.
Chomsky, Noam. 1965. *Aspects of the Theory of Syntax.* Cambridge, MA: MIT Press.
———. 1977. *Language and Responsibility.* NY: Pantheon.
Chugani, Harry. 1994. In "To Lift Intelligence, Intervention is Needed in the First Three Years." *Wall Street Journal,* by Rochelle Sharpe, April 12, B1.
Dewey, John. 1958. *Art As Experience.* NY: G. P. Putnam's Sons.
Downing, John. 1973. "Is Literacy Acquisition Easier in Some Languages than in Others?" *Visible Language* 7 (2): 145–154.
Edman, Irwin. 1948. *Arts and the Man: A Short Introduction to Aesthetics.* NY: G. P. Putnam's Sons.
Edwards, Betty. 1979. *Drawing on the Right Side of the Brain: A Course in Enhancing Creativity and Artistic Confidence.* Los Angeles: J. P. Tarcher.
Eisner, Elliot. 1992. "The Misunderstood Role of the Arts in Human Development." *Phi Delta Kappa* April, 1992: 591–595.

FIELD, TIFFANY. 1991. "Quality Infant Day-Care and Grade School Behavior and Performance." *Child Development* 62: 863–870.

GAGNÉ, ROBERT MILLS. 1977. *The Conditions of Learning.* NY: Holt, Rinehart, and Winston.

GARDNER, HOWARD. 1981. "Do Babies Sing a Universal Song?" *Psychology Today* December, 1981: 70–76.

———. 1993a. *Frames of Mind: The Theory of Multiple Intelligences.* 2nd ed. NY: Basic Books.

———. 1993b. *Multiple Intelligences: The Theory in Practice.* NY: Basic Books.

GOODMAN, KENNETH S. 1982. *Language and Literacy: The Selected Writings of Kenneth S. Goodman,* vol. 1, *Process, Theory, Research.* Ed. Frederick V. Gollasch. London et al: Routledge and Kegan.

———. 1982. *Language and Literacy: The Selected Writings of Kenneth S. Goodman,* vol. 2, *Reading, Language, and the Classroom Teacher.* Ed. Frederick V. Gollasch. London et al: Routledge and Kegan.

GOODMAN, KENNETH S., LOIS BRIDGES BIRD, and YETTA M. GOODMAN. 1991. *The Whole Language Catalog.* Santa Rosa, CA: American School Publishers.

GOODMAN, YETTA. 1981. "Print Awareness in Pre-school Children: A Working Paper. A Study of the Development of Literacy in Pre-school Children." Occasional Papers, Program in Language and Literacy, Arizona Center for Research and Development, College of Education, University of Arizona, September, no. 4.

GORDON, EDWIN E. 1980. *Learning Sequences in Music: Skill, Context, and Patterns.* Chicago: G.I.A. Publications.

GREEN, BARRY. 1986. *The Inner Game of Music.* Garden City, NY: Doubleday.

HANNA, ELIZABETH and ANDREW N. MELTZOFF. 1993. "Peer Imitation by Toddlers in Laboratory, Home, and Day-Care Contexts: Implications for Social Learning and Memory." *Developmental Psychology*, 29 (4): 701–710.

HONEGGER, ARTHUR. 1966. Trans. Wilson O. Clough and Allan Arthur Willman. *I Am a Composer.* NY: St. Martin's Press.

KATZ, DAVID. 1950. *Cognitive Psychology: Its Nature and Significance.* NY: Ronald Press.

KEETMAN, GUNILD. 1974. *Elementaria.* London: Schott.

KODÁLY, ZOLTÁN. See Choksy; and Wheeler and Raebeck.

LANGER, SUSANNE K. 1953. *Feeling and Form: A Theory of Art.* NY: Charles Scribner's Sons.

———. 1951. *Philosophy in a New Key.* NY: Mentor Press.

LERDAHL, FRED and RAY JACKENDOFF. 1983. *A Generative Theory of Tonal Music.* Cambridge, MA: MIT Press.

LEVIN H. and J. P. WILLIAMS, eds. 1970. *Basic Studies on Reading.* NY: Basic Books.

LIBERMAN, MARK. 1979. *The Intonational System of English*. NY: Garland.

MOOREHEAD, GLADYS and DONALD POND. 1944. [Reprinted 1993.] *Music of Young Children*. Book III, *Musical Notation*. Santa Barbara, CA: Pillsbury Foundation for the Advancement of Music Education.

MORGENSTERN, SAM. 1961. *Composers on Music*. NY: Bonanza.

NEISSER, ULRIC. 1967. *Cognitive Psychology*. NY: Appleton-Century-Crofts.

ORFF, CARL. See Keetman; Wheeler and Raebeck.

PAYNE, SUSAN I., 1995. Incorporating Children's Home Language into the Daily Curriculum." Master's thesis, University of Idaho.

PIAGET, JEAN. 1966. Trans. Margaret Cook. *The Origins of Intelligence in Children*. NY: International Universities Press.

RAUSCHER, FRANCES. 1994. Paper presented August 13, 1994 at annual meeting of the American Psychological Association. Reported by Malcolm Ritter, Associated Press, August 14.

SESSIONS, ROGER. 1965. *The Musical Experience of Composer, Performer, Listener*. NY: Atheneum.

———. 1970. *Questions About Music*. Cambridge, MA: Harvard University Press.

SLOBODA, JOHN. 1985. *The Musical Mind: The Cognitive Psychology of Music*. Oxford: Clarendon Press.

SMITH, FRANK. 1982. *Understanding Reading: a Psycholinguistic Analysis of Reading and Learning to Read*. 3rd ed. NY: Holt, Rinehart, Winston.

TSENG, OVID J.L. and HARRY SINGER, eds. 1981. *Perception of Print*. Hillsdale, NJ: Lawrence Erlbaum Associates.

WHEELER, LAWRENCE and LOIS RAEBECK. 1985. *Orff and Kodály Adapted for the Elementary School*. Dubuque, Iowa: Brown.

Appendix A: Suggested Book List

Books with music as a component in the subject matter
ACKERMAN, KAREN. 1988. *Song and Dance Man.* New York: Knopf.
ARDLEY, NEIL. 1991. *The Science Book of Sound.* San Diego: Harcourt Brace Jovanovich.
BARBER, DAVID W. 1986. *A Musician's Dictionary.* Chicago and New York: Contemporary Books.
———. 1986. *Bach, Beethoven, and the Boys; Music History as it Ought to Be Taught.* Toronto, ON: Sound and Vision.
BARRETT, MARY BRIGID. 1994. *Sing to the Stars.* Boston: Little, Brown and Co. (Beautiful illustrations by Sandra Speidel. Story of an African American boy with his violin and his friend, a former famous jazz pianist now blind.)
BORNSTEIN, RUTH. 1978. *The Dancing Man.* New York: Seabury.
BOTTNER, BARBARA. 1987. *Zoo Song.* New York: Scholastic.
BRETT, JAN. 1991. *Berlioz the Bear.* New York: GP Putnam's Sons.
CHILD'S PLAY INTERNATIONAL, LTD. 1993. *The Musical Life of Gustav Mole.* Singapore: Child's Play International, Ltd.
CLÉMENT, CLAUDE. 1988. *The Voice of the Wood.* New York: Penguin. (Beautiful illustrations by Frédéric Clément. Mythical tale about a magic 'cello. Better for older elementary students.)
COLE, JOANNA, and STEPHANIE CALMENSON. 1991. *The Eentsy-Weentsy Spider: Finger Plays and Action Rhymes.* New York: Mulberry.
COSGROVE, STEPHEN. 1987. *Melody Moth.* Los Angeles: Price, Stern, Sloan. (Why musicians need to practice.)
DEVERELL, CATHERINE. 1992. *Stradivari's Singing Violin.* Minneapolis: Carolrhoda Books, Inc.

ELLIOT, DONALD. 1976. *Alligators and Music*. Boston: Gambit.

GALDONE, PAUL. 1985. *Cat Goes Fiddle-i-fee*. New York: Clarion. (Music to song not included.)

HART, AVERY, and PAUL MANTELL. 1993. *Kids Make Music: Clapping and Tapping from Bach to Rock*. Charlotte, VT: Williamson Publishing.

HASELEY, DENNIS. 1983. *The Old Banjo*. New York: Aladdin (Macmillan). (Fantasy; wistful story; lovely black-and-white illustrations by Stephen Gammell.)

HURD, THACHER. 1985. *Mama Don't Allow*. New York: HarperTrophy. (Music to song included.)

ISADORA, RACHEL. 1979. *Ben's Trumpet*. New York: Scholastic. (jazz)

JEUNESSE, GALLIMARD and CLAUDE DELAFOSSE. 1992. *Musical Instruments: A First Discovery Book*. New York: Scholastic.

KEATS, EZRA JACK. 1971. *Apartment 3*. New York: Macmillan. (Beautiful illustrations by the author: collage-effect, realistic impressions of inner-city tenement environment.)

KENT, JACK. 1974. *The Bremen-Town Musicians*. New York: Scholastic.

KOMAIKO, LEAH. 1987. *I Like the Music*. New York: HarperTrophy.

KOVALSKI, MARY ANN. 1987. *The Wheels on the Bus*. Boston: Little, Brown. (Music to song included.)

KRULL, KATHLEEN. 1993. *Lives of the Musicians; Good Times, Bad Times, and What the Neighbors Thought*. San Diego: Harcourt Brace Jovanovich.

KUSKIN, KARLA. 1982. *The Philharmonic Gets Dressed*. New York: HarperTrophy.

LANGSTAFF, JOHN. 1983. *Frog Went a-Courtin'*. San Diego: Harcourt Brace Jovanovich. (Music to song included.)

MAYERHOFER, FELIX. 1993. *Tommy, Sticks, and the Big Bass Drum*. Dallas: Macie.

MILLAY, EDNA ST. VINCENT. 1991. *The Ballad of the Harp-Weaver*. New York: Philomel. (Attractive illustrations by Beth Peck.)

NICHOL, BARBARA. 1993. *Beethoven Lives Upstairs*. New York: Orchard Books.

NORWORTH, JACK. 1993. illus. and text, Alec Gillman. *Take Me Out to the Ball Game*. New York: Four Winds Press (Macmillan). (Includes music to the song and some history of baseball, with a bibliography.)

PEEK, MERLE. 1985. *Mary Wore Her Red Dress, and Henry Wore His Green Sneakers*. New York: Clarion. (Music to song included.)

RAFFI. 1983. *Baby Beluga*. New York: Crown. (Music to song included. Environmental message.)

———. 1988. *One Light, One Sun*. New York: Crown. (Music to song included.)

———. 1987. *Shake My Sillies Out*. New York: Crown. (Music to song included.)

———. (Other books in Raffi *Songs to Read* series.)

ROUNDS, GLEN, illus. 1990. *I Know an Old Lady Who Swallowed a Fly*. New York: Holiday House. (Bold, humorous illustrations, but music to song not included.)

SAGE, JAMES. 1991. *The Little Band*. New York: McElderry Books.

SEBASTIAN, JOHN. 1993. *JB's Harmonica*. San Diego: Harcourt Brace Jovanovich.

SHANNON, GEORGE. 1982. *Dance Away*. New York: Mulberry. (Includes a simple, useful dance step.

STADLER, JOHN. 1983. *Hector, the Accordion-nosed Dog*. New York: Aladdin (Macmillan).

STAINES, BILL. 1989. *All God's Critters Got a Place in the Choir*. New York: Penguin. (Music included.)

SUNDGAARD, ARNOLD, and DOMINIC CATALANO. 1992. *The Bear Who Loved Puccini*. New York: Philomel.

VAN KAMPEN, VLASTA, and IRENE C. EUGEN. 1989. *Orchestranimals*. New York: Scholastic.

WESTCOTT, NADINE BERNARD. 1990. *There's a Hole in the Bucket*. New York: HarperTrophy.

———. 1980. *I Know an Old Lady Who Swallowed a Fly*. Boston: Little, Brown. (Music to song included. Humorous illustrations.)

WILLIAMS, VERA B. 1984. *Music, Music for Everyone*. New York: Mulberry. (Pleasant story about a child who starts a community band.)

WINTER, JEANNETTE. 1988. *Follow the Drinking Gourd*. New York: Dragonfly (Alfred A. Knopf). (Authentic story about slaves escaping to the North by following the instructions hidden in the song. Fine illustrations by the author.)

Books about making musical instruments

BARTON, JILL. 1991. *The Happy Hedgehog Band*. Cambridge: Candlewick Press. (Instruments you can make; body percussion.)

BOER, AFKE DEN, and MARGOT DEZEEW. 1989. *Making and Playing Musical Instruments*. Seattle: University of Washington Press.

CLINE, DALLAS. 1976. *Homemade Instruments*. New York: Oak Publications.

HUNTER, ILENE, and MARILYN JUDSON. 1977. *Simple Folk Instruments to Make and Play*. New York: Simon and Schuster.

WARING, DENNIS. 1981. *Folk Instruments: Making Folk Instruments in Wood*. New York: Sterling.

WISEMAN, ANN. 1979. *Making Musical Things: Improvised Instruments*. New York: Charles Scribner's Sons.

WYLER, ROSE. 1987. *Fun with Drums, Bells, and Whistles*. New York: Julian Messner.

Songbooks

BEALL, PAMELA CONN, and SUSANN HAGEN NIPP. 1979. *Wee Sing* series of songbooks and cassette tapes. Los Angeles: Price Stern Sloan.

CHAPIN, TOM. 1989. *Family Tree.* New York: Cherry Lane Music Co.

HACKETT, PATRICIA. 1992. *The Melody Book: 300 selections from the world of music for autoharp, guitar, piano, recorder, and voice.* 2nd ed. Englewood Cliffs, New Jersey: Prentice Hall.

NELSON, ESTHER. 1981. *The Funny Songbook.* New York: Sterling.

———. 1981. *The Silly Songbook.* New York: Sterling. (Songbooks and cassette tapes.)

RAFFI. 1987. *The Everything Grows Songbook.* New York: Crown.

SEEGER, RUTH CRAWFORD. 1948. *American Folk Songs for Children.* Garden City, New York: Doubleday. (a classic)

SEEGER, RUTH CRAWFORD. 1993. *Animal Folk Songs for Children.* Hamden, Conn.: Linnet Books.

SIMON, WILLIAM L., ed. 1985. *The Reader's Digest Children's Songbook.* New York: Reader's Digest Association.

WARREN, JEAN. 1983. *Piggyback Songs.* Everett, Washington: Totline Press, Warren Publishing.

———. 1985. *More Piggyback Songs.* Everett, Washington: Totline Press, Warren Publishing.

Beat, rhythm, alliteration, rhyming

AYLESWORTH, JIM. 1992. *Old Black Fly.* New York: Henry Holt and Co. (Children love Stephen Gammell's "splattery" illustrations.)

COLE, JOANNA. 1989. *Anna Banana: 101 Jump-rope Rhymes.* New York: Beech Tree.

———. 1990. *Miss Mary Mack, and Other Children's Street Rhymes.* New York: Beech Tree.

DEGEN, BRUCE. 1983. *Jamberry.* New York: HarperTrophy. (Also a counting book.)

DR. SUESS. (Theodore Geisel). 1968. *Horton Hatches the Egg.* New York: Random House.

———. (Any works by this author are equally worth while.)

FLEISCHMAN, PAUL. 1988. *Joyful Noise: Poems for Two Voices.* New York: Harper and Row. (Excellent for older elementary students.)

GUARINO, DEBORAH. 1989. *Is Your Mama a Llama?* New York: Scholastic. (Pleasant illustrations by Steven Kellogg.)

HOBERMAN, MARY ANN. 1982. *A House is a House for Me.* New York: Puffin.

MAYER, MERCER. 1973. *What Do You Do with a Kangaroo?* New York: Scholastic. (Appealing illustrations.)

MILNE, A. A. (1927.) 1970. *Now We Are Six.* New York: Yearling.

———. (1924.) 1992. *When We Were Very Young.* New York: Puffin (Penguin).

PATZ, NANCY. 1983. *Moses Supposes His Toeses Are Roses.* San Diego: Voyager/HBJ (Harcourt Brace Jovanovich).

SHAW, NANCY. 1989. *Sheep on a Ship.* Boston: Houghton, Mifflin.

SILVERSTEIN, SHEL. 1981. *A Light in the Attic.* New York: Harper and Row.

———. 1996. *Falling Up.* New York: HarperCollins.

———. 1974. *Where the Sidewalk Ends.* New York: Harper and Row. (Silverstein books are masterpieces for children. Both illustrations and text will convert any child to poetry.)

VAN LAAN, NANCY. 1990. *Possum Come a-Knockin'.* New York: Dragonfly (Knopf). (Delightful rhythmic poetry in Appalachian-type dialect. Wonderful illustrations by cartoonist George Booth.)

YOLEN, JANE, ed. 1992. *Street Rhymes Around the World.* Honesdale, PA: WordSong.

For original drama and musical theater

DR. SUESS. (Theodore Geisel). 1968. *Horton Hatches the Egg.* New York: Random House.

———. (See *all* other works by this author.)

HAYES, JOE. 1995. *The Day It Snowed Tortillas: Tales from Spanish New Mexico.* Santa Fe, NM: Mariposa.

HEIDE, FLORENCE PARRY. 1971. *The Shrinking of Treehorn.* New York: Holiday House. (A story with which many children can identify: a child who is benignly overlooked. Appealing illustrations by Edward Gorey.)

LOWELL, SUSAN. 1992. *The Three Little Javelinas.* Flagstaff, AZ. (Southwestern adaptation of *The Three Little Pigs* has an excellent introduction to the culture of the Southwestern United States. Delightful illustrations by Jim Harris.)

OFFEN, HILDA, illus. 1981. "The Three Billy Goats Gruff," from *A Treasury of Bedtime Stories.* New York: Simon and Schuster. (or any other source)

SENDAK, MAURICE. 1963. *Where the Wild Things Are.* New York: Harper and Row. (Appealing illustrations by the author suggest costumes for a dramatization.)

———. (See *any* other works by this author.)

VAN LAAN, NANCY. 1990. *Possum Come a-Knockin'.* New York: Dragonfly (Knopf).

Poems and stories for sound effects, movement, creating songs, and participation in repeated phrases

ANDREAS, BRIAN. 1993. *Mostly True; Collected Stories and Drawings.* Decorah, IA: StoryPeople.

AYLESWORTH, JIM. 1992. *Old Black Fly.* New York: Henry Holt and Co.
BAYLOR, BIRD. 1982. *Moon Song.* New York: Charles Scribner's Sons. (Mood-evoking black and white illustrations by Ronald Hunter capture the moonlight.)
JOHNSTON, TONY. 1987. *Whale Song.* New York: G.P. Putnam's Sons. (Beautifully illustrated. Also a counting book.)
KATZ, BOBBI. 1991. *Ghosts and Goose Bumps: Poems to Chill Your Bones.* New York: Random House.
KRAUSS, RUTH. 1945. *The Carrot Seed,* illus. by Crockett Johnson. New York: Scholastic.
LITTLEDALE, FRYA. 1985. *The Magic Fish.* New York: Scholastic.
MONCURE, JANE BELK. 1982. *Sounds all around.* Chicago: Children's Press. (Good source for listening and sound.)
MUNSCH, ROBERT. 1982. *Love You Forever.* Ontario, Canada: Firefly Books.
———. 1992. *Mortimer.* Toronto, ON: Annick Press. (Beloved by early childhood classes, who can chime in with the repeated punch line, which fits the Ur-song. Other participatory opportunities. Amusing illustrations by Michael Martchenko.)
PHILIPS, NEIL, ed. *Songs are Thoughts: Poems of the Inuit.* New York: Orchard. (Unusual illustrations by Maryclare Foa.)
RATZESBERGER, ANNA. 1954. *Farm Pets.* New York: Checkerboard Press.
STEELE, MARY Q. 1989. *Anna's Garden Songs.* New York: Scholastic. (Words for creating songs.)
STEVENSON, JAMES. 1983. *The Great Big Especially Beautiful Easter Egg.* New York: Scholastic. (Fantasy; seasonal; create a play.)
WOOD, NANCY. 1993. *Spirit Walker.* New York: Delacorte Press. (Native American spirituality and bonds with the earth; word pictures of sound. Beautiful paintings by Frank Howell.)

Movement and games (See also "How-to books for teachers")

BEALL, PAMELA CONN, and SUSAN HAGEN NIPP. 1979. *Wee Sing and Play: Musical Games and Rhymes for Children.* Los Angeles: Price Stern Sloan. (Book and cassette.)
———. (Also other *Wee Sing* books.)
FULTON, ELEANOR, and PAT SMITH. 1978. *Let's Slice the Ice: A Collection of Black Children's Ring Games and Chants.* St. Louis: MMB Music, Inc.
HART, AVERY, and PAUL MANTELL. 1993. *Kids Make Music: Clapping and Tapping from Bach to Rock.* Charlotte, VT: Williamson Publishing.
JONES, BESSIE, and BESS LOMAX HAWES. 1972. *Step it Down: Games, Plays, Songs, and Stories from the Afro-American Heritage.* New York: Harper and Row.
JOYCE, MARY. 1980. *First Steps in Teaching Creative Dance to Children.*

Mountain View, CA: Mayfield.
MAGUIRE, JACK. 1990. *Hopscotch, Hangman, Hot Potato, and Ha Ha Ha.* New York: Simon & Schuster.
PALMER, HAP. 1987. *Songs to Enhance the Movement Vocabulary of Young Children.* Van Nuys, CA: Alfred Publishing Co.
SHOTWELL, RITA. 1984. *Rhythm and Movement Activities for Early Childhood.* Van Nuys, CA: Alfred Publishing Co.
WEIKART, PHYLLIS S. 1989. *Movement Plus Music: Activities for Children 3 to 7.* Ypsilanti, MI: High/Scope.
———. 1987. *Round the Circle: Key Experiences in Movement for Children.* New York: High/Scope.
———. (Recordings, videos, and other books by this author.)

"How-to" books for teachers (See also "Movement and games")

ANDRESS, BARBARA L., and LINDA MILLER WALKER. 1992. *Readings in Early Childhood Music Education.* Reston, VA: Music Educators National Conference.
BRADY, MARTHA, and PATSY T. GLEASON. 1994. *Artstarts: Drama, Music, Movement, Puppetry, and Storytelling Activities.* Englewood, CO: Teacher Ideas Press.
BOS, BEV. 1982. *Don't Move the Muffin Tins: a Hands-off Guide to Art for the Young Child.* Roseville, CA: Turn-The-Page Press.
LEVENE, DONNA B. 1993. *Music Through Children's Literature: Theme and Variations.* Englewood, CO: Teacher Ideas Press.
SEEGER, RUTH CRAWFORD. 1948. *American Folk Songs for Children.* Garden City, New York: Doubleday. (Classic collection also contains helpful commentary and suggestions.)
WHEELER, LAWRENCE, and LOIS RAEBECK. 1985. *Orff and Kodály Adapted for the Elementary School.* Dubuque, IA: William C. Brown.

Recordings

(Because there are endless possibilities here, according to the objectives of the teacher, this is only a sampling of artists who make fine recordings for children.):

Gemini	Fred Koch	Hap Palmer
Ella Jenkins	Fred Penner	Raffi
Rosenschontz	Sharon, Lois, and Bram	

Stories on cassette; videos

Beethoven Lives Upstairs (cassette, CD, and video)
Mozart's Magic Fantasy (cassette, CD)
Mr. Bach Comes to Call (cassette, CD)
Tchaikovsky Discovers America (cassette, CD)
Vivaldi's Ring of Mystery (cassette, CD)

Appendix B: Songs

String String Bass

A good way to get children to internalize beat and rhythm patterns is the "string string bass." Give each child a length of string (kite string or hard-surface cord is best) about a yard long. One end of the string is held firmly to the floor by one foot; the other end is stretched over the tip of the index finger and held to the ear. The child then strums the string with the other hand, with a resulting effect in the ear of a string bass. The more tightly the string is held, the higher the pitch. Holding the string more loosely produces a lower pitch.

The "players" can play along with a recording of music with a prominent beat. Country western and bluegrass are good for this. After they get the beat going, they can experiment with rhythmic "riffs" and changing of pitch.

A Colorful Story

(An integrated lesson in color identification and sound awareness.)

One day, Clarence, a very shy little boy, hurried out of school to enjoy the Spring day. The sky was very *blue*; the sun bathed everything in a warm, *yellow* light. The landscape was turning *green*. Clarence was very happy, and began to pretend that he was the Masked *Purple* Avenger. As he rounded a corner, he saw Frankie, the class bully. Frankie was very large, and swaggered around wearing a *black* leather jacket and *brown* "shades," pushing people around. Clarence, the Masked *Purple* Avenger, saw that Frankie had picked up a little *brown* kitten and was hanging it by its tail. Clarence saw *red*, but was afraid of Frankie, who was twice as big as Clarence, even if Clarence *was* the Masked *Purple* Avenger. But Clarence said to himself, "I'm no *yellow* coward." He took a deep breath and started toward Frankie. "Put that cat down, Frankie," he managed to choke out, his face *green* with fear.

"W-e-l-l-l," said Frankie evilly. "If it isn't little Clarence." Frankie began to swing the little *brown* cat by its tail; it mewed piteously. Clarence saw *red* again and lunged toward Frankie. At that point, Clarence stumbled over his *green* shoelaces that his brother had given him for his birthday. As he fell, his head rammed Frankie right in the mid-section, knocking the breath out of him and causing him to drop the little *brown* cat, which made a *blue* streak for its home. Clarence wisely did the same thing before Frankie recovered. At home, the Masked *Purple* Avenger rubbed his knees, which were *black*, *blue*, and *red*, and happily savored his rescue of the little *brown* kitten.

by Lois Blackburn

For this story, the children choose sound effects to accompany the color words. A selection of classroom instruments should be available, from which the students decide which would best represent, for example, a green sound. (Children often choose a triangle or bell for this.)

Class Story

This story was composed by a fifth-grade class. After the opening phrase, "One dark Halloween night" (provided by the teacher), each student in turn added something to the story. The teacher wrote the story on the chalkboard as it developed, with a student scribe copying it for future reference. After the sentence ending with, " . . . falling into a hole in the ground that was covered by leaves," the ending committee (selected in advance) took over and devised an ending. Sound effects were added, for which students invented notation. Later, from the student scribe's copy, the teacher then typed the story, adding the notation, and made copies for the class members.

HALLOWEEN STORY

One dark halloween night, there were cats screeching all around. As the wind howled through the trees, I could hear footsteps coming toward me. They weren't footsteps of an ordinary person. The shuffling was coming from the dark graveyard. And with the shuffling came the sound of chains. I looked up and saw ghosts floating all around. I was so scared I took off running. The wind blew a large tree in front of my path. When I fell, I could hear the chains coming closer and closer. I began to scream. As I lay there in the wet weeds, I searched for a new way out of the woods. The footsteps were getting closer, and I could hear an owl hooting in the distance. I decided I had better run. Faster and faster I ran. I was so frightened that I began to cry. Suddenly, a cat jumped on my back. I screamed as a ghost hit me with a chain, falling into a hole in the ground that was covered by leaves. And just when I thought I would pass out, I heard dogs barking in the distance. I screamed, and my mother woke me from my dream.

- cat sounds
- windy sound
- tramping footsteps
- frightened, shivering sounds
- sandblocks
- bells
- ghostly sounds
- fast footsteps
- sound of wind howling in trees
- drum
- scream
- owl sounds
- weeping
- dogs barking

APPENDIX B · · · 181

Dynamics

The concept of dynamics, or loud and soft sounds, can be experienced by being incorporated into other games and activities, such as "Body Machines" (see section on "Movement") and "Sound Circle" (see section on "Listening").

A game involving dynamics that is a favorite of children is built around the song *Oh, Where, Oh, Where Has My Little Dog Gone?* This game requires first a stuffed toy dog, and second, that children learn to sing the song (below). The students practice singing it loudly, then softly. Then a volunteer to be "it" goes out of the room while the class agrees on a hiding place for the toy dog. The class then sings the song softly when "it" is not near the hiding place, louder when "it" is hot on the trail. "It" can be rewarded by hiding the dog for the next turn.

OH, WHERE, OH, WHERE HAS MY LITTLE DOG GONE?

Traditional

Oh, where, oh, where has my little dog gone? Oh, where, oh, where can he be? With his ears cut short and his tail cut long, Oh, where, oh, where can he be?

Kodály Rhythm Symbols

| | tah (quarter note)
⊓ | ti-ti (paired eighth notes)
𝐙 | rest (quarter rest)
⌒
⊓ | ta-ah (soon, introduce ♩)
♪ | ti (eighth note)
|. ♪,♪ |. tah-i-ti, ti-tah-i (dotted quarter with eighth)
⊓⊓ tiri-tiri (4 sixteenth notes)
⊓⊓ , ⊓⊓ ti-tiri, tiri-ti (sixteenth notes with eighths)
♪| ♪ syncopah (syncopated pattern)
⊓. , ⊓. tim-ri, ri-tim (dotted eighths with sixteenth)
⊓⊓ triple-ti (triplet)
| | | | tah-ah-ah-ah (soon, introduce 𝐎)
| | | tah-ah-ah (soon, introduce ♩.)

APPENDIX B···· 183

Apples and Bananas

1. I like to eat . . . apples and bananas.
2. I like to ate . . . aypuls and banaynays.
3. I like to eet . . . eepuls and baneenees.
4. I like to ite . . . eye-puls and banyenyes.
5. I like to ote . . . opuls and banohnohs.
6. I like to ute . . . uples and banunus.

Apples and Bananas, by Frank Scott
Copyright © 1964 PolyGram International Publishing, Inc.
Copyright Renewed
International Copyright Secured. All Rights Reserved.
Used by permission.

The Bus Song

The people in the bus go up and down, up and down, up and down. The people in the bus go up and down, all around the town.

From *EYE WINKER TOM TINKER CHIN CHOPPER: Fifty Musical Fingerplays*, by Tom Glazer. Garden City, New York: Doubleday & Company, Inc. © 1973 by Tom Glazer. Used by permission 1997.

The Bus Song (continued)

2. The wiper on the bus goes, "Swish, swish, swish,
   Swish, swish, swish, swish, swish."
   The wiper on the bus goes, "Swish, swish, swish,"
   All around the town.

3. The brake on the bus goes, "Roomp, roomp, roomp,
   Roomp, roomp, roomp, roomp, roomp!"
   The brake on the bus goes, "Roomp, roomp, roomp!"
   All around the town.

4. The money in bus goes, "Clink, clink, clink,
   Clink, clink, clink, clink, clink!"
   The money in the bus goes, "Clink, clink, clink!"
   All around the town.

5. The wheels on the bus go 'round and around,
   Round and around, 'round and around.
   The wheels on the bus go 'round and around,
   All around the town.

6. There's a baby in the bus goes, "Wah, wah, wah,
   Wah, wah, wah, wah, wah!"
   There's a baby in the bus goes, "Wah, wah, wah!"
   All around the town.

v. 1: Children go up and down in their seats.
v. 2: Hold arms out and imitate wipers by waving forearms.
v. 3: Pull an imaginary hand-brake up three times to "roomp, roomp, roomp."
v. 4: Tap thumb against forefinger (same hand) three times to "clink, clink, clink."
v. 5: Describe circles with both hands to "round and around."
v. 6: "Rock" a baby in one's arms.

The Eensy, Weensy Spider in Spanish

La araña pequeñita
Subió, subió, subió.
Vino la lluvia
Y se la llevó.
Salió el sol y todo se secó.
Y la araña pequeñita
Subió, subió, subió.

Used by permission
Wilma Salzman
MY BIG BOOK
Table Top Press, 1993
PO Box 640296
El Paso, TX 79904

The Inchworm

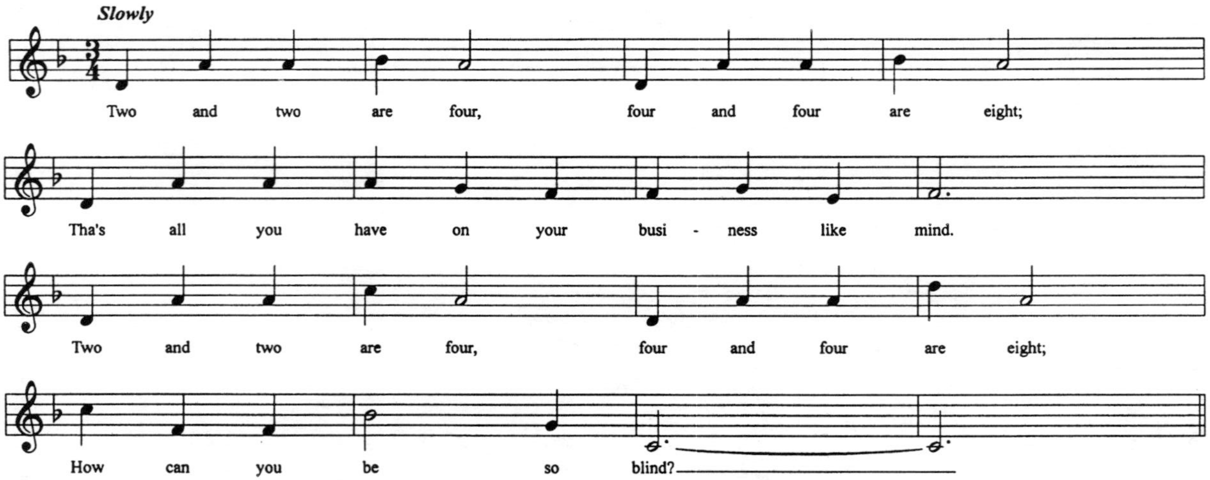

Slowly

Two and two are four, four and four are eight;

That's all you have on your busi-ness like mind.

Two and two are four, four and four are eight;

How can you be so blind?

The Inch Worm, by Frank Loesser
© 1951, 1952 (renewed) FRANK MUSIC CORP.
All rights Reserved. Used by permission.

The Inchworm *(continued)*

Refrain

Two and two are four, four and four are eight,
Inch-worm, inch-worm, measuring the marigolds,

Eight and eight are six-teen, six-teen and six-teen are thir-ty two
You and your a-rith-me-tic, you'll prob-a-bly go far.

Two and two are four, four and four are eight,
Inch-worm, inch-worm, measuring the marigolds,

Eight and eight are six-teen, six-teen and six-teen are thir-ty two
Seems to me you'd stop and see how beau-ti-ful they are.

Land of the Silver Birch
and
My Paddle's Clean and Bright

Land of the sil-ver birch, home of the bea-ver, Where still the migh-ty moose wan-ders at will:

My pad-dle's clean and bright, flashing like sil-ver, fol-low the wild goose flight, dip, dip, and swing.

Blue lake and rock-y shore I will re-turn once more, Boom-di-a-da, Boom-di-a-da, Boom-di-a-da, Boo-oo-oom.

Dip, dip, and swing her back, flash-ing like sil-ver and in the pale moonlight, dip, dip, and swing.

These two songs, both probably Canadian in origin, fit together beautifully as partner songs. Since they are folk songs—that is, passed by ear from one person to another, usually at camp—there are occasional variations of the words from one version to another. However, both of the simple, appealing tunes invariably appear as they are written. Singing them as partner songs is less common but very effective. Ostinatos and bordurns based on D and A can be added using barred or other instruments. Drums are an appropriate accompaniment to the "Boom-di-a-da" words in the first song. Both songs are also excellent examples for study of minor scales.

190 · · · · APPENDIX B

Mi chacra
(My Farm)

© 1961 Max T. Krone, renewed 1989 by Neil A Kjos Music Co. Used with permission, 1996.

Mi chacra (My Farm) (continued)

1. Vengan a ver mi chacra que es hermosa, (bis)
   el perrito hace así: guq-guq. (bis)

   Come see my farm which is beautiful, (repeat)
   The little dog does like this: arf-arf, (repeat)

Estribillo *(Refrain)*
   O ven camarad, o ven camarad, o ven, o ven. (bis)
   Oh come, my friend, oh come, my friend, oh come, oh come, oh come. (repeat)

2. ......El pollito hace así: pi-pi-rí,
   The little chicken does like this: peep-peep,

3. ......El burrito hace así: ji-jo,
   The little donkey does like this: hee-haw,

4. ......El gatito hace así: miau-miau,
   The little kitten does like this: meow-meow,

5. ......El cerdito hace así: cué-cué,
   The little pig does like this: oinck-oinck,

6. ......el patito hace así: cuac-cuac,
   The little duck does like this: quack-quack

My Hat (Mein Hut)

Eng: My hat it had three cor-ners, three cor-ners had my hat;
Ger: Mein Hut er hat drei Eck-en, drei Eck-en hat mein Hut;

And had it not three cor-ners, It would not be my hat.
Und hät er nicht drei Eck-en, Dann ist er nicht mein Hut.

After this song is sung through once, it is repeated, each time omitting another key word and substituting the following motions during the silent pause:

"my" - point to self
"hat" - indicate a hat on the head by joining fingertips of both hands to form a pointed hat
"three" - hold up three fingers
"corners" - point to elbow

During the silent pause when a motion is substituted for a word with a pitch, the singer "thinks" the omitted pitch, enabling him/her to resume on the correct pitch after the interruption. This is inner hearing, or audiation (Edwin Gordon's term).

APPENDIX B · · · · 193

Orchestra Song

The vi - o - lin's ring - ing like love - ly___ sing - ing, The
The clar - i - net, the clar - i - net makes doo - dle, doo - dle, doo - dle, doo - dle det, The
The trum - pet is sound - ing ta ta ta ta ta ta ta ta ta ta ta ta ta ta, The
The horn, the horn a - wakes me at morn, The
The drum's play - ing two tones and al - ways the same tones, Five
The bas-soon it makes a point of coun - ter - point la la la la la la la la la la, The bas -

Orchestra Song (continued)

"Das Orchester" Text: engl. Version (Originalurheber Willy Geisler)
Musik: Willy Geisler
© Voggenreiter Verlag, Bonn
Used by permission

196···· APPENDIX B

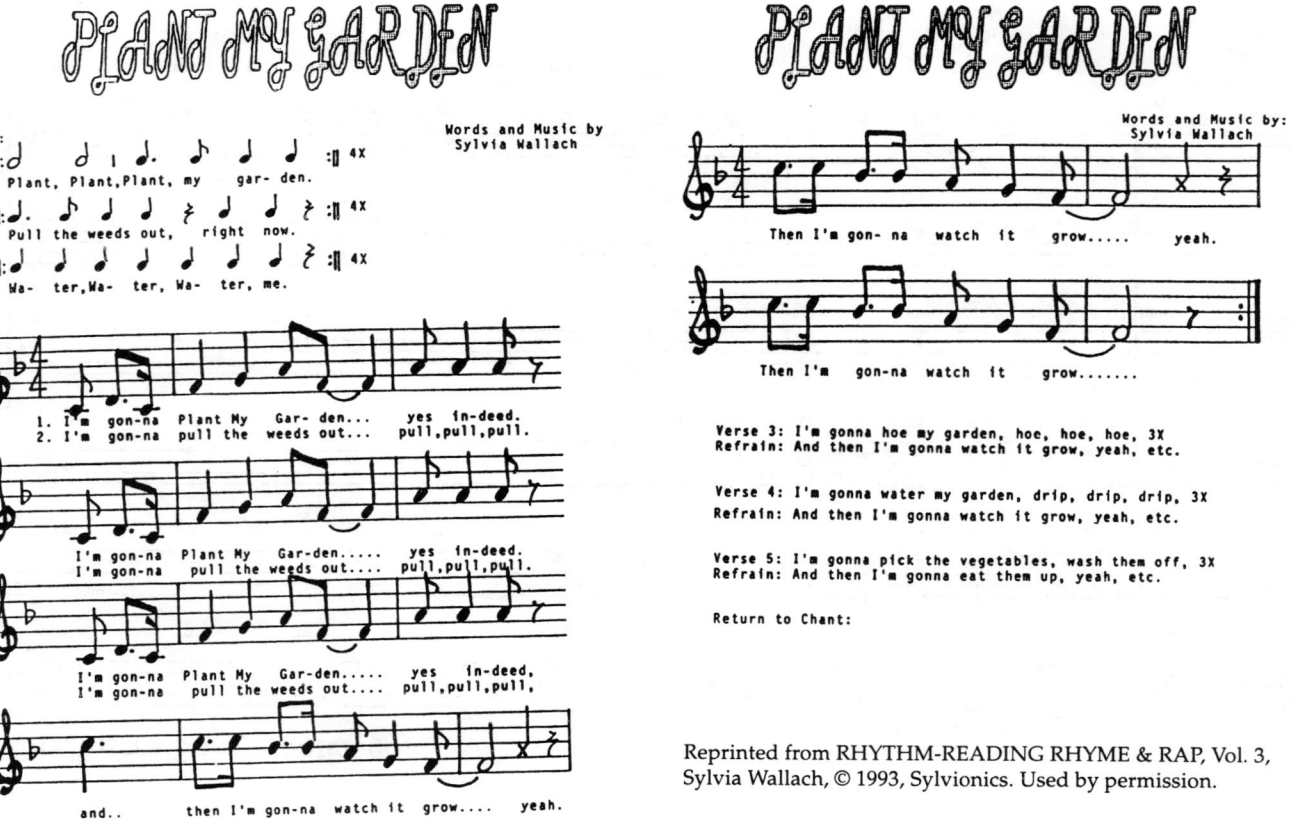

Rain, Rain

Rain, rain, go a-way! Come a-gain some o-ther day.
Rain, rain, go a-way! Lit-tle John-ny wants to play.

Scotland's Burning

Round

Scot-land's burn-ing, Scot-land's burn-ing, Look out! Look out!
Fire! Fire! Fire! Fire! pour on wa-ter, pour on wa-ter!

APPENDIX B · · · · 197

Ebeneezer Sneezer

E - be - nee - zer Sneez - er, Top - sy - tur - vy man,
Walks up - on his el - bows Eve - ry - time he can,
Dress - es up in pa - per Eve - ry - time it pours
Whis - tles "Yan - kee Doo - dle" Eve - ry - time he snores.
Oh, E - be - nee - zer, what a man!

EBENEEZER SNEEZER, by Georgia E. Garlid and Lynn Freeman Olson
© 1986 Belwin Mills Publishing Corp.
All Rights Reserved. Used by Permission.
WARNER BROS. PUBLICATIONS U.S. INC., Miami, FL 33014

Tony Chestnut

[musical notation]

To - ny Chest - nut knows I love you, To - ny knows, To - ny knows.

To - ny Chest - nut knows I love you, That's what To - ny knows.

Accompanying motions for this song:

"To-ny"—touch toe, then knee
"Chest..."—touch chest
"...-nut"—touch head
"knows"—touch nose
"I"—point to eye
"love"—hand over heart
"you"—point to someone else

TONY CHESTNUT (a/k/a "Toe-Knee-Chest-Nut") by Roy Jordan
© 1949 (Renewed) EMI Robbins Catalog Inc.
All Rights Reserved. Used by Permission.
WARNER BROS. PUBLICATIONS U.S. Inc., Miami, FL 33014

Miss Mary Mack: Hand Jive

Hand jive can be easy enough to be great fun, as with the motions below. Exhilaration increases when the song and motions are speeded up. With a little alteration, the pattern below can be fitted to a great many other children's songs besides *Miss Mary Mack*. In the "hands" of a skilled practitioner, hand jive can also be very elaborate, producing complex percussive effects and rhythmic variations. Many African American musicians have taken this art to a high level. Tyrolean male folk dancers also do a type of hand jive (not so named!) involving the kicked-up heels of the shoes as well as thighs, arms, and hands.

[Miss Mary] Mack, Mack,

Patsch twice

Mack, all dressed in

Clap twice

black, black,

Pass palm of one flattened hand over top of the other, twice

black, with silver

Same, with hand reversed.

buttons, buttons,

Bump fists together, twice

buttons down her

Same, other fist on top.

back, back,

Point thumb over shoulder twice.

back. She asked her.

Same, with other thumb, other shoulder.

200···· Appendix B

Miss Mary Mack

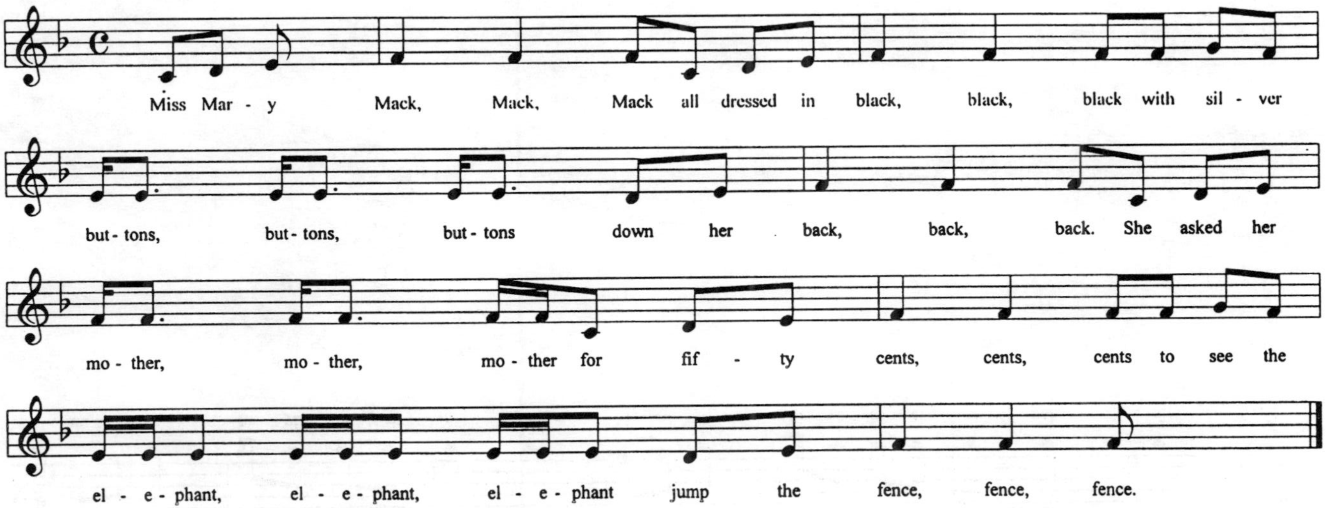

Miss Mar-y Mack, Mack, Mack all dressed in black, black, black with sil-ver but-tons, but-tons, but-tons down her back, back, back. She asked her mo-ther, mo-ther, mo-ther for fif-ty cents, cents, cents to see the el-e-phant, el-e-phant, el-e-phant jump the fence, fence, fence.

He jumped so high, high, high
He reached the sky, sky, sky
And didn't come back, back, back
'Til the fourth of July-ly-ly.

Navajo Happy Song

202 · · · · APPENDIX B

The Elephant

One el-e-phant went out to play out on a spi-der's web one day.
He had such e-nor-mous fun, he called to a-no-ther el-e-phant to come.

One child begins as the first elephant, walking as follows while the other children sing: On beats one, two, and three, take three steps forward; then, on the fourth beat, stop and cross the free foot in the air over the other foot, putting it down again on the next "one." The first elephant then chooses another elephant, who walks behind the first one holding onto his/her shoulders. Each succeeding elephant attaches to the previous one until there is a group snaking around the room in a line.

Bill Grogan's Goat

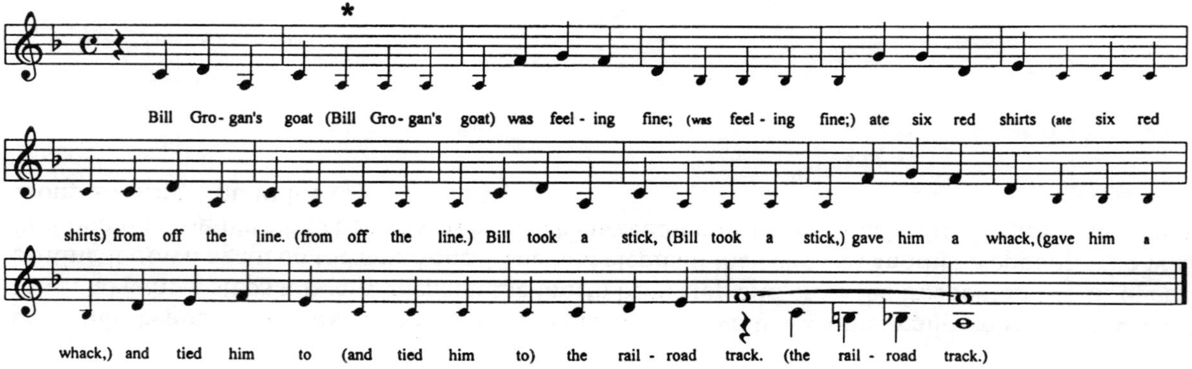

Bill Gro-gan's goat (Bill Gro-gan's goat) was feel-ing fine; (was feel-ing fine;) ate six red shirts (ate six red shirts) from off the line. (from off the line.) Bill took a stick, (Bill took a stick,) gave him a whack,(gave him a whack.) and tied him to (and tied him to) the rail-road track. (the rail-road track.)

* when using the echo, hold the melody note through the measure.

The whistle blew,
The train drew nigh.
Bill Grogan's goat
Was doomed to die.
He gave three groans
Of awful pain,
Coughed up the shirts,
And flagged the train!

One Bottle of Pop

A song with three separate tunes, each with different words, all sung simultaneously.

This song is an excellent exploration of harmony: two or more different pitches played or sung simultaneously, resulting in an enrichment of the musical texture. It is an accessible form of part-singing, in which each singer or group of singers is singing a different part at the same time. This requires—and develops—two different levels of concentration. The first is the ability to focus on one's own part without being distracted by the parts being sung by others. The second level of concentration is the ability to maintain one's own part while at the same time hearing and enjoying the effect of the blended parts.

These skills are developed by repeating a part until it is completely familiar and can be sung with little thought. "One Bottle of Pop" has three little tunes with nonsense words. These minisongs are "catchy," amusing, and easy to memorize quickly. After the three minisongs have been learned separately, the singers can begin the blending by first singing two of them simultaneously, and finally all three. The effect is really quite musically sophisticated, both more challenging and more satisfying than a round.

One Bottle of Pop

1. One bot-tle of pop, Two bot-tles of pop, Three bot-tles of pop, Four bot-tles of pop. Five bot-tles of pop, Six bot-tles of pop, Seven bot-tles of pop, Pop!

2. Don't throw your junk in my back-yard, my back-yard, my back-yard. Don't throw your junk in my back-yard, My back-yard's full.

3. Fish and chips and vin-e-gar, vin-e-gar, vin-e-gar, Fish and chips and vin-e-gar, vin-e-gar, Pop!

Reprinted with the permission of Little Simon, an imprint of Simon & Schuster Children's Publishing Division from the FIRESIDE BOOK OF FUN AND GAME SONGS by Marie Winn and Allan Miller. Text copyright © 1974 Marie Winn and Allan Miller.

Appendix C: Classical Music for Listening Activities

BARTÓK, BÉLA. *Rumanian Dances.*
BEETHOVEN, LUDWIG VAN. *Symphony no. 5,* first movement.
———. *Symphony no. 8,* second movement.
———. *Symphony no. 9,* last movement.
BERLIOZ, HECTOR. *Symphonie Fantastique,* fourth movement, "March to the Scaffold" and fifth movement, "Dream of a Witches' Sabbath."*
———. *Roman Carnival Overture.*
BIZET, GEORGES. *Carmen,* overture.
———. *Children's Games.*
———. *L'Arlesienne Suite no. 1,* Minuet.
———. *L'Arlesienne Suite no. 2,* Farandole.
BORODIN, ALEXANDER. "Polovtsian Dances," from *Prince Igor.*
———. *In the Steppes of Central Asia.*
BRAHMS, JOHANNES. *Hungarian Dances.*
———. *Symphony no. 3,* third movement.
———. *Violin Concerto in D, Op. 77,* first movement.
COATES, ERIC. *London Suite,* "Knightsbridge."
COPLAND, AARON. *Appalachian Spring.*
———. *A Lincoln Portrait.*
———. *Rodeo,* "Hoedown."
———. *El Salon Mexico.*

*May be objectionable to some parents because of subject matter (witches, supernatural).

DEBUSSY, CLAUDE. *Children's Corner Suite.*
———. *La Mer.*
DUKAS, PAUL. *The Sorcerer's Apprentice.*
DVORÁK, ANTONIN. *Symphony no. 9 in e minor, The New World.*
GERSHWIN, GEORGE. *An American in Paris.*
———. *Porgy and Bess.*
———. *Rhapsody in Blue.*
GLIÈRE, REINHOLD. *The Red Poppy,* "Russian Sailors' Dance."
GRIEG, EDVARD. *Peer Gynt Suite no. 1,* "In the Hall of the Mountain King."
GROFÉ, FERDE. *Death Valley Suite.*
———. *Grand Canyon Suite.*
———. *Mississippi Suite.*
HANDEL, GEORGE FREDERICK. *The Messiah.*
———. *Royal Fireworks Music.*
———. *Water Music.*
HANSON, HOWARD. *Symphony no. 2,* second movement.
HAYDN, FRANZ JOSEF. *Symphony no. 94 ("Surprise"),* second movement.
HOLST, GUSTAV. *The Planets.*
HONEGGER, ARTHUR. *Pacific 231.*
HOVHANESS, ALAN. *And God Created Great Whales.*
HUMPERDINCK, ENGLEBERT. *Hansel und Gretel.* [opera]
JOPLIN, SCOTT. "The Entertainer." [rag]
———."Maple Leaf Rag."
KABALEVSKY, DMITRI. *The Comedians.*
KHATCHATURIAN, ARAM. *Gayne Ballet Suite no. 2.*
KODÁLY, ZOLTÁN. *Háry János Suite.*
MENOTTI, GIAN-CARLO. *Amahl and the Night Visitors.*
MOZART, WOLFGANG. *The Marriage of Figaro,* overture.
———. *Piano Concerto no. 21 in C,* second movement.
———. *Symphony no. 40 in g minor,* first movement.
MUSSORGSKY, MODEST. *Pictures at an Exhibition.*
———. *Night on Bald Mountain.**
PROKOFIEV, SERGE. *Cinderella.*
———. *Classical Symphony.*
———. *Lieutenant Kije Suite.*
———. *Peter and the Wolf.*
RAVEL, MAURICE. *Mother Goose Suite.*
RESPIGHI, OTTORINO. *The Birds.*
———. *The Fountains of Rome.*
———. *The Pines of Rome.*
ROSSINI, GIOACCHINO. *William Tell,* overture.

*May be objectionable to some parents because of subject matter (witches, supernatural).

SAINT-SAENS, CAMILLE. *Carnival of the Animals.*
———. *Danse Macabre.**
SCHUBERT, FRANZ. *String Quartet no. 14 in d minor (Death and the Maiden),* second movement.
SCHUMANN, ROBERT. *Album for the Young.*
———. *Scenes from Childhood.*
———. *Symphony no. 4,* second movement.
SIBELIUS, JEAN. *Finlandia.*
———. *Symphony no. 2,* first movement.
SMETANA, BEDRICH. *The Moldau.*
STRAUSS, RICHARD. *Till Eulenspiegel's Merry Pranks.*
STRAVINSKI, IGOR. *Firebird Suite.*
———. *Petrouchka.*
———. *Sacre du Printemps (Rite of Spring).*
———. *The Soldier's Tale.*
TCHAIKOVSKY, PETER. *Nutcracker Suite.*
———. *Romeo and Juliet.*
———. *Symphony no. 4,* third movement.
VERDI, GIUSEPPE. *Aida,* "Triumphal March."
VILLA-LOBOS, HEITOR. "Little Train of the Caipira."
VIVALDI, ANTONIO. *The Four Seasons.*
WAGNER, RICHARD. *Die Meistersinger,* prelude, "Dance of the Apprentices." "Entrance of the Meistersingers."
———. *Lohengrin,* overture to act one, prelude to act three.
———. *Die Walküre* from *Ring of Nibelungen,* "Ride of the Valkyries."

*May be objectionable to some parents because of subject matter (witches, supernatural).

Index

audiation, 67–70. *See also* inner hearing

beat, 36–38, 58–65, 145–147
Beethoven, 143
Bernstein, Leonard, 12, 14, 45–47, 68, 92
Bruner, Jerome, 11, 14, 117

calling tune (vocative tune), 35, 46–48, 51
Chomsky, Noam, 11–12, 45, 113, 121, 137, 142, 145
Cloze procedure, 55
cognitive psychologists, 14
conducting, 64, 70–71, 76, 146
courtesy, audience, 75–76, 98, 100
Cunningham, Merce, 33

Dalcroze (Emile Jaques-Dalcroze), 33–34, 71
dance, 39–40, 158–159
Dewey, John, 5, 6, 10
drama, 36, 40–41
Dr. Suess (Theodore Geisel), 38, 41, 111, 150
Duncan, Isadora, 8
dynamics, 70, 71, 145, 182

Edman, Irwin, 140
Edwards, Betty, 14
Eisner, Elliot, 8
environment, music, 15–20

form, 77, 146–147

Gagne, Robert, 11, 14

Gardner, Howard, 7–8, 10, 43–45, 110, 154
Gestalt psychologists, 13
Goldovsky experiment, 139
Goodman, Kenneth, 6, 113–115, 136–140
Goodman, Yetta, 6, 116
Gordon, Edwin, 67
Green, Barry, 26

hand-jive, 38
harmony, 78–80, 92–95
hearing impaired, music for, 101–102
Heide, Florence Parry
  The Shrinking of Treehorn, 112
homemade instruments, 16–17, 73
Honegger, Arthur, 122, 147

inner hearing, 67–70. *See also* audiation
intervals, 66–68, 87
invented notation, 104–110, 135. *See also* notation

Jackendoff, Ray, 12, 14, 142
job cards, 18–19

kazoos, 50–51, 73
key signatures, 87–91
Kodaly, Zoltan, 42, 47, 52–54, 62, 66–69, 81, 83–86, 111, 128–132, 136

Langer, Susanne K., 8, 121, 162
learning activity packages (LAP), 18
learning centers, 18–19
Lerdahl, Fred, 12, 14, 142
Lieberman, Mark, 46
"lining-out", 53

211

melody, 65, 68–69, 95
meter, 61–65, 82–86
Milne, A. A., 38, 63, 82–83
Mozart, 17, 57
Munsch, Robert
　I'll Love You Forever, 111–112, 150
　Mortimer, 48

Neisser, Ulric, 11, 14
notation, 96, 104–110, 113–143
　sequence for teaching, 135

Orff, Carl, 16–17, 34, 47, 60, 69, 71, 74, 77, 79, 94, 147
ostinato, 79

partner songs, 79
Payne, Susan, 152–153
Piaget, 117
Pillsbury Foundation for the Advancement of Music Education, 47
pitch, 49–55, 65–68
project contracts, 20
puppets, 16, 48

recorder, 19–20, 103
rhythm, 59–61, 81–82, 145–147

scales, 45–47, 69–70, 75, 86–92
secondary level, whole music for, 17–18, 25–28, 146
Seeger, Ruth Crawford, 158
Sendak, Maurice, 41
sequence (order), 41, 53
Sessions, Roger, 14, 122, 142–143
shape notes, 123–124
Silverstein, Shel, 38
singing
　development in children, 12, 44–45
　technique, 49–50, 55–56
Sloboda, John, 12, 14, 138
Smith, Frank, 6, 113–115, 118–119
string string bass, 60

teaching a song, 55–56
tempo, 71, 145
timbre, 71–76

Ur-song, 45–48, 51

Van Laan, Nancy
　Possum Come a-Knockin', 41

Weikart, Phyllis, 39–40